Eritrea

THE BRADT TRAVEL GUIDE

THE BRADT STORY

The first Bradt travel guide was written by Hilary and George Bradt in 1974 on a river barge floating down a tributary of the Amazon in Bolivia. From their base in Boston, Massachusetts, they went on to write and publish four other backpacking guides to the Americas and one to Africa.

In the 1980s Hilary continued to develop the Bradt list in England, and also established herself as a travel writer and tour leader. The company's publishing emphasis evolved towards broader-based guides to new destinations – usually the first to be published on those countries – complemented by hiking, rail and wildlife guides.

Since winning *The Sunday Times* Small Publisher of the Year Award in 1997, we have continued to fill the demand for detailed, well-written guides to unusual destinations, while maintaining the company's original ethos of low-impact travel.

Travel guides are by their nature continuously evolving. If you experience anything which you would like to share with us, or if you have any amendments to make to this guide, please write; all your letters are read and passed on to the author. Most importantly, do remember to travel with an open mind and to respect the customs of your hosts – it will add immeasurably to your enjoyment.

Happy travelling!

Hilary Bradt

Hilary Bradt

19 High Street, Chalfont St Peter, Bucks SL9 9QE, England
Tel: 01753 893444; fax: 01753 892333
Email: info@bradt-travelguides.com
Web: www.bradt-travelguides.com

Eritrea

THE BRADT TRAVEL GUIDE

Third Edition

Edward Denison
Edward Paice

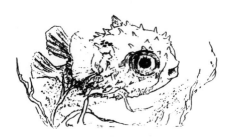

Bradt Travel Guides Ltd, UK
The Globe Pequot Press Inc, USA

Third edition published in 2002 by Bradt Travel Guides Ltd,
19 High Street, Chalfont St Peter, Bucks SL9 9QE, England
web: www.bradt-travelguides.com
Published in the USA by The Globe Pequot Press Inc, 246 Goose Lane,
PO Box 480, Guilford, Connecticut 06437-0480

First published in 1994 by Bradt Publications

British Library Cataloguing in Publication Data
A catalogue record for this book is available from the British Library

ISBN 1 84162 057 2

Library of Congress Cataloging-in-Publication Data applied for

Photographs
Front cover Woman pouring tea (Edward Denison)
Text Edward Denison

Illustrations Hilary Harvey, Annabel Milne
Maps Steve Munns. Regional maps based on ITM *Eritrea*

Typeset from the author's disc by Wakewing
Printed and bound in Italy by Legoprint SpA, Trento

Authors

Edward Paice first visited Eritrea in 1993 as an antidote to ten years of working in investment banking. He now spends up to half of each year in Africa researching for his books on aspects of the colonial history of the east and south of the continent. His latest tome, the best-selling *Lost Lion of Empire: The Life of Cape-to-Cairo Grogan*, was published to critical acclaim in April 2001; he is now working on a comprehensive history of World War I in East Africa. Edward Paice is a Fellow of (and regular lecturer at) the Royal Geographical Society, and an active member of the Africa Group of the Royal Institute of International Affairs.

Based in China and the UK, **Edward Denison** is a freelance design consultant and photographer, specialising in the social and environmental responsibilities of design practice. The context of this work is founded on the need to secure and maintain local culture, while encouraging the boundless potential of globalisation. This work takes him around the world, especially to countries that face critical change due to development.

He has previously written books on packaging and environmental design, and is currently working on publications covering architecture and urban development in Eritrea and Shanghai. His love for Eritrea was sparked during an independent trip from Cape Town to Alexandria in the 1990s. Since then, Eritrea has become very much a part of his life and work; he continues to devote his time to the preservation of its culture and built environment, and the promotion of its architectural heritage.

Contents

LIST OF MAPS

Acknowledgements

To Heden, may your life be always full of peace and happiness.

This third edition would not have been possible without the unreserved help of a great many individuals and organisations. Firstly, I would like to thank Ato Mohiadin Shengeb from the National Union of Eritrean Youth and Students for his early backing and ongoing support throughout my visit. The book could not have been completed without the help of Dr Negusse Araya at the British Council and his superb team. I also wish to thank Dr Naigzy Gebremedhin and all those at the Cultural Assets Rehabilitation Programme, whose support and friendship were enormously appreciated; Yitbarek Habtegiorgis and Mekuria at the Ministry of Information; Dr Yoseph Libsekal at the National Museum; John, Terje and all those working at the British Consulate; The Ministry of Tourism; Ian Martin and those many others at the United Nations Mission to Ethiopia and Eritrea; Gerda, Beth, Peter, Ben, David Wright, Amanuel Sahle and Tanja.

I am particularly indebted to those many individuals who gave their all during a period when a great many other things were occupying their time. Moges, Donica (and of course Noah) for your trust and friendship; Weini; Bereket – see you in Bar Diana!; Abdu and Doggy, Ruth and Charlotte in the pink building; AW and Renee, your work and kindness are an inspiration. My greatest debt of gratitude goes to Salahadin, Semira and Heden for their support, friendship and immeasurable help throughout my visit in Eritrea. In spite of the great many pressures that they, like so many others, have to bear they always remained cheerful, energetic and the truest of friends. Thanks, of course, also to my friends and family for their faith and encouragement. Finally, the freaks that had their own obstacles and dreams and persevered against all odds – this edition is yours, Magnus (Sesen at 7), Peder and, beyond all measure, my fiancée Guang Yu, to whom I will forever be indebted and without whose support none of this would have happened.

Thanks also go to those who have taken the time to write in and contribute to the improvement of the book from the second edition. These include: Katie Baker; Chris Caul; John F Griffiths; Markus Haeflinger; Richard Hotchkiss; Paul Liquorish; George Mandel; Colin McCorquodale; Tanja Muller; Dr S Munro-Hay; Jolanda Roth; Mike Roycroft; Michael Shaw; David Tremlett; Chris Shewen; Cyril Wensley; and M E Winter.

Introduction

Eritrea is a country characterised by substantial cultural and environmental diversity and an infamously turbulent past. Above all else, what endears most visitors to this country is the remarkable kindliness and unreserved humanity of the Eritrean people. Making friends in Eritrea is an unavoidable pleasure. If you begin to comprehend the immeasurable suffering that these people have had to endure and the degree of success with which they have been able to put this tragic history behind them, it makes it even more remarkable that their compassion towards visitors is so resolute.

My first impression of Eritrea was forged when I stepped off the bus that had brought me across the Eritrean border from Ethiopia to Asmara. It was late and the journey, like so many African bus journeys, had been exhausting. I was struggling to gather the energy to prepare myself for the other infamous African experience – the bus station reception, where you are greeted by what often appears to be thousands of people of all ages trying to offer a million and one different products and services. It was dark and the only light came from the dimly lit stalls skirting the bus station. It was difficult to see what was awaiting me beyond the doorway, so I prepared for the worst and strode out into the unknown. I was dumbfounded by the tranquillity. There was no one, not a soul. Having prepared myself for a time-honoured mêlée I stood alone in the bus station almost disappointed. After a minute or two a young man came to me and asked me where I was headed. I thought this might be the start of the more subtle approach adopted be the Eritreans, so I assured the man that I knew where I was going, thanked him for his concern and began to walk towards the centre of town. He followed me and insisted on carrying my bags. This was more like it. I was used to this old trick and many more besides. He even insisted on taking me to the hotel that I had said I was planning to stay at. Weariness grew to frustration as I faced the inevitability that he would not leave me alone and I would be expected to pay out a hefty tip for his troubles. We marched to the hotel with him carrying all my baggage and me too tired to protest. On arriving at the hotel I thanked him and reached for my wallet to pay the tip. His expression became puzzled when he realised my insinuation and he stopped me from going any further. 'No, please!' he said, 'It is my pleasure, welcome to Eritrea.' He smiled, turned around and left the hotel. For the second time in half an hour, I stood alone, dumbfounded.

I had reached Asmara, the almost mythical city of calm and civility. In the morning I stopped in a local snack bar for breakfast. A group of old men recommended I try *ful* – a local bean dish. I accepted their recommendation and we began to talk about their country, the war, the peace, and the future. It was an enlightening tale, full of courage, hope and optimism. After some time, I got up to pay my bill but was stubbornly prevented from doing so. I was their 'guest'. For the third and by no means the last time in Eritrea I was dumbfounded.

I wouldn't expect everyone to have the same experiences as this, but I am certain, especially if you have travelled in other African countries, that you will often be surprised, shocked even, by the unmitigated friendliness of the Eritrean people and their determination to develop their country. It was this determination that characterised the optimism and passion with which Eritrea gathered itself together after the 30-year struggle, when it achieved independence from Ethiopia in 1991. From 1991 to 1997 Eritrea consistently had one of the fasted growing economies in Africa. Infrastructure developments were catapulting the country into the 21st century. It was becoming known as the newest and most exciting travel destination, offering uncharted diving, one of the highest concentrations of early 20th-century architecture, astounding bird watching, and literally thousands of unexcavated archaeological sites. In addition to this it has vast mountains, lowland deserts, coral islands, and virgin rainforests. Eritrea's temperatures range between below freezing in the highlands to some of the hottest recorded on earth in the infamous Danakil Depression. Eritrea does not offer the *best* diving, or the *best* food, or the *largest* rainforests, or the *biggest* mountains, or the *most* astounding architecture, or *particularly* inspiring archaeological sites. That it has all of these, of whatever standard, is surprising enough for most visitors.

The road from independence was always likely to be fraught. Tragically, since my first visit, Eritrea has been engaged in a three-year conflict with its neighbour, Ethiopia. A ceasefire agreement was signed in December 2000, which, it is hoped, will mark the start of the road to peace. Compounding this tragedy is the fact that this war is like a viscous family feud on a devastating magnitude and scale. This is not just a war between friends or neighbours, but a war between integrally related societies. The war between Ethiopia and Eritrea was, at the time, the largest war on the planet and constituted the amassing of the largest number of soldiers and sophisticated technology in any field of conflict. The cost of waging such a war was being borne by two of the poorest countries in the world. The consequences to both country's economies, infrastructures and societies have been devastating. Between the two countries, an estimated 150,000 soldiers died, while over $1 million a day was being spent on sustaining the unsustainable. Now the Eritrean economy stands in ruins, while hundreds of thousands of men and women still remain on the frontline, depriving the economy of a vast potential workforce. Development projects have been put on hold as emergency relief and re-settling displaced communities become the priority. Poverty is more noticeable now than it was after independence. The war has cost this country dear, and it is the one country least able to afford it. In addition to this, the implementation of Eritrea's much-anticipated democratic constitution has been delayed and still awaits ratification.

The road to peace and democracy remains a troubled one, but whatever obstacles the people of Eritrea still have to face, for the visitor the same endearing features will always remain. The people of Eritrea will always make you feel welcome and the country will always provide a diversity of activities and experiences that will have you wanting to come back for more. The first years of Eritrean independence saw an almost fanatical romanticism emerge amongst those who had been lucky enough to experience its infancy. The country might have now passed through a troubled adolescence, but maturity is just around the corner. It would be foolish to consider Eritrea more exceptional than any other country, but it *is* different and it adds a whole new dimension for those familiar with the rest of the African continent.

KEY TO STANDARD SYMBOLS

—·—·—	International boundary	🏰	Historic building
······	District boundary	✝	Church or cathedral
-----	National park boundary	♣	Buddhist temple
✈	Airport (international)	🏠	Buddhist monastery
✦	Airport (other)	♨	Hindu temple
✛	Airstrip	Ç	Mosque
🚁	Helicopter service	⚑	Golf course
▭▬▭	Railway	🏃	Stadium
--🚗--	Car ferry	▲	Summit
--🚢--	Passenger ferry	△	Boundary beacon
⛽	Petrol station or garage	◉	Outpost
🅿	Car park	✕═✕	Border post
🚌	Bus station etc	⌂	Rock shelter
🚲	Cycle hire	▭–○–▭	Cable car, funicular
M	Underground station	»	Mountain pass
⌂	Hotel, inn etc	○	Waterhole
⛺	Campsite	☀	Scenic viewpoint
♦	Hut	✾	Botanical site
♇	Wine bar	♧	Specific woodland feature
✕	Restaurant, café etc	🗼	Lighthouse
✉	Post office	≍	Marsh
☏	Telephone	🌴	Mangrove
e	Internet café	🦅	Bird nesting site
✚	Hospital, clinic etc	🐢	Turtle nesting site
⚱	Museum	〰〰	Coral reef
🐘	Zoo	⛏	Beach
i	Tourist information	✒	Scuba diving
$	Bank	🐟	Fishing sites
⚱	Statue or monument		
⸪	Archaeological or historic site		

Other map symbols are sometimes shown in separate key boxes with individual explanations for their meanings.

Part One

General Information

ERITREA FACTS

Government Transitional government prior to implementation of Constitutional Democracy

Population 3.5 million (estimated)

Capital Asmara (population c400,000)

Currency Nakfa (Nfa)

Language Tigrinya and Arabic. Italian still spoken; English is widely taught and understood.

Time GMT +3

International dialling code +291

Weights and measures Metric system

Electricity 220 volts, 50Hz (110 volts, 60Hz in some areas)

Flag Rectangle composed of three triangles of green, blue and red. The central red triangle contains a gold laurel wreath and olive branch.

Emblem The camel, which played an instrumental role in moving supplies around the country during the war

Background Information

1

GEOGRAPHY AND CLIMATE

Eritrea lies between 12° and 18° north, and 36° and 44° east. It covers an area of 125,000km² (over 48,000 square miles) and is thus approximately the size of England. Its Red Sea coastline is 1,200km long with approximately 350 islands. It is bordered by Sudan to the north and west and by Ethiopia and Djibouti to the south. Saudi Arabia and Yemen are its closest neighbours across the Red Sea.

There are essentially three different topographic regions in Eritrea. The central highland plateau stretching from the Ethiopian border in the south to the Sudanese border in the north includes parts of the Central, Dubub and Anseba zones. Amba Soira (3,010m), the tallest peak in Eritrea, stands to the southeast of Asmara. The western lowlands take in land from the Gash Barka and Anseba zones and comprise all of the land between the highlands and the Sudanese border to the west. The coastal plains extend from the Red Sea coast of Sudan to the border of Djibouti, encompassing the Northern and Southern Red Sea zones and the 350 or so islands.

As far as the soil is concerned it is varied in both structure and origin. The soils of the highlands are of volcanic and sedimentary rock and have relatively

---

WHY THE 'RED' SEA?

While the original naming of the Red Sea and Eritrea has never been fully explained, Cyril Crossland, travelling in the area in 1907–1915, put forward an interesting explanation:

> The salt pools found here and there on these arid coasts soon evaporate to a slush of salt crystals, and in these a red microscopic alga flourishes to such an extent as to colour the whole pool. Whether the name 'Red Sea' is given from this alga, or from the pelagic form which occasionally makes a scum as if of iron rust over large areas of the sea during calms, or from the brown Xenidae which carpet the harbour sides, is indeterminable: any one of these is a striking phenomenon, the first being obvious to shore dwellers, the second to sailors. Perhaps, after all, the name was given by landsmen who noted the appearance of red colour in the hills which border the sea along its length.

high clay content when on flat ground, but with shallow soil and rock outcrops in the more mountainous areas. The soils of both the eastern and western lowlands and the flood plains of the Barka, Anseba, Gash and Setit rivers are sandy alluvial deposits as a result of soil erosion, exacerbated by war, and soil transportation by the flood water (when this occurs). The water retention of this soil is thus poorer than in the highlands. The coastal plains are mostly sand.

Climate

Eritrea can be divided into three major zones: the central highlands, the coastal region, and the western lowlands. Each has a different climatic pattern.

In the highlands, the hottest month is usually May with highs around 30°C. Winter is between December and February with lows at night that can be near

A NATURALIST'S CIRCUIT

Derek Schuurman

I went to Eritrea with the preconception of the country featuring little more than dreary desert and camels, so I was amazed at the varied natural habitats. The country is perfect for naturalists of all kinds. The route detailed below took eight hours with numerous stops, but if completed in two or three days with camping along the way would be most rewarding.

We left Asmara in the early morning and made our first stop at Weki-Zager, some 20km from the capital. En route to Weki-Zager is a small lake where waterfowl is plentiful. At Weki-Zager we turned off the main, tarred road on to a rutted dirt road, heading for Sabur mountain. I'd call the vegetation here sub Afro-alpine, since it lacks the giant lobelias and other typical Afro-alpine plants, but there are numerous aloes and small ground orchids. The trees average 7–10m in height and are covered in 'beard moss', or 'old man's beard', which hangs in woolly strands from the branches and trunks of the trees.

After Sabur we continued on a narrow but good asphalt road for Mount Meglo. This was truly mind-boggling: evergreen montane forest and lots of it. The road winds its way around numerous hairpin bends and the view over the valleys from the steep mountain slopes is breathtaking. Included in the abundant birdlife here was the beautiful Narina trogon and the equally stunning, near-endemic white-cheeked turacou, both sought-after 'lifers' for many birders. Amongst many other exciting species, we saw several tropical boubou shrike and Bruce's green pigeon.

The valley area from Mount Meglo to Mount Medhanit and to a valley called Filfil is dominated by these montane forests, alternating with cultivated fields. There seemed to be very few, if any, villages, the farmers apparently coming all the way from Weki-Zager to tend their crops of maize and potatoes here. The farmers here informed us that bushpigs are a pest.

freezing point. Asmara itself enjoys a pleasant climate all year round, although it can be cold at night in winter. There are two rainy seasons: the short rains in March and April and the main rains from late June to the beginning of September.

On the coast, the months from June to September are extremely hot with daily temperatures ranging from 40°C to 50°C (and hotter in Denkalia). In winter the daily temperature ranges from 21°C to 35°C. The rainy season on the coast north of Denkalia falls in the winter months; in Denkalia itself rain is extremely rare.

In the western lowlands, the high temperatures are comparable to those on the coast in the hottest months of April until June. December is the coldest month with temperatures falling as low as 15°C. The rainy seasons are the same as for the highlands.

From Filfil we drove out of the Semienawi Bahri, or 'green belt', to Mount Solomuna where the moist montane forest is replaced by lighter deciduous woods. This was, if anything, even better for birding. The woods soon give way to dense thornbush and, as you leave the mountains, there's a long drive through semi-desert dominated by flat-topped acacia trees. The road ends at a tiny, vibrant roadside settlement, Ghatelai, on the junction with the Asmara–Massawa road. Though the semi-desert was eerily silent, we saw black bush robin and several slender hares with very large ears. There are also reports of jackal, gazelle and spotted hyena for this area.

The direct route from Massawa back to Asmara was just as enjoyable: no evergreen montane forest, but more low deciduous woodland and, on the sheer rock faces, aloes and other succulents are plentiful. There are also baboons, and leopards are said to roam in the mountains.

Whichever route you take from Asmara to Massawa, it will soon become apparent that Eritrea presents exciting opportunities for birders, botanists, lepidopterists and hikers.

The main vegetation or topographical patterns are:

• the afro-montane or *Juniperus procera* forests on the Red Sea watershed
• the East African evergreen and semi-evergreen bushlands and thickets that cover the escarpments and the highland provinces
• the Somali-Maasai *Acacia commiphora* deciduous bushlands and thickets which form a strip adjacent to the sandy coastline of the Red Sea
• the Northern Sahel semi-desert grassland and shrubland covering parts of Barka and Sahel
• the Sahel acacia wooded grassland and shrubland covering parts of Barka and Sahel
• the Red Sea coastal desert in the Assab area
• the gravel/stone desert in Denkalia.

ENVIRONMENT

Eritrea has a very fragile environment and every care should be taken not to further impact the already considerable damage that man has wrought on this part of the world (see *Terracing and deforestation,* pages 164–5). Eritrea was revered by the ancient Egyptians for being a land of plenty, rich in minerals and wildlife. Nearly all the major species of mammal common to Africa could be found in this small but diverse environment, including elephant, lion, rhinoceros, hippo, leopard, giraffe and zebra. Now, after extensive clearance of natural habitats and the unsustainable hunting methods introduced by European settlers, there is little or nothing left of the once plentiful wildlife. In addition to this tragic loss, Eritrea has also suffered from drought and deforestation, resulting, amongst other things, in massive loss of precious topsoil in each rainy season. As a result, the condition of the environment today is a poignant reminder of how destructive humankind's capacity is to neglect and render infertile the land on which we depend.

Since independence the Eritrean government has attempted to tackle these most urgent issues and establish an environmental protection plan. Although much of this has not yet been implemented, it has at least been highlighted as a top priority for the country. A substantial tree-planting campaign is underway and you will often be amazed by the avenues of trees along each road connecting the highland towns. Other measures include the prevention of grazing in certain areas, terracing the hillsides to prevent water and soil loss, and banning the felling of trees for construction or firewood.

Eritrea has yet to designate any land for national parks, although it is being discussed. This is unfortunate, as the little remaining wildlife left in Eritrea is in desperate need of safe sanctuary. Even the 20 or so remaining Eritrean elephant are common targets for the wrath of local farmers who understandably get upset with having their crops destroyed. It is vital that certain areas be assigned national park status in the near future to attempt to preserve and even build on the numbers of animals that still exist in the country.

GOVERNMENT AND ADMINISTRATION

Eritrea finally became an independent country after the referendum held from April 23–25 1993 in which 1,100,260 voted for independence and 1,822 against. There was a 98.5% turnout of those eligible. This followed over 30 years of war against Ethiopia and its various allies, a war that ended in total victory for the Eritreans with the capture of Asmara in 1991. The referendum for independence was, as the figures show, a formality. But Eritrea had also indicated a clear preference for independence following World War II, and such status was denied them. The second time round there would be no room for misinterpreting their wishes.

Following the referendum in 1993, a new government was created with a four-year mandate to draft a democratic constitution and thereafter hold full elections. This transitional government was naturally heavily influenced by the political beliefs of the EPLF (Eritrean People's Liberation Front). Isaias Afewerki, the

EPLF leader during the armed struggle, was, and still is, the country's president. The first moves towards a democratic system were announced at the 3rd EPLF Congress held in Nacfa in February 1994. At this congress the EPLF dissolved and then reconstituted itself as a political party with the name People's Front for Democracy and Justice (PFDJ). Isaias Afewerki was its chairman.

Ten years since independence there have still been no formal elections in Eritrea and though the constitution has been drafted it has yet to be implemented. Isaias Afewerki remains president, though the various ministerial posts appear to change frequently. There is little doubt that the recent war with Ethiopia which started in 1998 has affected constitutional and democratic reform but now that peace has been established, one remains hopeful that the democratic process will be allowed to continue.

Major towns

Asmara (population c400,000) is by far the most important city, not least because – with the exception of Assab – it suffered the least war damage. The capital of Eritrea, it lies in the centre of the Eritrean highlands. Massawa and Assab are the two key ports, the former lying to the east of Asmara and the latter in the extreme south of the country, almost on the border with Ethiopia and Djibouti. Other important towns are, in no particular order, Keren, Agordat, Barentu, Tessenei, Decemhare, Adi Keih, Mendefera (Adi Ugri), Adi Qala, Senafe, Afabet and Nacfa.

THE SIX ZOBAS

Province	Capital	Location
Dubub	Mendefera	Region of central Eritrea bordering Tigray in northern Ethiopia
Central	Asmara	Small region containing the capital, Asmara, and 20km surroundings
Southern Red Sea	Assab	The large southern leg of the country covering the region from Ras Andadai to the Djibouti border and the northeastern Ethiopian border.
Northern Red Sea	Massawa	The northeastern Eritrean coastline from Ras Andadai to Sudan, including parts of the northern Sahel mountains.
Gash Barka	Barentu	Areas north of Setit River to Anseba region. This region covers the vast lowland area bordering northern Ethiopia and central-eastern Sudan.
Anseba	Keren	Bordering eastern Sudan to the north and the Gash Barka region to the south, this region covers the northern highlands of Eritrea and northwestern lowlands.

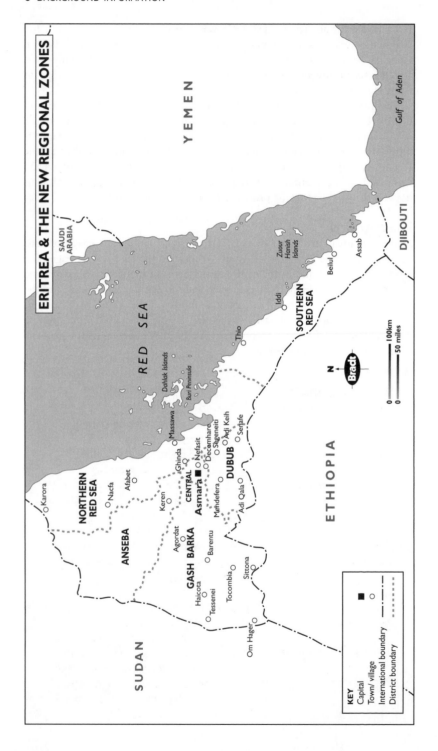

Administrative divisions

Following the Eritrean People's Liberation Front's (EPLF) commitment in their 1994 Congress to abolish old 'colonial' provincial boundaries and reconstitute them according to development and resources, the new boundaries were established in 1995. This had a considerable affect on local government as the new seats were established: six *zobas* (zones) replaced the ten provinces that had more closely marked ethnic boundaries, thereby contributing to the desired process of mixing the different cultures and the breaking down of divisions between these groups. See box on page 7.

ECONOMY

Eritrea's economy relies primarily on agriculture, though certain other industries are becoming increasingly important. Fisheries, mining and the potential to exploit oil deposits represent key areas of economic development in the future, as does the steady growth in the service sector, including tourism, banking, transport and aviation. In terms of future industrial potential, Eritrea is well positioned strategically between Africa, Europe and the Middle East.

Eritrea has enjoyed periods of great economic development in the last hundred years, both under the Italians and in the early years of the British Military Administration, and this experience has left its mark. In the 1940s Eritrea's exports topped US$100m, but by the end of the war for independence they amounted to no more than a fraction of this. The years following independence saw a marked rise in economic growth, which proved a good indication of Eritrea's formidable determination to rebuild the country after 30 years of destruction. This growth peaked in 1997 before a devastating return to war with its neighbour Ethiopia in 1998. The full cost of this war will not be measured for many years but the immediate effects are obvious. The economy has suffered greatly as a result of three years of fighting and the human and social cost of supporting up to 100,000 soldiers on the frontline is vast. Eritrea also relied heavily on trading with Ethiopia, which was its largest export market. This has now all but dried up and the inflated prices of basic goods in Eritrea, once imported from Ethiopia, testify to this.

Though the country is starting to rebuild again it will take some time before the economy is back to how it was in the mid-1990s. Aid in Eritrea is now a big business and the number of aid organisations working in the country is astonishing. With their emblazoned four-wheel drives it makes the average car park look like an annual conference of the world's NGOs. Nonetheless the development agenda is well established in Eritrea and the necessary expertise imported from overseas appears to be steadily filtering through the system. Many highly educated Eritreans living abroad have now returned, providing the country with a valuable skills base. With this, continued peace and the unique determination of the Eritrean people it is reasonable to assume that the Eritrean economy will eventually prosper.

PEOPLE AND LANGUAGES

There still remains considerable ambiguity as to the exact population of Eritrea, though a census to establish the precise figure is said to be underway. Many of the half-million refugees from camps in Sudan have now returned, as have many Eritreans living overseas, though the recent war with Ethiopia has considerably complicated this issue. Official statistics quote a total figure of around 3.5 million, which includes approximately 200,000 or so Eritreans still living overseas.

Population density is low at 22.7 people/km², based on a population of 3.5 million. The annual growth rate is currently estimated at 0.8%, which has been reduced significantly by the war. Life expectancy is 51. About 20% of Eritreans live on the high plateau, 30% in areas of elevation between 1,000m and 2,000m and the remainder in the lowlands.

Language

The official working languages in Eritrea are Tigrinya and Arabic. Italian is also still spoken, particularly by the older generation in areas formerly inhabited by Italians, and English is widely taught and understood.

Tigrinya is by far the most extensively used, representing the numerical dominance of this group. Tigrinya is an African Semitic language and the mother tongue of most southern Eritrean highlanders, as well as certain regions in northern Ethiopia. The spoken language was derived from the ancient Axumite language of Ge'ez around the 13th century AD and developed to a written language during the 19th century AD. For practical information, see *Appendix 1*, page 201.

There are nine ethnic groups in Eritrea, a number that has remained the same since the arrival of the last of the waves of migrants in the middle of the 19th century (the Rashaida). However, a possible tenth group does exist, though their eligibility as the tenth ethnic group has not yet been aired. These are the Tokharir, who arrived from Nigeria having made the pilgrimage to Mecca many centuries ago and did not have the means to get themselves home, so they stopped where they stood (in Eritrea) and have remained here ever since. They are found in the western lowlands, especially around Tessenei, and in some areas around Keren. For the nine official groups, and their respective languages, see box opposite.

Religion

The population is described as being equally divided between Christians and Muslims, with a small percentage of animists (5%) among some tribes such as the Kunama.

The Christian population is divided between the Orthodox Church, who represent the vast majority, Roman Catholics and Protestants.

The calendar

The calendar of the Orthodox Church has 13 months; 12 months have 30 days each and the thirteenth month has five days (six in a leap year). In Eritrea you

ETHNIC GROUPS

Group	*Language*	*Area*
Afar	Afar	Afar inhabit areas of southern Eritrea and spread into Djibouti and into Ethiopia. They are Muslim and organised in clans.
Bilen	Bilen	Bilen populate Keren and its immediate surrounds. There are equal numbers of Christians and Muslims and they are organised in clans.
Hedareb	To Bedawi (Beja)	Hedareb are found in the Western Lowlands. They are descendants of the Beja kingdom.
Kunama	Kunama	Kunama reside in villages between the Gash and Setit rivers and in Barentu. They are Nilotic and traditionally animists, but some have been converted to Christianity and Islam.
Nara (or Baria)	Nara	Nara are also Nilotic and live in the region east of the Gash river. They follow Islam.
Rashaida	Arabic	Rashaida are Eritrea's newest ethnic group, arriving from the Arabian peninsula in the 19th century. They are Muslim.
Saho	Saho	Saho occupy the territory on the southeastern slopes of the highlands as far as the coastal plains south of Massawa. Saho are predominantly Muslim, with some Christians among them.
Tigre	Tigre (derived from the ancient language of Ge'ez)	Tigre cover a large area of northern, northeastern and western Eritrea. They are predominantly Muslim, though there are some Christians amongst this group.
Tigrinya	Tigrinya (derived from the ancient language of Ge'ez)	Tigrinya populate the highlands of Eritrea and share their language with the Tigray of northern Ethiopia. They are mostly Coptic Christians, with a few converts to Catholicism and Protestantism. A small group of Muslims (Jiberti) also form part of the Tigrinya, differentiated only by religious belief.

want to check that the year is in the Roman not Orthodox calendar. In practice there is little scope for confusion since the Roman calendar is nearly always used in business.

VERNACULAR ARCHITECTURE
Cultural Assets Rehabilitation Project
edited by Mebrahtu Abraham and Edward Denison
Source: 'Eritrea Profile (Culture and Arts)' December 1997–January 1998

Most of the houses in rural Eritrea are constructed in a traditional way using construction materials obtained from the surroundings such as soil, dried branches or logs, ropes, stones and mats. They are mainly **hidmo** *(adobe-looking dwelling place found mainly in the highlands)*, **agudo** (thatch-roofed hut common in the lowlands), **agnet** (a sort of make-shift nomad tent, preferred by nomads), **gebaza** (round or rectangular dwelling made of sticks and branches) and **merebae** (brick house with corrugated iron sheet for a roof).

The Hidmo

Hidmos are made of wood, stone and clay. The main frame is constructed from thick tree trunks or branches and then filled in using smaller branches and clay. The roof is made up of layers of twigs and branches and reinforced with earth, supported by thick, dry-stone walls (sometimes up to 0.7m thick) and large tree trunks. An average sized hidmo uses 12 poles, six trans-beams. The method of construction is extremely resource-intensive and is a reflection of the once bounteous forests in this region. The size of a **hidmo** is determined by the owners' economic situation, and taste. Most have two rooms known as **midri-biet** and **wushate**, which are separated by eight to ten **koffotat** (cylindrical earthenware miniature silos for storing grain). While the midri-biet is used as a dining room, bedroom or dwelling-room, the wushate is partitioned in two parts. One is used as a kitchen and the other as a storeroom. The veranda known as gebela is used for relaxation during the day, and as a safe area for livestock during the night. There is no latrine inside the house, but on occasions a small latrine might be built inside the house to be used by a sick person, a bride or a mother with a newborn baby. Every hidmo also has a *gebela* (veranda).

The hidmo has two or three doors depending on its size. Windows, except for some narrow holes, are not common. In the wushate, a sort of chimney is built for both directing smoke and giving light. Usually, the door is fitted in such a way that it always opens to the right, even if the way the hidmo is constructed may become an obstacle for doing that. Most of the time, the hidmo is constructed in a manner that prevents direct sunlight from shining directly into the house.

The life span of a hidmo varies according to its location, the raw materials used in its construction, the style of construction and the frequency of maintenance. Most hidmos can keep intact for two generations or from 50 to 60 years. As for maintenance, while the beams, wooden colonnades, planks, etc. are taken care of when necessary, the roof is reinforced yearly with loose earth before the coming of the rains.

In the rooms one can find eight to ten cylindrical earthenware miniature silos, two raised platforms made of stone and clay which serve as beds, ovens, pottery, stone grinding mills, etc. Since there is always a difference in material possession between the poor and the rich, it is not rare to see that some rich farmers reinforce the roofs of their hidmos with cement and fix iron doors instead of the normal wooden doors. They might also use bricks or stone to construct some part of the walls and grain stores, which they would do by hiring professional masons.

The hidmo is traditionally the dwelling used by Tigrinya people. The name given to a Tigrinya community or hamlet is *Adi*. The preferred location for an Adi is at the foot of a hill or the top of a mountain in order to defend themselves from enemies (invaders), and avoid natural disasters and diseases (floods and malaria). The Saho ethnic group, who live in the highlands, also construct hidmos.

The Agudo (Tukul)

The construction of the agudo is similar amongst the Tigrinya, Saho, Tigre, Bilen, Kunama and Nara ethnic groups. For the construction of agudo, the raw materials used are timber, grass, tree barks, soil and stones. After identifying the site of construction, a circle is drawn on the ground using a stick and a rope. Once the circle is traced, digging starts for the foundation. Next the wall is built and is plastered with mud. Before starting the roof, the grass is soaked in water and the central column is erected. In some cases the agudo is constructed without a central column.

In highland Eritrea, after cutting the wood of the cactus tree into long and narrow strips, they are tied together with the soft grass and put over the roof. Owing to the circular shape of the building the roof is conical, though this is also true of the more modern square building design. Agudos may remain intact for about ten years. The highland agudo has one door and one window. In addition, it has two partitions, similar to the interior of the hidmo. The midri-biet and the wushate, again, are separated by cylindrical grain stores made of clay, known as koffo. Since the agudo is smaller in size than the hidmo, the koffos are accordingly fewer. The floor is reinforced and smoothened with a mixture of ash, dung and fine clay. There is a strong similarity between the agudo built in the highlands and those built by the Bilen ethnic group. The only difference is in the household goods, furniture and facilities used. For example, the inside walls of the Bilen agudo is draped with a mat known as *higag*. A curtain known as *aleget* is also used.

Among the Tigre ethnic group of Maria Tselam, two types of agudo are in use: the *resiet* built with wood, grass and ropes and the *tiket* made of stones, reeds, grass and ropes. In this community, men construct the risiet and tiket.

There is a great similarity in the way the Kunama and Nara build their houses. The houses resemble agudos but are different from those constructed in the highland in that the roofs and the walls of the Kunama and Nara agudos are not permanently fixed together. The roof, for example, is made to simply sit atop the cylindrical walls of the agudo just as one would put a lid on a pot.

The walls are made of wood or mud. Stone masonry is seldom used. The walls are buttressed with palm leaves and twigs so much so that the hut does not need any extra support from the inside. And during the rainy seasons, the house is generally sound.

The diameter of the agudo of the Kunama and Nara is usually between six and seven metres. These ethnic groups usually build three agudos, one for the owner, one for guests and one as a grain store. These tree agudos are often enclosed with fences of grass and bramble. In front of the agudo, a sort of veranda known as *togodat* is built, which is open on all sides so that it maintains constant temperature during both the cold and hot season.

The Agnet

The Agnet is a dwelling place of the Tigre, Hedareb and Rashaida ethnic groups. Agnet (a sort make-shift tent, preferred by nomads) is a temporary dwelling. The life span of an agnet is approximately one year. In some places, the agnet is also used among non-nomadic people. The agnet is a semi-circular hut without any particular door or formal entrance. The construction materials used to build agnets are: long dried branches, mats or quilts, ropes for keeping the mats or quilts stretched and pikes thrust into the ground to hold the structure firm.

Men are expected to prepare the building materials while the women do the construction work. Owing to the agnet's small size a man with more than one wife is obliged to construct more agnets. In the past, the agnet was draped with animal skins inside and outside, but with the introduction of a market economy, the demand for animal skins in factories increased and as a result the agnets had to be covered with mats and quilts instead. Depending on the relative wealth of the owner an agnet will be covered with anything between two to eight mats. Since the mats are light and full of holes for ventilation, nomads tend to prefer them to skins. It is also common to see modern blue plastic tarpaulin used to cover these structures. Partitions inside the agnet are made with mats or hides to separate the bedroom from the kitchen.

Because of the nature of their nomadic life the Hedareb ethnic group do not construct solid or permanent dwellings but are satisfied with agnets which can be easily dismantled and carried to other places. In fact, other than being light, the agnet is also well ventilated being made up of mats and light materials. This being the case, the Hedareb do not have problems with acquiring plots of land to build their houses on. They are always on the move, and whenever they feel like pitching their agnets they do so with little trouble. A Hedareb's agnet does not have a door or windows. To get inside one has to bend below the frame and almost crawl in.

The Gebaza

In the lowlands there are a number of different dwelling styles to suit the warmer temperatures, such as the agnet. Another common method of building is the Gebaza, made from wood and grass. The walls are constructed using upright sticks and occasionally lined with mud and dung. However, in the warmer areas, the walls are unlined to allow the breeze to pass through the building. Around Agordat and Barentu, where palm trees are plentiful, the walls and roofs will be made of palm leaves.

The Meadeni

Meadeni is a rectangular building and is made of wood with a column in the middle. It is a dwelling place of the Tigre and Saho ethnic groups. The houses in Hirgigo and Afabet are known as *meadeni*. There are special houses known as **Sendekat** which are characteristic of Hirgigo. A meadeni has two rooms, and in Afabet and its surroundings, one of them is used as a bedroom and the other as a guest room.

A meadeni has three windows and two doors. In Hirgigo, the doors are made to face east in order for the occupants to get brisk sea breeze during the hot season, and the latrine, an open ground in the middle of the meadeni is often situated behind the main room. When the waste is full, it is removed and used elsewhere. Some meadenis have their latrines dug in the open yard behind the main room, and as often as the holes are filled, they are covered with earth and new ones are dug nearby. In some communities an open field serves as a public latrine.

The life span of the meadeni is between five and ten years provided it is well maintained. The wooden houses of Massawa and Hirgigo are often eaten by termites and unless insecticide is used for their maintenance, they are certain to deteriorate early. One method used to prevent this type of attack is to dowse the base of the structure in kerosene.

The Merebae

At present in rural Eritrea, hidmos and agudos are being replaced by *merebaes*. Most of those who build merebaes are wealthy farmers, government employees and traders. They have the merabaes built with corrugated iron, stones, cement, wood, etc and hire professional masons. Such buildings are becoming more and more common as hamlets or small villages begin to assume a certain permanence as they begin to prosper. These rectangular buildings have less character than their earlier cousins, but are cheaper and quicker to build and easier to maintain.

Other styles

Further south, towards Assab, an entirely different style is used, closely resembling a beach hut from northern Europe. These buildings are made from wooden planks imported from the Middle East and are much more of a conventional style of wooden hut than the traditional dwellings. Nonetheless, the residents add their own style by painting these huts in all manner of different colours and patterns. This results in a very attractive array of coloured designs displayed throughout a village. The floors are usually unlined and therefore just sand. The roofs are made from corrugated iron.

History

There is not anywhere upon the globe a large tract of country which
we have discovered destitute of inhabitants, or where the first
populations can be fixed with any degree of historical certainty.

The History of the Decline and Fall of the Roman Empire,
Edward Gibbon

One of the earliest known references to the name Eritrea, derived from the
Greek word for red, is in *Fragment 67* of Aeschylus:

There the sacred waters of the Erythrean Sea break upon a bright red
strand, and at no great distance from the Ocean lies a copper-tinted
lake – the lake that is the jewel of Ethiopia – where the all-pervading
Sun returns again and again to plunge his immortal form, and finds
solace for his weary round in gentle ripples that are but a warm
caress.

It was not until the arrival of the Italians in the 19th century, however, that the
country was officially called Eritrea. The creation of the modern state was
contained in a decree of Umberto I, dated January 1 1890. It is no surprise that
in the context of trying to revive the greatness of the Roman era, an ancient
name was chosen. Before this it was not actually referred to as a distinct unit,
nor did it constitute one.

Despite the fact that its existence as a nation in its own right is fairly recent,
it is easier to refer to Eritrea than the continually changing kingdoms and
provinces within its present-day boundaries. Eritrea has for thousands of years
been a home for people of diverse living patterns, religions and traditions.
After the South Arabian immigrations in the first millennium BC, Eritrea and
much of Tigray were known as the Kingdom of the Habeshat. From the 3rd
to the 7th centuries AD much of the present-day territory lay within the
Axumite Kingdom. From the 11th to the 15th centuries it often appears as
Maekele Bahr and from the 16th century onwards Medr Bahr, deriving from
the ancient Ge'ez meaning 'land of the sea'. The different provinces were
usually known by the same name as their indigenous tribes. The western
lowlands were Midre Beja, the eastern escarpment Midre Saho, and Hamasien
referred to the region around the present-day capital Asmara. South of the
Mareb river was known as Mareb Mellash ('beyond the Mareb'). Maps from
the 15th and 16th centuries also refer to the region of Barnagasso, 'the land of

the Bahr Negash', the overlord from Abyssinia who exacted tribute from such parts of Eritrea as he was able. Even in 1816, the British traveller Henry Salt published maps of his *Voyage to Abyssinia* and mentions only provincial names: Hamazen, Debarua, Bisan, Massawa and Serae.

THE FIRST INHABITANTS

Archaeological sources date back as far as the 8th millennium BC. Microlithic tools found in the Tigray highlands and the Barka Valley are evidence of a 'stone age' in the 8th and 7th millennia BC. Animals such as cattle were bred along the Sudanese border in the 4th and 3rd millennia and by the 2nd millennium the Barka Valley was clearly inhabited by a nomadic and semi-nomadic indigenous population. Rock paintings from this period near Karora on the northern border with Sudan, and in Akele Guzai in the south, depict short-horned and humpless cattle and anthropomorphic figures.

The earliest inhabitants, according to the Italian historian Conti Rossini, were of the Pygmoid type. Nilotic people arrived from the middle course of the Nile; the Kushitic element of the population arrived with subsequent waves of Hamitic stock, and were forerunners of the Beja people. From 1000 to 400BC, the southern Arabian tribes introduced the Semitic element, settling in the highlands and in Tigray. It is very difficult to classify the present-day population by reference to these early arrivals, or by reference to linguistic groups, but broadly their origins are as follows:

Nilotic	Nara
	Kunama
Kushitic	Beja (mainly Beni Amer and Hidareb)
	Bilen
	Afar
	Saho
Semitic	Tigrinya (mainly in the highlands)
	Tigre

In addition, among the groups of recent Arab origin to have arrived are the Rashaida, settled on the coast. Conti Rossini rightly concluded: '*L'Abissinia e un museo di popoli*'.

PRE-AXUMITE CULTURE

There are two main periods: the South Arabian or Sabean period (1000 to 400BC), and the interrnediary period (300BC to 100AD). Little is known about the latter.

Sabean period

The most concentrated migrations occurred in the 7th to 5th centuries BC. For some time after their arrival these tribes may have remained under the authority of the Kings of Saba, on the Arabian Peninsula, for whom the local *negasi* (prince) acted as tax collector. With the decline of the Saba kings, the migrants and the indigenous populations became more independent and the negasi became the actual rulers, the Neguse Negast emerging as their overall leader.

Development in this period is evidenced by irrigation schemes, dams and terracing. Rectangular, stone-walled and roofed houses were used. The Mukarrib system was the basis of government and the main gods of the Arabian pantheon came with the migrants (Asthar, Almougah and Sharns). Their semitic language probably evolved into Ge'ez, from which Tigrinya and Amharic derive.

AXUMITE KINGDOM

Archaeological surveys show the kingdom of Axum as 'a vertical rectangle about 300km long and 160km wide, between about 13° and 17° north and 38° and 40° east', according to Anfray (*Les Anciens Ethiopiens*). The kingdom rose to prominence in the 3rd century AD, after it had been unified, and expeditions were sent as far as South Arabia and the Nile Valley. The first apogee was in the 4th century with the official introduction of Christianity and the evolution of Ge'ez, the development of a distinct architectural style, and the conquest of Meroe, probably by the king Ezana.

The second apogee was in the 5th and 6th centuries, but between these two periods, after the rule of Ezana, there is a long period shrouded in obscurity until the rise of Kalieb in the 6th century. Two of the significant events in this second period were the arrival of Syrian missionaries who made a major contribution to the church, which at this time translated the Bible into Ge'ez, and the Nagran expedition (to present-day Yemen) in about AD525, in defence of Christians. These enhanced the prestige of the Axumite kingdom, as did its presence as a major trading centre attracting Greeks, Egyptians and others.

The decline started in the second half of the 6th century. The historian Vasiliev describes the reign of Kalieb as 'the last brilliant page of Axum'. A combination of factors may have led to this decline: the Persian conquest of Yemen, Arabia and even some ports on the African shore; the rise of the Arab state, united under Islam; the eclipse of Adulis (it is possible that the port silted up; it was certainly sacked by the Arabs in AD640 and 703); and the occupation of the Dahlak islands by Arabs, an important event as it gave them control of the former trade routes into Adulis.

BEJA AND ISLAM: AD700-1300

Although the successors of the great Axumite kings were still minting coins in the mid 8th century, by the end of the 9th century they were overrun by the Agaws. As a result no Abyssinian king ruled the Eritrean plateau again for any length of time until the Solomonic kings. The coastal region fell increasingly under the influence of the Middle East, while the Beja migrated into Eritrea from the north.

The Beja are mentioned in Axumite sources as the target of, in particular, Ezana's military campaigns. Even earlier references are found in *Monumentum Adulatum*, dated to the 3rd century. They were a Kushitic people, settled between Aswan and northwestern Eritrea. The Zenafidj people, under

AXUM

Axum as a kingdom, rather than the city, is first mentioned in the *Periplus of the Erythrean Sea*. Current research dates this to the early 3rd century AD; it is interesting that it cites an earlier lost work by Marinus of Tyre. Zoscales, the ruler of the time, is also mentioned. Before this there are mentions of Adulis, the principal Axumite port (in Pliny the Elder's *Natural History*), and references to Axum, Koloe and Maste are found (in Claudius Ptolemy's *Geography* of the 2nd century AD). An inscription on a metal object found in Adi Galamo, belonging to the 2nd century, is the first actual Axumite source. Axum's importance is attested to by various mentions of it as being ranked third among the great powers of the world.

Islamic expansion in Eritrea remained limited in this period. The main converts were the Dahlak islanders in the 8th century, after which an independent kingdom of some size rose to prominence in the islands. Massawa was also inhabited by Muslims from the early 10th century; in the late 14th century it became part of the kingdom of the Dahlaks as well. The famous water cisterns and Kufic inscriptions found on Dahlak date from about the 13th century. The cisterns can still be visited in situ today; many of the Kufic inscriptions are in the National Museum in Asmara.

Throughout the 10th–14th centuries other migrants were also arriving in Eritrea. The Saho spread north and inland from the area south of Irafale Bay, leaving various sub-tribes behind them such as the Assaworta, the Irob (Christian Saho), Debra Mela and Haso Tor'a. In addition Agaw peoples arrived in the Anseba Valley in the second half of the 10th century.

pressure from a more northerly Hedareb Beja tribe and the early Arab settlements, began the expansion into Eritrea. It appears from Al Ya'qubi's account of this period and other sources to have encompassed the whole coast north of Arkiko, Sahel, the Barka and Anseba valleys and most of the highlands. They established five kingdoms: Nagic, Baklin, Bazen, Kata'a and Giarin. There are still traces of this migration in local traditions, for example the Begathay of Bilen, the Dina Fana of the Hamasien highlands and certain Sahelian traditions.

PRESOLOMONIC AND SOLOMONIC PERIOD

As far as the Abyssinians were concerned, after the decline of Axum, the northern part of their former kingdom was subject to completely different influences, principally the Beja inland and the Arabs on the coast. But their designs on the Red Sea as an outlet for trade never waned, and various attempts were made to regain influence in the region under the Presolomonic and Solomonic kings.

The Agaw established the Zagwe dynasty, which claimed descent from Moses, and which ruled in Abyssinia from 1135–1270. They established a power base at Debre Libanos, south of Senafe, as a foothold for further expansion in the Eritrean highlands. But it appears that their efforts were fairly fruitless, and Abyssinia was often in a state of disunity itself. The Italian historian Rossini wrote,

> the extension of the Abyssinian kingdom at the time of Zagwe...must have been fairly limited: Tigray, Lasta, Begemder or even only part of it, Amhara and probably the northern districts of Shewa. In the north, Dahlak had a king of its own. The Abyssinian Eritrean highlands were still inhabited by mainly Beja populations, checked by the Bilen and other populations migrating from Abyssinia.

The last Zagwe king was killed in 1270 by Yikuno Amlak, an Abyssinian who claimed descent from Solomon and Sheba and who founded the Solomonic dynasty.

The Solomonic kings from Amdezion (1314–44) onwards sporadically put in more determined efforts at annexation of the region. Amdezion's opportunity came in about 1325 with an autonomist rebellion in Tigray. There is evidence that after this he moved his army as far as the Red Sea and appointed an overlord with authority from Tigray to the seaboard. Due to internal dissension it does not appear that Amdezion's immediate successors followed up on this expansion.

There was another attempt at colonisation under Zera Yaeqob (1434–68) with the settlement of military posts on the Eritrean plateau and the grouping of the provinces of Shire, Seraye, Hamasien and Akele Guzai in one region under the Bahr Negasi. A port was also built at Gerar.

From the 15th century date the first associations of the kingdom of Abyssinia with the legend of Prester John:

> the name given in the middle ages to an alleged priest and king, originally supposed to reign in the extreme Orient...but from the 15th century generally identified with the king of Ethiopia or Abyssinia

Oxford Companion to English Literature

and an all-powerful kingdom in the interior; mention was made of this by Venetian and Genoese mapmakers. In the 16th century the Portuguese Alvares' book was called *The Prester John of the Indies: A true relation of the lands of Prester John, being the narrative of the Portuguese Embassy to Ethiopia in 1520.* Despite such a legend, Abyssinian influence on the Eritrean regions between the decline of Axum and the arrival of the Turks was only strong when there was a powerful ruler. This influence was also virtually limited to the highlands and was only for short periods. The area was sometimes a tributary but was not integrated in any wider sense into an Abyssinian sphere of influence. It is equally dubious to consider that Eritrea itself had any semblance of being a unified political entity in this precolonial period.

THE ARRIVAL OF THE TURKS

The 16th century is marked by continual attempts by the Turks to extend their influence from the Eritrean coast. The degree of success waxed and waned according to the strength of Abyssinian and other kingdoms further south. By the time of the arrival of Francisco Alvares, chaplain of the first Portuguese mission to Ethiopia (1520–26), the Turks already controlled Massawa and most of the important islands as far north as Suakin. Their presence on the coast dated from 1517, and was facilitated by the invasion of Abyssinia by the Gragns, ferociously led by Imam Ahmed Musa, also known as Ahmed Gragn (Ahmed the Left Handed), the Sultan of Harar; but their ambitions were initially thwarted when Gragn went on to conquer Seraye in 1535, and later the provinces of Hamasien and Akele Guzai.

In 1543, a combined army of Portuguese, Tigrayan and imperial troops, led by Emperor Claudius of Abyssinia, defeated Gragn and killed him. Although the Turks returned to Massawa and made Debarua, south of Asmara, their capital, they were again ousted when Claudius sent an army north under Yeshaq, who defeated them and repossessed Massawa and Arkiko.

The Turks did not give up, and returned to Massawa in 1560, coinciding with a rebellion against Emperor Minas (1559–63). Ironically, the rebellion was led by Yeshaq – loyal to the previous emperor, but not to Minas; he was defeated on the plain of Wagara in July 1561, and fled to join the Turkish leader, Zemur Pasha.

In 1562, Yeshaq was defeated once more by Minas but the emperor died soon after, and for the next 15 years the Turks were left in control of much of Eritrea in alliance with Yeshaq, now overlord or 'Bahr Negash' of former Abyssinian territories in Eritrea. In 1577, Emperor Sarsa Dengel Malak Sagad I (1563–97), after being distracted for many years with problems elsewhere in the Abyssinian kingdom, turned his attention north. In November 1578 he defeated Yeshaq and the Turks near Debarua. Both Yeshaq and the Pasha were beheaded. This did not, however, end Turkish occupation of the coast, and in 1589 they attacked the army of the governor of Tigray, reoccupying Debarua. Sarsa Dengel retaliated by marching north and routing the Turks, who retreated again to Arkiko. He then marched against Wolde Ezum, a local chief, and killed him. The Turkish Pasha agreed to peace but the Turks were to remain as an effective power on the coast for the next three centuries.

Despite the Turkish presence and that of rebellious Bahr Negashes, the 16th century did witness some major changes in the relationship between the Abyssinian kingdom and the provinces that make up today's Eritrea. The *enda* emerged as a unit of residence and political loyalty and was in some ways a primitive form of democracy, although the overall nature of Abyssinian power was to remain predominantly feudal. As an example of the latter, the *gulti* system of granting land to loyal retainers was increasingly used after the Abyssinian emperors moved their capital to Gondar. Being closer to Eritrea they began to reward Eritrean friends with land and gradually other more feudal power structures replaced the *endas*. The historian Longrigg says of this period:

The events of the 16th century had brought the monarchy, and all the patronage and privileges within its gift, closer to far-off Eritrea; military garrisons appeared more regularly, lands were allotted to them, more royal officials were seen at work and their favour sought by local aspirants to greatness.

Nevertheless the demise of the role of the Bahr Negash, once the third highest position of authority in the Abyssinian Empire, is indicative of the inability of the emperors to establish any lasting control.

17TH-CENTURY MIGRATIONS

With the establishment of some sort of status quo in Eritrea between the Turks and Abyssinians, further migrations also took place. During the 17th century most of Semhar came to be ruled by the Belu although technically they were Naibs, or deputies, to the Turks. The tribes of Semhar witnessed continuous change, with the arrival of refugees from the Galla invasions in territory that is now in southern Ethiopia, and of Somalis, and Arab and African traders. But the Turks held the reins in this coastal region, and continued to interfere with Abyssinian trade, hence the increased Abyssinian interest in alternative ports like Beilul, just north of Assab, which was no more than a village at the time. Such alternatives never came to anything as the ports were too far from population centres, and may well have been as difficult to exert and retain control over as Massawa.

In the Keren region more Bilen arrived from the south during the 17th century, again as a result of Galla expansion in the south which was pushing migrants into the coastal Semhar region. There was also continual migration from Tigray into Senhit and Sahel. In the west the Beni Amer fell under the Funj dynasty of Sudan. Such continuous change makes it easier to understand why the Bahr Negash, whose power had largely been eclipsed anyway after the Solomonic era, never extended his authority into Beni Amer territory, the Barka Valley north of Agordat being its centre. Further west the Kunama and Baria were settled in the Gash-Setit Valley and were constantly harassed by invaders and slave traders, but they were not subject to any permanent outside authority.

TIGRAY IN THE 18TH CENTURY

Abyssinian influence in Eritrea remained patchy in the 18th century, superseded by Tigray. The Gondar-based empire of Fasil and Iyasu was a thing of the past, Iyasu having died in 1706. Abyssinian emperors in the 18th century were usually weak. James Bruce, a British traveller in Abyssinia at this time, described the continual intrigues at court which eventually led him to leave in disgust. Local princes (*rases*) were the key men with power. Ras Mikael Suhul of Tigray (c1735–80) was the undisputed ruler of Tigray and the Eritrean highlands for most of the century. After Ras Mikael, Wolde Selassie ruled the same area until his death in 1816. Tigrayan overlordship in the Eritrean highlands thus continued unbroken for some

80 years. Like Ras Mikael, Wolde Selassie was a powerful figure at court, particularly championing Abyssinian Christianity against Galla influence. There was an ever-increasing rivalry between the southern, Galla-influenced Shoa and the Tigrayan northerners. In 1807 Wolde Selassie actually had to defend Tigray, successfully, against attack from the Galla leader Gugsa.

19TH CENTURY: EGYPTIANS, BRITISH, FRENCH AND ITALIANS

By the middle of the 19th century there was a new threat to the region – Egypt. Ali Pasha invaded Sudan in 1820, and in the next decade he edged closer and closer to the western lowlands of Eritrea. In 1840 he built a fort at Kassala, occupied Metemma within Ethiopia and threatened Gondar. By 1850 his successors had claimed the western lowlands and had obvious designs on Bogos, the area around Keren. In 1853 the Bilen were attacked there and the whole area was conquered with the help of the Beni Amer. On the coast Ali Pasha also secured a foothold by obtaining a lease on Massawa from 1846–49.

Dedjazmatch Wubie, the current overlord in the highlands, countered any Egyptian attempts to move further inland from Massawa, but the ferocity of his raids in the territory he was trying to defend actually had the effect of alienating him from the population in the north and west, ultimately facilitating much greater Egyptian influence.

European involvement remained small in the first half of the 19th century but grew with the rise of Tewodros and Neguse in Abyssinia. The British opened their consulate in Massawa in 1849, the year that Ali Pasha died, and the Turks consequently repossessed the port. The French were already there. The Italians had also arrived in Eritrea, in the shape of Catholic missionaries in the Keren area, the most famous being Abuna Yacob. But it was two British envoys who played a particularly important role in the politics of the area in the middle of the century. John T Bell and Walter C Plowden arrived in Abyssinia from Egypt, Bell becoming an adviser to Ras Ali of Gondar. Later they both became advisers to Emperor Tewodros II (1855–68); both died in 1860. The importance of their five years as advisers is that they coincided with Tewodros, almost succeeding in reunifying the old Abyssinian Empire. The influence of Bell and Plowden secured British support for the emperor in his fight against the rebel leader, Neguse (supported by the French), whom he defeated in Tigray in 1860.

That the reunification attempt faltered was partly due to Tewodros' cruelty and ruthlessness: in his last years Tigray and Shoa broke away. In 1866 a rebel from Lasta, Gobazie, conquered Tigray and chose Ras Kassa as its ruler; by 1867 he had joined the opposition to the emperor and unified Tigray under his banner. In 1868 General Sir Robert Napier landed at Zula, south of Massawa, and marched inland to Magdala in Ethiopia, with the open support of Gobazie and Ras Kassa. His mission was to release the British Consul, Charles Cameron, and a number of missionaries of various nationalities held prisoner by Tewodros as retribution for receiving no reply to a letter to Queen Victoria, in which he had requested her assistance against the Turks. Following Tewodros' defeat by Napier, Ras Kassa got most of the arms from his camp, while Gobazie secured the throne and was crowned Takla Giorgis II. His reign was short, as he was himself defeated by Ras Kassa, at Axum, in 1871. Ras Kassa was then crowned Yohannes IV (1872–89).

As far as Abyssinia was concerned the Egyptian expansion became more serious under Khedive Ismail Pasha, the viceroy of Egypt from 1863. His predecessor Khedive Sa'id had been rather more moderate. By 1875 Egypt had pushed south from Suakin on the Red Sea coast, occupying much of the territory between there and Berbera in present day Somalia. In October they occupied Harar, and later a force from Massawa reached the Mareb, threatening the emperor.

Emperor Yohannes was now encircled. He found himself unable to enlist any European support and was forced to rely solely on his foremost general, Ras Alula. Their first encounter with the Egyptians was at Ghundet, south of Adi Qala and today a border post, where they outmanoeuvred the Egyptians and secured a total victory. The Khedive then sent a second army led by his son Hassan Pasha and an American, Colonel Loring. They landed at Massawa in December 1875 and marched to Gura, near Decemhare. Yohannes mustered 70,000 men and the support of the people and won this second battle as well, killing more than 4,000 of the enemy and taking Hassan Pasha prisoner. The battle of Gura marked the end of Egyptian interference with Abyssinian territory, although they remained on the coast and as overlords of Bogos (Keren). Following the victory at Gura, Ras Alula was made the new governor of Hamasien province and *Koraj* (prince) of Eritrea.

In 1879 the Khedive was deposed and succeeded by Khedive Tewfik, who sent General Gordon to Abyssinia to make peace. Yohannes demanded the return of Bogos and Senhit, control of the Denkalia coast and £2 million, which left Gordon speechless, but the demands were not pursued militarily.

ECLIPSE OF EGYPT

In May 1881 the rule of Egypt, now a British Protectorate, was overthrown in Sudan by the Mahdi. In 1884 Khartoum was besieged, and Egyptian garrisons on the Sudanese coast were under attack. Admiral Sir William Hewett negotiated a treaty with Yohannes. Ethiopian soldiers were to help evacuate Egyptian garrisons in the interior of Sudan in return for the stores and arms therein. In addition Bogos was to be returned to Abyssinia and the emperor was to be allowed free transit of goods at Massawa, also now under British protection. Ras Alula kept the Ethiopian side of the bargain (the British didn't), relieving Gallabat and Khartoum. In June 1885 the Mahdi died, following the murder six months earlier of Gordon. His successor was Khalifa Abduhalli, who retook Kassala and then threatened western Eritrea. The Gash Delta was occupied and his Dervishes went on the rampage, leading all those potentially in his path to seek refuge with the latest arrivals in Eritrea – the Italians.

WERNER MUNZINGER

One of the more colourful figures involved in the growing conflict between Egypt and Abyssinia was Werner Munzinger, a Swiss adventurer. He had arrived in Massawa in 1854 and sometimes acted as French consular agent. He moved to Keren in 1855, married one or more Bilen and learnt Tigre and Arabic. In 1865, he was back in Massawa, this time as a British agent and political adviser during the Napier expedition. In 1871 he became governor of Massawa and improved the region, for example building the two causeways which link the islands with the mainland. But during his time in Massawa, Munzinger still harboured a keen interest in Keren, his former home. He occupied the town in June 1872, fortified the fort of Senhit and declared the territory Egyptian. After buying land inland from Massawa, he planned to lay a telegraph line between Massawa, Keren and Kassala. His buccaneering career ended when he was leading Egyptian forces across the Danakil to take charge of the Egyptian eastern campaign; he was murdered by Danakil warriors (or, some say, by jealous Egyptians).

THE ITALIANS (1885–1941)

The Italians were the last of the European powers to join in what has become known as the 'Scramble for Africa'. This intensified following the completion of the Suez Canal in 1869. Great Britain had already secured Aden as a Red Sea base in 1839, controlling Egypt by 1882 and the eastern coastline to Zeila and Berbera, in present-day Somalia. The French had established a foothold in Djibouti. Among the first Italians was Fr Giuseppe Sapeto who had established a mission at Adua in 1840, and later one at Keren. He was also the main negotiator for the Italian government in its purchase, for 8,100 Maria Theresa dollars, of a tract of land near Assab (then a small village) on behalf of the Società di Navigazione Rubattino (see page 155) in November 1869. No doubt he had also been the prime source of information for the government in deciding the merits of a foothold in Eritrea. Further land was bought from the Sultan of Rahaita in 1879 and 1880, and in 1882 the Italian government purchased all the land from the shipping company and began to administer Assab directly, moving a garrison there. From these small beginnings they were to leave a lasting impression on Eritrea, indeed one that has lasted much longer than their colonial presence.

The opportunity for seizing more land appeared to improve with the Mahdist uprising which severely weakened Egypt. Following the Hewett Treaty of 1884 it appeared that Abyssinia might pre-empt Italian designs on former Egyptian territories on their northern boundaries and they made strenuous diplomatic efforts in London to enlist British support for their own cause. However, the British were largely indifferent to the fate of this land, apparently in contravention of the treaty, and even encouraged the Italians to take Massawa at the same time in order to avert a return of the port to Turkish rule. The British also saw Italy as a potential buffer against the French presence in Djibouti. A letter by Sir Gerald Portal, written in 1891, illustrates British thinking at the time: 'It is enough to say that the Egyptians wished to evacuate the place (Massawa); the Sultan of Turkey, to whom it would naturally revert, was not prepared to take over charge of it; the English did not want it; and the Italians stepped in.'

On February 5 1885 Admirale Caimi duly landed at Massawa and the Egyptian governor yielded to him. By November Generale Gene had taken full control of the port, ordered the Egyptians out and started actively to recruit local *askaris* (soldiers). The Naib accepted the new arrivals, as did the local Saho people. The Habib of Sahel and some Beni Amer tribes actually approached the Italians for protection against the twin threats of the Dervishes and Abyssinian counter-attacks. They were also joined by some chiefs in Hamasien and Akele Guzai provinces who were engaging in their own private quarrels with Ras Alula, Emperor Yohannes' governor of Hamasien.

Back in Abyssinia, Yohannes was surprised and annoyed with the British for encouraging these new entrants to the scene, in contravention of the Hewett Treaty, and he encouraged Ras Alula to attack any chiefs who sided with the Italians. His fears about Italian intentions increased markedly when in September 1886 the Italians marched inland from Massawa and occupied Sa'ati. This prompted Ras Alula to surround the expeditionary force in January 1887, and massacre a relief battalion at Dogali. The Italians withdrew. General Portal tried to negotiate with Yohannes for a peaceful settlement and to persuade him to accept Ghinda, inland from Massawa, as the Ethiopian border. Yohannes found this unacceptable, rightly assuming (as it turned out) that if given an inch the Italians would take a mile. He even tried appealing, unsuccessfully, to Queen Victoria.

In 1888 Generale San Marzano arrived in Massawa. Like his predecessor he marched inland and retook Sa'ati, building a rail link from there to the port. Yohannes mustered a large army (some 80,000 men) to meet San Marzano, relations between Abyssinia and the Italians having deteriorated further when the latter demanded Ailet, Ghinda and all of the coastal lowlands. The Dervish threat from Sudan, however, meant that Yohannes had to divert his army to face them, and the Italians realised that, as long as the Dervishes were providing another source of danger to the emperor, they were in a strong position. They were indirectly assisted by Menelik, the general upon whom Yohannes had depended to stop the Dervishes at Begemder, but who was himself negotiating with the Italian Count Antonelli for arms, and was therefore rather half-hearted in his attempts to help the emperor.

In 1889, therefore, Yohannes was in a quandary. He faced problems with Menelik, the Italians and the Dervishes. Where to turn first? Whichever way he turned the other two protagonists were liable to take advantage of his decision. In the end, he moved first against the Dervishes and was captured and killed on the verge of victory at Gallabat. Italian diplomatic efforts then supported Menelik in his claim to be Yohannes' successor (he had supposedly been promised the title some ten years earlier), rather than Ras Mangasha who had been declared the deathbed successor. The fact that Yohannes's ally Ras Alula had also withdrawn to Tigray on the emperor's death enabled the Italians to push inland to Keren with the help of various local chiefs. Their flag was raised there by Balambras Kafel, Ras Alula's bitter enemy, in July 1889. An Italian garrison arrived a year later, and on August 3 1889 they took Asmara and pushed on along the Mareb and Belesa rivers.

Menelik had taken the throne in March 1889, by which time he was virtually accepting the Italian presence north of the Mareb as a *fait accompli*. In May he signed, with Count Antonelli, the Treaty of Uccialli. Article 3 stated: 'The line of the plateau will mark out the Ethiopian-Italian boundaries. To begin from Arafali-Halai, Segeneiti and Asmara will be the three villages of the Italian boundaries. Addi Nefas (northeast of Asmara) and Addi Yohannes (west of Asmara) on the part of the Bogos (Keren) will be within the Italian boundaries. From Addi Yohannes a straight line extended from east to west will trace the Italian Ethiopian boundaries'. In other words, most of Akele Guzai and Seraye were in Ethiopia, and most of Hamasien, Senhit and Semhar were in Italian hands. In October 1889 the Ethiopian Ras Makkonen was sent to Rome to put the treaty into effect. A dispute arose over Article 17 and whether it, in effect, made Ethiopia an Italian Protectorate. Emperor Menelik had signed an Amharic version which he did not consider stated this and in February 1893 he renounced the treaty altogether.

In 1889 the Italians took Adua and Mekalle, both well within Abyssinia's borders, on the pretext of supporting Emperor Menelik against Ras Mangasha in Tigray. In December 1891 Ras Mangasha met secretly with Generale Gondolfi, the governor of Eritrea, and signed a treaty giving Italy more land in southern Eritrea. After this Italy finally abandoned Menelik, although the break was not entirely clear-cut as this period was characterised by internal Italian differences of opinion between the local commanders and the government and its envoys. It was not unknown for them to be scheming against each other. Each new government at home would proclaim a new policy for the colony, thus weakening its authority and the efficacy of its governors. In 1891 Senator Borgnini was sent to review the situation.

In the same year Britain and Italy signed a treaty for the Sudanese Eritrean border which allowed them both to chase each other's enemies across those borders. In effect this gave the Italians a good opportunity to stake their claim on territory in west and north Eritrea that had hitherto not been under their control. After many skirmishes with the Dervishes, Generale Baratieri did indeed lead his forces across the border to Kassala in early 1894. By this time they were again looking closely at Tigray which they intended either to annex peacefully or through cooperation with Ras Mangasha. But the inconsistency of their negotiations with both Mangasha and Yohannes in previous years had by now forced those two into the same camp (Mangasha had made his peace with the Emperor Menelik, unbeknown to the Italians, in May 1893); they had publicly supported Menelik while negotiating with his vassal, and intrigued with Mangasha while refusing him the arms he needed to challenge the emperor. In 1894, when Bahta Hagos of Akele Guzai seized the Italian residence at Segeneiti, south of Asmara, the Italians rightly suspected the hand of Abyssinia.

Partly as a result of this incursion, Generale Baratieri moved once more into Adua, in Tigray, in December 1894. He defeated Mangasha and then announced the annexation of both Adua and Axum. He also occupied Adigrat and Mekalle. This culminated in one of the biggest battles in African history, a battle that was to leave scars on the Italian army for the next 40 years: the battle of Adua. Although the numbers are, as ever, not verifiable, the Abyssinian army which routed the Italians was probably some 73,000 strong. The Italians fielded a force of about 27,000. All the great Abyssinian leaders came together under the emperor – Rases Mikael, Mangasha, Alula, Wolie and Makkonen. After the defeat, Generale Baldiserra evacuated Adi Keih and Segeneiti and prepared to defend Ghinda, inland from Massawa, but Menelik did not press his advantage. Why he didn't is the subject of much debate. It may have been that he was prudent enough not to overplay his hand, especially when his supply lines were already stretched. It was also difficult to keep the rases together in the field for any length of time, Abyssinian casualties were high and Tigray was not favourably disposed to having such a huge army on its soil. The decision was a correct one since, one month after Adua, 40,000 Italian reinforcements arrived at Massawa with 60 cannon. Menelik therefore signed a peace treaty with the Italians, the independence of Eritrea was reaffirmed and the boundary put at the Mareb-Belesa-Muna river line.

The building of a colony

Italy then set about building a colony. The first civilian governor, Signor Martini, was appointed in 1898. The principal aims were to secure power, to develop the colony with Italian immigrants, to develop the natural resources to the advantage of Italy and to equip it as a base for further expansion in the area when the opportunity arose.

By 1910 Eritrea had its present provincial shape, following boundary agreements with the Sudan (1901) and Ethiopia for Gash-Setit (1907) and the partition of the Danakil (1908). Initially they relied for administration on local chiefs but this form of indirect rule was not regarded as a success, the Italians doubting the loyalty of these chiefs, and therefore a new provincial structure was formed: Hamasien, Bassopiano Orientale (Massawa, Semhar, Dahlak, Denkalia and Ghinda), Akele Guzai, Serae, Keren (including Nacfa) and Bassopiano Occidentale (Tessenei, Barentu and Agordat). An elaborate Italian hierarchy was established under the governor, who until 1900 ruled from Massawa (although by 1899 most government offices were in Asmara).

The Italian colonial era can be divided into three phases: conquest, with its consequential expropriation of land (1885–96); consolidation (1896 to the late 1920s); and the fascist period (1922–41). After conquest was completed the economy certainly remained much the same, based on agriculture and pastoral forms of production. The Italians concentrated on demographic colonisation and commercial and political consolidation. They also sought raw materials and markets for industries at home. This strategy was actively pursued by Martini who was the most influential of the colonial governors. From 1912 onwards the authorities also actively started to recruit soldiers as part of the process of making Eritrea a base for its wider geographical aspirations. There was therefore a readiness to invest more in Eritrea than was often the norm for European colonial powers in Africa and elsewhere. Imports always exceeded exports and there was massive state subsidisation. The emphasis on social stability, however, served largely to freeze social relationships. Eritreans were never treated as equals and there was no emergence of a petty bourgeoisie, although it was not until the fascist era that active discrimination was practised.

The most extensive period of land expropriations ended in 1909 by which time much of the *kebessa* (highland) land was in Italian hands. After the turn of the century attention also turned to granting private agricultural concessions in the lowlands, around Keren and along the eastern escarpment.

The most important projects undertaken in the economy after the land expropriations were the construction of a large state-sponsored irrigation project in Tessenei (begun in 1923), and the building of the railway, which reached Asmara in 1909 and Keren in 1922. The Agordat-Keren stretch was completed in 1920. The construction of primary and secondary roads was also a priority, as was the rebuilding of Massawa following the earthquake of 1921. On the agricultural front, cotton growing around Tessenei began after the irrigation works were completed in 1927. Citrus and sisal production began in Bahri Medri and Keren, as did salt production at Assab and the mining of potash in Denkalia.

After the fascists took power in Italy in 1922, a period of even more ambitious development began. *Pax Italiana* had brought with it a surge in the Italian population (from 330,000 in 1900 to 760,000 in 1941), putting increased pressure on the availability of land for Eritreans. Thus, coinciding with increased fascist intervention, more and more Eritreans were forced to seek alternative means of subsisting, often conveniently provided by the army. It is worth noting that there was continual small-scale resistance from Eritreans to their subjugation. Nevertheless, a total of some 60,000 Eritreans served in the Libyan campaigns of 1911–32, also working on infrastructure projects.

The Fascist years

In 1934 a decade of enormous expansion in the economy and Eritrean society began. By 1929 Massawa had become the largest port on the east coast of Africa. In 1934 the road network was expanded and military recruitment increased once again. In January 1935 Generale de Bono arrived and recruited 50,000 Italians (the overall population was still less than 700,000) to rebuild the roads to the Ethiopian border and to build an aerial tramway from Massawa to Asmara to augment the supply route (the largest of its kind in the world, later dismantled by the British).

In May 1935 Italy defeated Abyssinia. By 1937 Eritrea was the centre of a regional transport network that employed some 100,000 people. In 1938 the road linking Assab to Addis Ababa was completed. As a result of all the state contracts being undertaken Asmara had grown from a city of 3,500 European inhabitants in 1934 to 55,000 by 1940. By the mid 1930s, 20% of Eritreans lived in urban centres, their number in Asmara growing from 15,000 to 120,000 in 1934–41. Only with the defeat of Italy in Eritrea by the British in 1941 did the artificial nature of such a boom become apparent.

Italian defeat

In 1941 Italy had some 300,000 soldiers in East Africa, 200 aircraft and many tanks. In July 1940 they attacked Kassala and Gallabat in the west, but did not press on further for fear of overstretching their supply lines. It is also likely that they considerably overestimated British strength. By September the British had reinforced and started to push the Italians back into Eritrea. The latter withdrew from Tessenei in January 1941. General Platt, commanding the British forces, moved his army up to Agordat, capturing it on February 1, and Fort Dologorodoc, further east, on March 16. On March 27 he entered the plain of Keren and the Italian commander Generale Lorenzini was killed. The Italians withdrew to a last line of defence at Adi Teclesan, on the Asmara-Keren road, but were defeated. Asmara surrendered on April 1 1941.

The speed of British success against such high odds surprised them and meant that they were faced with huge problems. Eritrea was run by demoralised Italians and the British were wholly undermanned for the task of taking over the running of the economy. It was therefore largely left to Italian officials, the police being the only department subject to wholesale change. There were great dangers associated with this reliance but there was no real choice and the British took on a 'care and maintenance' programme. Some substantial changes took place however – officials were instructed not to enforce the colour bar operated by the Italians, Eritreans started to be trained for the civil service and in 1943 the first teacher-training institution was established, there having been only 24 public primary schools in the fascist period and no secondary education.

Such changes aside, it is not true to say that the British, however awesome the task, fostered democracy, education and social progress, and their inability or unwillingness to do so was compounded by the depression which inevitably followed the fascist boom. After the Italian defeat the state-subsidised economy virtually collapsed, with far greater ramifications for the Eritreans than for Italians. As previously mentioned, the British Military Administration (BMA) continued to employ Italian officials, paid social security payments to Italians and encouraged entrepreneurs to develop import substitution industries (food processing, glass and shoe manufacture) and agricultural estates. This created a second mini-boom until 1944, while the area was still of strategic importance for the Allies' North Africa campaign. In addition, while Arabia remained cut off from Europe there was a ready-made marketplace. Many of the historically 'household' names in Eritrean industry date from this period although eventually most were emasculated during the Ethiopian occupation. Among them were the Maderni match factory, the Sava glassworks, the Melotti brewery, the Tabacchi cement factory and the Da

Nadai agricultural estates. But this development was more limited than that which took place under the fascists and was largely facilitated by the vast build-up of raw materials in the country by the Italians prior to the outbreak of World War II.

When the course of the war changed, most military projects were closed down in 1944, and by the following year most of the raw material stocks had been exhausted. The British then engaged in removing lock, stock and barrel most of the (movable) infrastructure, apparently taking with them some US$86m of equipment and supplies by the end of the decade. These included the Massawa dry docks, the cement factory at Massawa, Gura airport and the aerial cableway from Massawa to Asmara (although some sources say that the cableway survived the British occupation and was, in fact, removed by Haile Selassie). Da Nadai was the only serious export business to weather this storm, crops being largely immovable.

1946–1950

By 1946 the economy was in serious depression (and may well have complicated future spurious debates when deciding the nation's future as to whether it was economically viable as an independent entity). The effects on Eritreans were drastic. There was considerable social unrest and xenophobia flourished. The Italians, due to their favoured treatment, were particular targets for this: *shifta* (bandit) attacks concentrated on Italian landowners who had benefited from the British policy of land alienation and the replacement of the traditional elite with British appointees.

The next two decades were to see a modernised colonial economy under severe political pressure, exacerbated by the fact that the pre-war boom had seen the development of a fully-fledged working class. Urban unemployment reached critical levels, with the industrial workforce shrinking from over 30,000 in 1947 to just over 10,000 in 1962. During 1948, at the height of the post-war crisis, 637 businesses closed and 10,000 Eritreans and 4,000 Italians became unemployed. This was the background against which the future of Eritrea, for the next 40 years, was decided.

The British Military Administration, which governed Eritrea from the time the Italians were defeated in 1941 until the country was federated to Ethiopia, was set on partitioning Eritrea. Such a plan would have given the west and the north to Sudan and the rest to Ethiopia. This suited Emperor Haile Selassie's designs well as he had a strong interest in controlling the Red Sea ports and in the mineral and industrial wealth of the country which had previously been developed by the Italians. His intention to expand his empire is further evidenced by his simultaneous claim to Italian Somaliland. Beginning in 1945 he consistently lobbied the United States in an attempt to advance such claims.

The future of all the former Italian colonies was first formally discussed at the Paris Peace Conference in July 1946. Article 23 stated that the issue had to be resolved by the Four Powers within one year otherwise it would be put to the UN General Assembly. In May 1948 the report of the commission of investigation was submitted but there was no consensus of opinion.

In April 1949, at the third session of the UN, the Bevin-Sforza plan worked out between Italy and Britain was put to the Assembly as a blueprint for the partition of Eritrea. Although this clearly suited Britain, Italy, Ethiopia and the United States, the plan came under attack on the basis that this was largely an agreement between the two former colonial powers rather than a resolution moulded by international opinion with due consideration of the wishes of Eritreans themselves.

At the fourth session the future of both Libya and Italian Somaliland, the two other principal Italian colonies, was decided. In marked contrast to what was to happen in Eritrea, Libya was given immediate independence and Italian Somaliland was granted a ten-year period of trusteeship followed by independence. That Eritrea was treated differently points to the influence in the UN of something of a hidden agenda among the interested parties. The UN set up a Commission of Enquiry, comprising representatives from Pakistan, Norway, Guatemala, South Africa and Burma. Their brief was 'to ascertain the wishes of the Eritrean people and the means of promoting their future welfare'. The enquiry presented its report on June 28 1949.

Burma and South Africa recommended a close association between Eritrea and Ethiopia under the sovereignty of the latter. Norway pressed for unconditional union. The other two recommended a solution the same as that decided for Italian Somaliland – a ten-year trusteeship followed by independence. None of the parties accepted partition as a solution. The whole process of information gathering also seems to have been dominated by misinformation fed by the British to the commission, namely that the Christian majority favoured union with Ethiopia, which was a simplification of a very much more complex matrix of aspirations on the part of the Eritrean people. That this information was erroneous was later demonstrated by the fact that in the local elections in 1952 parties that favoured independence gained 55.2% of the vote. Similarly, after federation with Ethiopia, in the first elections for the Eritrean parliament, non-unionist parties won over 50% of the vote.

FEDERATION WITH ETHIOPIA: 1950

The debate was thrown into an even more international context with the outbreak of war in Korea on June 25 1950. Haile Selassie sent troops from the imperial bodyguard to fight alongside the Americans in Korea, illustrating the strengthening of links between the two countries. American ambitions were to be further realised when they signed a 25-year treaty with Ethiopia, commencing in 1953, to use Eritrea as a strategic base. That such an ambition had existed for some years is shown by the fact that the United States had first gained permission from the British to build a complex communications centre in Asmara, which came to be known as Kagnew Station, before federation. With such close ties developing between the United States and Ethiopia it was indeed unlikely that Eritrea would be treated within the bounds of the UN's stated policy of 'assuring the right of peoples and nations to self-determination'. Resolution 390A(v) was thus accepted by the UN on December 2 1950, making Eritrea an autonomous unit federated to Ethiopia.

The very different aspirations of Eritreans and the Ethiopian regime were bound from the outset to cause problems. One of the most fundamental flaws in the federation was that in the event of disagreement Eritrea had no means of appeal to the international community. While the imperial head of state in Eritrea was supposedly there to ensure that the Eritrean Assembly did not contravene the federation 'agreement', the first three such governors were sons-in-law of Haile Selassie and treated Eritrea as simply another fiefdom. A systematic policy of creeping control ensued.

ANNEXATION AND AFTER: 1955–1961

In 1955 Tedla Bairou was forced by the Ethiopian regime to resign as chief executive of the Eritrean government. Four years later Tigrinya and Arabic were barred as the official teaching languages and were replaced by Amharic, erecting a major obstacle to further education for Eritreans. Resistance to such moves continued throughout the 1950s. Student boycotts, and protests from officials and in the workplace, were all met with an increase in police brutality; many people were jailed or forced into exile. A number of industries were closed and transferred to Ethiopia as part of a process of undermining the economic independence of Eritrea.

In 1958 there was a general strike, but there was little interest from the outside world even though its suppression left many dead and wounded. When Eritreans tried to protest to the UN they couldn't gain access to the assembly. It increasingly appeared to many that the only hope of resisting Ethiopian domination was through armed struggle; this is exactly what happened, the first act of armed resistance occurring on September 1 1961. This formed part of the pretext for the Ethiopian annexation of Eritrea. In late 1962 Asmara was put under a state of siege by Ethiopian troops when the assembly was supposed to vote on the future of Eritrea. Intimidation and bribery made the outcome on November 14 a foregone conclusion. Order number 27 dissolved the Eritrean Assembly even though it wasn't legally empowered to dissolve itself and, with the building occupied by soldiers, it was under duress. Some historians and participants maintain that there wasn't even a vote *per se*. Either way, the federal agreement had not provided Eritrea with any means of preventing such treatment. The country was now formally annexed to Ethiopia.

ERITREAN RESISTANCE AND THE GROWTH OF NATIONALISM
Eritrean Liberation Movement (ELM): the late 1950s

The first organised opposition to the adverse conditions of Ethiopian rule, dedicated to liberating the country, was provided by the Eritrean Liberation Movement (ELM). Centred on Asmara and the lowlands it attracted teachers, students, intellectuals and small tradesmen. It was widely popular, although being the first such organisation, it was rather short-lived as there was no clear organisational structure and no clear political programme.

The movement was started in Port Sudan by exiles about whom not much is known. This is one reason why there is something of a scarcity of information about the ELM. The highland cadre was known as *Mabber Shewate* and the lowland cadre as *Harakat' Atahrir Al Eritrea*. The founders had been influenced by rising nationalism in Sudan in the 1950s and its independence in 1956, and by the seeming futility of seeking any form of external redress (for example through the United Nations) to the escalation of Ethiopian repression in Eritrea. Such sentiment increased markedly after the suppression of the general strike in March 1958.

The five founders of the ELM were all Muslims who wanted to build an organisation to oppose Ethiopian encroachment in Eritrea. Most of the initial members were also Muslims although they soon tapped a surprisingly deep-seated resentment against Ethiopia among Christian workers and students as well. The highland movement was predominantly Christian, reflecting their demographic superiority in that region, but the ELM always sought to try to avoid major divisions along religious lines.

They soon encountered difficulties with opposition from the 'old guard' of pro-independence parties from the 1940s and early 1950s, who were mostly in exile in Cairo. Idris Mohammed Adam was in the process of forming the Eritrean Liberation Front (ELF), and he and others were suspicious of the motives of the younger generation; their suspicion was exacerbated by the communist links of some of the ELM's founders (which manifested themselves, for example, in the characteristic cell structure of the organisation). Only Woldeab Woldemariam, who had made famous radio broadcasts of exhortation to Eritreans from Cairo earlier in the decade, received them with any openness and he later became their representative in Egypt. The ELM was dedicated to freeing Eritrea from Ethiopia by any means, including through armed struggle, possibly drawing on support in the Eritrean police and army.

The ELM only had one congress, held in Asmara in September 1960, just one year before the fighting actually began. But without cooperation from Ibrahim Sultan, former head of the Muslim League in Eritrea, and Idris Mohammed Adam, they found it difficult to expand as they wished; such sectionalism was to dog the various nationalist movements for over twenty years. In particular the ELM's welcoming of Christians into the fold alienated them from the others.

The beginning of the armed struggle was effected by neither the ELM nor the ELF, but by a *shifta* leader called Hamid Idris Awate, who fought with police in September 1961 at Amba Adal, in the western lowlands, and thereby passed into folklore. The date of this first conflict is commemorated with a national holiday in Eritrea. The authorities, aware of the ELM not least because of its rather public arguments with the nascent ELF, moved to round up the leaders in 1961. Although they continued to try to participate in the armed struggle through 1962 the fabric of the movement had been fatally undermined. In future years there was also actual conflict between the ELM and the ELF, for example at Ela Tada in 1965.

The encourangement of participation of members of all religious factions by the ELM was a characteristic which in twenty years' time was to be one of the strengths of the Eritrean People's Liberation Front (EPLF). But in these early days the ELF commanded greater influence and therefore came to dominate the struggle for independence, despite showing an equally obvious lack of organisational cohesion – a factor which ultimately resulted in their demise as well.

Eritrean Liberation Front (ELF): 1960

While ELM's roots were in Port Sudan among Eritrean exiled youth, ELF was based in Cairo and founded by some of the veterans of pro-independence opposition in the 1940s. They were well supported by Eritrean students in exile as well. Woldeab Woldemariam was the first of the leaders to arrive in Cairo in 1954. Ibrahim Sultan (founder of the Muslim League) and Idris Mohammed Adam (former president of the Eritrean Assembly) arrived in 1959. The latter is actually credited with announcing the formation of ELF in July 1960. He, his deputy Idris Osman Galadewos, and Osman Saleh Sabbe were to dominate it for the next ten years although they themselves were not without disagreements.

The immediate necessity was to obtain arms, an aim that was often frustrated by the alliances of those whom they approached. They were advised by veterans of the Moroccan war for independence, including Abdelkrim al-Khattabi, that in order to secure support they first had to show that they were actually engaged in fighting in Eritrea. The first force in the field operated in the Barka and Gash lowlands, drawing on recruits from the followers of Hamid Idris Awate, the Eritrean contingent in the Sudanese army, and others. With an increase in the activity of these bands their popularity among exiles grew, and fundraising, at which Osman Saleh Sabbe was a master, became easier.

Syria was the first external supporter in material terms, anxious to extend its influence in the region. The political ambitions of neighbouring countries, and their rivalries and alliances, always determined the extent of support for nationalism in Eritrea. In the mid 1960s both the desire to oppose the United States, due to its role in the Arab-Israeli conflict, and a continuing desire to extend Arabic influence, were prevalent. In 1963, 30 Eritreans went to Syria for military training; 70 more went two years later, returning to Eritrea with arms. Similar support later came from Saudi Arabia. As a result, by 1965, the ELF had about 1,000 fighters in the field. Growth, however, brought problems such as the concentration of the field force in the strategically more isolated west of Eritrea and conflicts between the original fighters and the rather more sophisticated revolutionaries who joined with the benefit of overseas training and secondary education.

The zonal commands

Responding to this, the ELF reorganised in 1965, dividing the fighting force zonally: one in the western lowlands, one in northern Senhit/Sahel, one on the plateau, and one in the coastal provinces of Semhar and Denkalia. Each zone had

Left The rugged beauty of Gash Barka

Below left Traditional lowland dwelling at Adi Ghider, near Tessenei

Below right A vital job in the Sahel mountains

Above Imperial Palace in Massawa, built in the late 19th century

Right Haile Selassie's personalised Lion of Judah gates still hanging by the Imperial Palace

Below left Ottoman tombs on the road to Narrow: one of the many intriguing legacies in Eritrea left by past empires

Below right The beautiful and commanding campanile of Asmara's central Catholic cathedral

a patron-amongst the ELF leadership. The Revolutionary Command was placed in Kassala, in Sudan, but it was never able to exert much influence in the field. The whole system was destined to have difficulties associated with parochialism and sectarianism. Despite the intended formation of a proper command structure, in practice most zone commanders carried out their own military planning, recruitment, and taxation of the local population; in short they acted largely independently of one another. They also relied heavily on their individual sponsors in the leadership rather than on the leadership structure as a whole.

Idris Mohammed Adam was a native of Barka province and supported the first zone; the second zone was the domain of his deputy, Idris Osman Galadewos, a Bilen. The third zone was strategically the most important since it was in the plateau area that essentially controlled the country, a fact apparent in later years, but it was weakened by not having the support of the Christian peasantry and it lacked a patron. The fourth zone was represented in the leadership by Osman Saleh Sabbe, who had formerly been a schoolteacher in Arkiko, south of Massawa. Thus the rather parochial nature of the zonal forces was reinforced by being reflected in the ELF leadership structure.

The problems inherent in such a structure came to the fore during the Ethiopian offensive in 1967, when in each zone the commanders succeeded in alienating another interest group within the zone. For example in the first zone the fighters were actually encouraged to attack the Kunama, in alliance with Beni Amer and Baria tribesmen. In zone three the Christian peasantry were in conflict with the Saho. Such actions were clearly predicated upon the virtual absence of Christians in the movement at this stage. Arabic was the ELF's official language and it printed its literature in that language. All the leaders and zonal commanders were Muslim and its power-base was in traditionally Muslim strongholds.

But on the plateau and elsewhere Christian discontent with the Ethiopian regime was also growing, and they began to join the ELF after about 1965, in protest at many things, including the deliberate stunting of economic growth in Eritrea which limited their livelihoods. There was at the time no other conduit for their discontent than the ELF, although because of Muslim dominance, and because many of these new recruits were well educated, they often found getting into the ranks a very difficult process. Nevertheless it was the ELF that was conducting the fight for their country. The leadership, whatever the distrust among some of them of Christian participation, was not blind to the need to respond to changing circumstances. A new, fifth zone was set up in 1966 and was known as the 'Christian Zone' centred on Hamasien province, on the plateau, and including Asmara. This not only recognised the increasing number of Christian recruits but also the crucial importance of Asmara as the capital city and major industrial and population centre. Wolday Khasai, hitherto the only Christian in any position of seniority in the ELF, was made its leader.

The fifth zone

The fifth zone was not accorded the financial autonomy which the other zones had *de facto*, and it also encountered hostility among the highland Christian peasantry due to old animosities caused by ELF raids. The fifth zone's force was overwhelmed by the Ethiopian offensive in 1967, before it could find its feet. Yet this area was to remain crucial to the success of the nationalist movement; until pressure was exerted on the Ethiopian regime in its heartland it was inclined to ignore insurrection in the hinterlands. To some degree the very creation of the fifth zone alerted Ethiopia to the need to take civil disturbances more seriously, and it enlisted both American and Israeli help in training troops more suited to fighting a guerrilla war than its normally cumbersome tactics allowed. When the 1967 offensive was launched, after a number of senior Ethiopian officials had been assassinated, it moved into the west after destroying the fifth zone. It did not meet much resistance but exacted high retribution among the civilian population, leading to the first substantial wave of refugees from Eritrea (some 20,000 fled to Sudan).

Recriminations among the ELF: 1967

Although the ELF had survived largely intact by avoiding confrontation during the 1967 offensive, it faced severe difficulties later in the year with the defection of Wolday Khasai to Ethiopia, following the execution of 27 of his men for failing in their duty in the first offensive. All the men were Christians. He was joined by a number of others from his command presumably all fearing a similar fate due to sectarian retribution. The Reform Movement (*Eslah*) also grew out of a general dissatisfaction with the efficacy of the zonal system. In response, the Supreme Council of the ELF elected three new members with the intention of broadening its appeal and appearing to put its house in order, but this was a largely token gesture. Further pressure on the leadership was caused by the increasing difficulty in securing external support in the wake of the closure of the Suez Canal, although some headway was made with China (where the current president, Isaias Afewerki, was trained), Cuba and South Yemen.

The increase in the ELF ranks of student radicals and those trained abroad manifested itself in the pressure for change. They added a new dimension, one of professionalism, and revolutionary rhetoric and thought. With the increase in their numbers the struggle became more profound. The 'cause' became a wider one. At the forefront of such developments were Isaias Afewerki and Abraham Tewolde, the new commander of the fifth zone, as well as Ramadan Mohammed Nur and Mohammed Ali Omero in the fourth zone.

Responding to change: the late 1960s

A meeting was convened in Aredaib, in Barka province, in June 1968; the call for greater unity in the ELF met with much approval. Issues which had not previously been aired were raised, such as the often harsh treatment of civilians by the fighters. This meeting marked the beginning of complex and far-reaching changes in the ELF. Following a disastrous attack by the second zone on Halhal, northwest of Keren, zones two, three and four united in the Tripartite Unity Force. All zones then attended another meeting in 1969. Not only did this ultimately bring about the downfall of the Supreme Command, but the quarrelling led to embarrassing, not to say horrifying, incidents such as the massacre of 300 new Christian recruits. Wolday Giday and Kidane Kinfu, two prominent Christian ELF members, were also killed in Kassala by comrades.

Many Christians fled, fearing for their lives; others went with Isaias Afewerki and Abraham Tewolde to Ala in Akele Guzai province, breaking away completely. Factionalism also increased among the other zones with various splinter groups forming, such as Obel, led by Adam Saleh. In spite of all this, military success was still being achieved and by 1970 the Ethiopians seem to have realised that the situation was worsening and appointed the first military governor of Eritrea, General Debebe Haile Mariam.

While a new force, the Labour Party, was pushing for reform of the ELF at their conference in October 1971, Osman Saleh Sabbe announced the formation of another liberation movement, the People's Liberation Front (PLF). The latter was intended to provide a conduit for Christians' desire to become further involved in the armed struggle. Soon after, Obel also announced, rather confusingly, the birth of the Eritrean Liberation Force (another ELF) which joined Sabeh's group in 1972, the coalition being named ELF-PLF.

ELF-PLF: 1972

This was a strange marriage between a traditional Muslim rural force, Obel, the Christian radicals at Ala, and Sabbe's supporters, which even included elements of the old ELM. Although the Ala group was seemingly beleaguered, their statement of objectives was to prove the code that eventually secured their pre-eminence in the nationalist movement. Initially they chose to fight both the ELF and the external enemy but needed the support of Sabbe for arms. The combined forces of the ELF-PLF were at its inception less than 500 men, compared with an ELF force over four times the size. It is interesting that even combined the two fronts numbered surprisingly few considering that within five years they were to control most of Eritrea and be on the brink of victory. This attests to the fundamental changes brought about by the formation of the new group, and also to certain external influences which helped the cause of all those who sought the freedom of Eritrea.

Changing times: 1970s

In the years leading up to 1974, Haile Selassie was himself under increasing pressure at home to maintain control of his country. There were a number of mutinies in the Ethiopian army which not only encouraged the Eritreans to fight even harder, but also encouraged those who had previously not taken part in the struggle to do so. Eritrean members of the Ethiopian parliament resigned in 1974, the police in Eritrea demonstrated in support of independence (ironic, considering their usual role in retaliating against civilians after military setbacks) and a flood of new recruits joined the fighters, most of them Christians.

Yet even when the Derg (Military Committee) took power in Ethiopia in 1974, the Eritrean fighters were still just as preoccupied with battling with each other as with the common enemy. In October 1974 ELF and ELF-PLF, both trying to surround Asmara, fought a sizeable battle at Zagher, north east of Asmara. This actually prompted a mass demonstration by the population of Asmara demanding that the factions put their house in order. A truce ensued and both fronts collaborated in an attack on Asmara in January 1975, a move unimaginable five years earlier. After the customary brutal retaliations Ethiopia lost any last vestiges of support in Eritrea and there was another flood of converts to the fighters' cause. The swelling of their ranks again highlighted the fact that there was a simultaneous civil war. Various negotiations took place in 1975 including the ELF's second conference and a parley with Sabbe who committed the ELF-PLF to a coalition without its members knowing. The ELF-PLF commanders met at Zagher at the end of the year, and by March an irreparable and acrimonious split was riven between Sabbe, the founder of the PLF, and those commanders. Henceforth the field force was known as the Eritrean People's Liberation Front (EPLF). The guerrillas were, however, to continue fighting internally for much of the next ten years.

The ELF had a purge in 1977, begun by radical Christian highlanders who saw the organisation's defects as a threat to its very survival. However, military successes against the Derg continued unabated. The EPLF had routed the Ethiopian 'Flame' Division's offensive in the Anseba Valley north of Keren in 1976, enabling the ELF to overcome almost all the garrisons in Barka province. Karora, on the northern border with Sudan, fell to the EPLF early in 1977, and they then moved on to Nacfa, Afabet, Keren, Elabored and Debarua. The ELF captured Mendefera, Tessenei, Agordat and the hills surrounding Barentu in the same year.

This offensive put the fighters in a decisive position, poised to seize control of their country despite internal differences. But they were to have to wait another fourteen years to seize the victory which appeared to be theirs on the eve of 1978, frustrated by the intervention of the Soviet Union on the side of Ethiopia. In the second half of 1977, Ethiopia's new ally injected US$850–1,000 million in military aid into the country. Both the EPLF and the ELF had 20,000 fighters in the field by now, a staggering number when one considers their combined number was some 2,500 at the time the ELF-PLF was formed in 1972. (Some sources, however, estimate that the EPLF had already reached substantial numerical superiority by a factor of 3 to 1, with an overall total of 40,000 fighters.) Had their combined forces succeeded in winning at this stage, though, it is clear that there may well have been an all out civil war. Understandably, the response to the Soviet intervention was for the EPLF and ELF to withdraw to their heartlands in 1978.

EPLF's first congress

The EPLF's congress in Nacfa in 1977 seemed to show that they were destined to prove the more powerful force. The National Democratic Programme was a mélange of the idealist aspirations of their disparate supporters, but it demonstrated that unity was a paramount concern. From this conference sprung the EPLF's insistence on proper government within its occupied areas of Eritrea, even when faced with poor odds in the decade ahead; everything was considered from land reform to schooling, to the protection of rights for women. The conviction with which these tasks were undertaken was matched by the determination to have a secure and dependable leadership. From the original members of the coalition the Politbureau included Isaias Afewerki, later to become the first President of free Eritrea, Mesfin Hagos and Ramadan Mohammed Nur.

Demise of the ELF

The ELF continued to be beset by defections to the EPLF and by internal rifts, although it also continued to score important victories in the field. It was not, however, always a reliable partner in operations depending on the current state of relations with the EPLF. For the latter the final straw, which ended any semblance of cooperation, came in 1980, when a joint EPLF-ELF force was occupying Karora. In the summer ELF forces suddenly withdrew to Barka leaving the EPLF exposed. Alone, they were not able to prevent the Ethiopians from reoccupying the town. Simultaneously the ELF was holding peace talks in Russia and Ethiopia which threatened to leave the EPLF isolated.

Therefore, in the last three months of the year, they harried ELF forces west out of Eritrea into Sudan, often with fierce skirmishes being fought. By the end of the summer of 1981 the last of the ELF forces were pushed out and although its leadership continued to strive for a resurgence its field force was by now a spent one. In addition its heartland, Barka province, was now in EPLF hands and most of its fighters who wished to continue the struggle defected to this rival force, which was left free to carry the fight alone to the Ethiopian occupying force.

The Struggle: 1961–91

The armed conflict between Ethiopia and Eritrea lasted just under 30 years. It is a remarkable story of human resilience on the one hand, and on the other of the terrible cost that two Ethiopian regimes (those of Haile Selassie and President Mengistu) were prepared to inflict upon Eritreans and Ethiopians alike to further their own cause, and that of their strategic allies, first the United States (until the mid 1970s), and then the Soviet Union. The war went largely unheeded in the western press; Eritrea for the most part fought alone, with the overwhelming majority of its supplies being captured from the Ethiopian army.

What made the conflict even more terrible, bearing certain similarities to the internecine fighting in Afghanistan during the Soviet occupation of that country, is that for the majority of the war Eritreans were fighting themselves as well. While all in the pro-independence movement were united in their desire to gain control of their own country, Eritreans had to concertina a phase of enormous political development into a very short time period. From the emergence of the ELM to the pre-eminence of the EPLF in carrying the struggle to the Ethiopians took barely twenty years. Considering Eritrea's history, one of disparate peoples, three religions, different lifestyles (ranging from the urban bourgeoisie to the pastoralists and nomads), unification was a difficult task – complicated by the different perceptions of the future for which the various parties were fighting. It was achieved, by the EPLF, due to two fundamental factors: that the people were united in their desire for independence, and that the EPLF was sufficiently politically adroit to reconcile the differences of various groups by supporting the basic tenet of rights for all those people.

Although not without internal disagreements themselves (surely a characteristic of any political party), the EPLF, following the collapse of the ELF, was able to fight out the last ten years of the war without having to watch its flank. Victory was never a certainty; what was a certainty, in the minds of the fighters, was that they wouldn't lose. Although, after the staggering assault by the EPLF on Afabet in 1988, many in the EPLF felt that victory was inevitable, they had also been on the brink of victory during the assault on Massawa in 1977, only to be thwarted by Soviet intervention. Who was to know what might rob them this time? In the end international events helped, with the demise of the Soviet Union, but in that final hour the EPLF were marching on their capital which still had some 140,000 Ethiopian troops in occupation. Had that final battle taken place, the toll of death and destruction of the war would have been considerably higher. As it is President Mengistu's position in Ethiopia was sufficiently precarious for him to flee to Zimbabwe on May 22 1991 (where he resides to this day as a personal guest of Zimbabwean President Robert Mugabe). Eritreans were thus spared from a possible bloodbath as the Ethiopian troops fled from Asmara west to Sudan, the southern retreat being blocked by the EPLF. Huge numbers died on the way, having no food and water, a final indignity in the story of the occupying Ethiopian army. Throughout it had been largely made up of conscripts; however well-equipped they were this always put them at a disadvantage in terms of morale and skill.

Chronology of the Struggle: 1961–91

The following is a brief overview of the major battles and offensives:

September 1 1961 Armed struggle commences with a group of eleven Eritreans under the leadership of Hamid Idris Awate attacking police posts in western Eritrea.

March 1967 Ethiopia launches a major offensive following an increase in Eritrean terrorist activities.

September 6–7 1968 ELF attacks Halhal unsuccessfully, sustaining heavy casualties, including the commander of the third zone, Omar Azaz.

1974 Haile Selassie is deposed in Ethiopia. The Derg (Military Committee) takes power.

January 31 1975 Combined ELF/EPLF forces attack Asmara, fighting for ten days.

December 31 1976 EPLF routs the Ethiopian 'Nebebal' (Flame) offensive north of Keren.

January 5 1977 EPLF takes Karora.

March and April 1977 EPLF captures Nacfa, Afabet, Keren and Elabored. ELF captures Tessenei, Agordat and the hills surrounding Barentu.

October 13 1977 Dogali on the Massawa-Asmara road falls to EPLF and the attack on Massawa begins on December 19. During the siege some 600 fighters die in a desperate attempt to capture the islands on which Massawa is built, but due to heavy fire from ships offshore they are held at bay. Ethiopian casualties during the siege number 4,000.

May to December 1977 Soviet Union injects an estimated US$850–1,000 million of military aid into Ethiopia, including 60 MIG-21 planes and 12 MIG-23s. Before the war ended the Soviet Union was to spend some US$12 billion on military training and equipment for Ethiopia.

1978 Soviet and other foreign assistance, on a vast scale, enables the Ethiopian army to launch the First Offensive. Having almost secured total victory in 1977 the ELF and EPLF are spread too thinly to be able to defend all the territory they captured.

July 1978 Following the ELF and EPLF's 'strategic withdrawal' from parts of Eritrea after the Soviet intervention, Ethiopia recaptures Tessenei and Mendefera and relieves the siege of Massawa and Barentu. EPLF suffers a defeat outside Decemhare.

August 1978 Agordat, Segeneiti and Digsa fall to the Ethiopian forces.

November 20 1978 Ethiopian Second Offensive. After heavy fighting EPLF decides to withdraw from Keren to the more mountainous terrain of Sahel.

January 1979 Third Ethiopian Offensive on the Anseba valley and northeast Sahel fronts, north of Keren. EPLF has built a vast trench network in the mountains stretching from the coast to the western lowlands.

March 30–April 11 1979 Fourth Ethiopian Offensive against Mersa Teklai, on the north coast, and Afabet. Ethiopian casualties in the first six months of the year are 8,000, totalling 25,000 during the first four offensives.

July 8 1979 After the Fourth Offensive fails to breach EPLF defences, the Fifth Offensive is launched with a three-pronged attack on Nacfa. EPLF claims to inflict 15,000 casualties, including 6,000 dead.

December 2 1979 Having successfully held on to Nacfa the EPLF counter attacks south towards Afabet.

January 1980 Fierce fighting continues in Sahel. On the northeast front a force of 30,000 Ethiopians is pushed back to Mersa Teklai. Pressure is maintained on Afabet.

Summer 1980 ELF forces withdraw from the EPLF-ELF line defending Karora, enabling Ethiopians to take the strategically important town guarding supply routes into Eritrea from Sudan. This brings the long-running antagonism between the two Eritrean forces to a head. EPLF harries ELF all the way west to the Sudanese border and this marks the end of the ELF as an effective force.

1981 EPLF continually attacks Ethiopian positions in an attempt to frustrate plans for the next large offensive. Pre-emptive strikes are made in the area surrounding Arezza in the south, against Aderde in Barka, in the Seraye lowlands and on the outskirts of Keren.

January 23 1982 EPLF attacks Asmara airport destroying two garrisons and the 35th Brigade headquarters in Asmara, as well as the Baratollo textile factory. Decemhare, Keren and Massawa are also briefly occupied.

February 1982 Red Star Campaign is launched, involving 90,000 Ethiopian troops on four fronts. The attack on Barka from Agordat collapses in a week. Fierce fighting takes place all along the 120km northeast Sahel front, inland from Mersa Teklai. Some 33,000 Ethiopians are killed or wounded. Casualties for the EPLF are variously estimated at 2,000–4,000. Tear gas is used by the Ethiopians at Trukruk, Alghena and Nacfa, an event witnessed by the western press. Following the failure of the offensive, Soviet Field Marshal Dimitrov takes charge of Ethiopian forces in the field.

March-August 1983 The Seventh ('Silent') Offensive.

August 1983 EPLF retakes Karora and the Barka Valley and key positions on the Agordat-Keren-Afabet road. EPLF offensive continues into the following year, liberating Tessenei and Ali Ghider in January 1984.

February 22 1984 EPLF makes an armoured offensive in northeast Sahel, breaking through Ethiopian lines to the sea and marking the first victory in a conventional tank battle for the Eritreans.

March 1984 Mersa Teklai is taken by the EPLF bringing a further 4,000km^2 under their control.

May 1984 EPLF attacks Asmara airport destroying ten planes and damaging 23 others.

July 6 1985 EPLF defeats two battalions of mechanised troops and two infantry divisions at Barentu killing 2,000 men and capturing 400. They withdraw in August, with substantial stocks of captured artillery, being unable to hold the town.

October 10–October 25 1985 The Red Sea Offensive is launched on most of the frontlines with the main aim of capturing Nacfa from the EPLF. Despite extensive air support and the use of airborne troops in northeast Sahel the Ethiopian forces fail to capture the town. A second unsuccessful attempt is made in November.

October 17 1985 EPLF captures Ghinda, on the Asmara–Massawa road.

January 14 1986 EPLF again attacks Asmara airport despite a substantial upgrading of its defences since the previous attack. Forty aircraft are destroyed and the ammunition and fuel depots set alight.

May 1986 EPLF bombards Massawa and blockades the Asmara road.

September 1 1986 EPLF attacks Asmara airport to mark the 25th anniversary of the war.

November 1986 Ethiopian position at Om Hager in the southwest is captured by EPLF.

1987 Extensive EPLF assaults on Ethiopian positions around Asmara, and on the Nacia Front.

March 17 1988 EPLF offensive commences from Nacfa.

March 19 1988 EPLF captures Afabet, the centre of Ethiopian military intelligence and their main supply depot in Eritrea. This offensive was described by Basil Davidson as 'one of the biggest (victories) ever scored by any liberation movement anywhere since Dien Bien Phu [the defeat by the Viet Minh of the French in Vietnam] in 1954'. Over the next few weeks Ethiopian forces flee from Tessenei, Barentu and Agordat leaving all of northern and western Eritrea in EPLF hands. Fifty tanks and a number of 'Stalin Organs' (multiple rocket launchers) are captured; these are then trained by the EPLF on Keren to the south. Although Ethiopia have 300,000 troops in Eritrea they are now, for the first time, judged to be at a disadvantage in terms of firepower.

April 23 1988 EPLF naval forces attack the oil refinery in Assab.

January 1989 The largest tank battle of the war; 37 Ethiopian tanks are destroyed on the coastal lowlands.

February 1990 EPLF captures Massawa.

May 19 1991 The last major battle of the war begins at Decemhare and after three days the Ethiopian lines collapse. EPLF commences the bombardment of Asmara.

May 22 1991 President Mengistu flees Ethiopia for Zimbabwe. Ethiopian troops start to flee Asmara.

May 24 1991 EPLF forces enter Asmara, which the day before had been defended by 140,000 troops. EPLF troops are required to hand in their weapons as they enter the city.

May 25 1991 EPLF fighters arrive in Assab.

April 23–25 1993 In order to provide a 'legal and democratic conclusion' to the struggle for independence Eritrea holds a referendum. 99.81% of the voting population votes for independence.

May 24 1993 Eritrea is formally declared independent.

There are many good books written about the armed conflict by authors who were involved in the field. For the last section of this brief history of Eritrea, they are the best places to tell the story of the heroic battle. These are some to recommend:

Against All Odds by Dan Connell
Eritrea: Never Kneel Down by Firebrace and Holland
Even the Stones are Burning by Roy Pateman
Revolution at Dusk by Robert Papstein
The Eritrean Struggle for Independence by Ruth Iyob

Many books are available from the Africa Book Centre, 38 King Street, London WC2 (tel: 020 7240 6649), and in all good bookshops in Asmara.

ERITREA AND THE UNITED NATIONS

President Isaias Afewerki's speech to the opening of the 48th session of the UN in September 1993 sums up the consequences of the political settlement imposed on Eritrea in the 1950s:

> I cannot help but remember the appeals that we sent year in and out to this Assembly and the member countries of the United Nations, describing the plight of our people. We appealed to the UN not only in its capacity as a representative of the international community, but also because of its special responsibility to Eritrea. For it was the UN that decided in 1950, at the beginning of the Cold War, to deny the colonised people of Eritrea their right to self-determination, thereby sacrificing their national and human rights on the altar of the strategic interest of the superpowers.

He went on to say that

> despite the repeated appeals of the Eritrean people, the UN refused to raise its voice in defence of a people whose future it had unjustly decided and whom it had pledged to protect. Not once in 41 years did Eritrea...figure on the agenda of the UN.

After 30 years of fighting to secure independence, Eritrea was confronted by the reality of a devastated country. More than 150,000 of its people died, 100,000 were disabled or orphaned and about a quarter of the population were forced to flee the country. These are the harsh realities in what historian Bereket Habte Selassie described as 'a colony singled out for denial of independence'.

POST-INDEPENDENCE

At the end of this section in the second edition it mentioned that 'The next chapter in Eritrea's history will judge the success with which they are able to tackle the (many) difficulties'. The next chapter can now be partially written, though only time will reveal what will mark the end of this phase. Eritrea was left devastated by the 30-year struggle and in 1991 was truly starting from nothing. The spirit and determination to develop was characterised by a dogged self-sufficiency. Owing to the little external support they had received throughout the 30-year struggle and the inevitable cost of accepting loans from international financial institutions, the government and the people set about building their country from scratch in the way that had brought them freedom in the first place; by doing it themselves, albeit with increasing overseas assistance latterly. This resolute attitude inevitably disgruntled many in the developed world, as here was a country that really appeared to prove there was an alternative to becoming servile to wealthier nations when developing one's own country. There is little doubt, however, that the early successes this new approach achieved brought much favour from many corners of the globe. Economic growth outstripped most other African nations throughout the period 1991–97 and infrastructure developments were providing a sound basis for future successes. Unconditional help and assistance began to flow into this fledgling nation, as talk of an African Renaissance led by countries in The Horn appeared tangible. Respect, though long overdue, was at last being paid to Eritrea.

The early-mid 1990s was Eritrea's honeymoon. It is common to hear people now talk of this period as 'the good old days'. Significant numbers of foreign Eritreans were coming back from the diaspora and whole suburbs in Asmara and Massawa were being built for them so as to maintain a 'Western standard of living'. The refugees from Sudan were returning and inhabiting new plots of land that could now be made productive. The demobilisation of over 90,000 fighters led to a huge input of manpower into a booming economy. Perhaps most importantly, political relations with their old enemy Ethiopia were now better than at any time in recent history, as the two leaders and close friends guided their countries on a path of peace. A constitution was drafted, elections were promised and a US-style clause that capped a Presidency's time in office at two terms was included – unheard of in many of Africa's dubious democracies. The rewards for this new direction were innumerable and the Eritrean people thrived in this new-found freedom and increased prosperity. It would be hard to find anyone who had a bad word to say about this period of Eritrean history.

THE RECENT WAR

Tragically the bubble was to burst and in 1998, after the introduction of the new currency that formally severed financial ties with their Ethiopian neighbour, and inflamed by other unsettled disputes, a war broke out, causing the country to descend back into the mire from which it had so famously arisen. War, with all its appalling consequences, shattered the dreams of this nation and forced it into another long period of suffering, from which it is still far from relieved.

There remains countless speculation regarding the causes of the war, but the sad fact remains that it was a war between two of the world's most impoverished countries and those certainly least able to afford such a conflict. It has been coined ostensibly as a 'border conflict', arising from the question of the administration of the tiny village of Badme situated near the border. However, as the conflict deepened other suggestions speculated that it was more to do with Ethiopian expansionism and access to the Red Sea - a claim arguably substantiated by their failed push to the port of Assab. Eventually, in 2000, Ethiopia made significant inroads into Eritrean territory.

What this overwhelming invasion did do was force the governments around the discussion table, which eventually led to a peace agreement signed between the two countries in December 2000. With a considerable United Nations presence now in the region and the drawing up of a Temporary Security Zone (TSZ), which runs the length of the entire border, 25km into Eritrean territory, peace is, for now, secured. However, it remains for the two countries to continue to build up the trust that would allow a normalising of relations and an opening of the border to trade and free movement if a lasting peace is to be guaranteed. Neither country can afford poor relations with the other when their economies and peoples are so closely interdependent.

As this book goes to press, the United Nations Border Commission in The Hague has announced its ruling that has formally delineated the boundary between Eritrea and Ethiopia. (It is important to note that the scale of the maps in this guide is such that these boundary changes cannot be precisely shown and therefore these maps are not official.) Both countries have signed a 'binding' agreement to accept this decision. In the meantime, the UN has extended its mandate in Eritrea until late 2002. This is designed to consolidate the steps made in securing peace and will support the Border Commission's ruling. The TSZ will likely remain in place until the UN leaves.

It would be impossible to speculate on the future at this stage, as too many things remain uncertain. There still remain many questions to be answered and the voices demanding answers are getting louder. Time will tell if the forces of emerging democratic institutions will prevail in this long and inevitably arduous process of democratic nation-building or whether there is a descent into the type of authoritarian state control experienced by so many other African states. With the Eritrean people so weary of war and so thirsty for justice and personal freedom, I would favour the former.

Practical Information

3

WHEN TO VISIT

There is no time of year that is unsuitable for visiting Eritrea. Asmara and the highlands have a very pleasant climate all year round, the hottest month being May with highs of about 30°C. There are little rains in March and April and big rains from late June to the beginning of September. These rains are unlikely to impede travel or general enjoyment of the highlands.

On the coast, September to January and April to early June are good months to visit: it is not insufferably hot and skies are likely to be clear. While it is always warm enough to swim, the winter months of February to April can be cloudy. Unless you are used to very hot climates, visiting between June and September is only for those who know what to expect: Massawa regularly has temperatures in the mid 40s°C and there is no significant fluctuation between day- and night-time temperatures. If rain does fall it is in winter.

Suggested itineraries

There still remains a marked paucity of information available overseas about Eritrea, though booking from abroad is now easier than it ever has been. Most large hotels accept bookings from overseas and certain travel agents will accept bookings and payment by credit card. With the increasing use of the internet in Eritrea it is likely that this process should get easier still. Nonetheless, when you arrive in Asmara it is never too far to visit different hotels or travel agencies around the town if you have not been able to make plans before arriving.

Asmara, Massawa and Keren are the absolute musts on any visit to Eritrea and you can enjoy all of them in quite a limited timeframe; beyond that ring usually requires more time and a little more money. Expeditions to Sahel north of Nacfa, to the Danakil, and to the southwest (south of the main Keren–Tessenei road) all require 4WD, plenty of time, and preferably a guide.

Be sure to consider the times of year in which you will be travelling. The temperatures in the western lowlands from April–June and in the coastal regions from May–September can reach 45–50°C. Similarly, from June to September, during the heavy rains in the highlands and northern and western lowlands, the roads to Nacfa and Tessenei can be blocked by flooding.

Here are some suggested routes, based on road conditions and distances, though if you are travelling on local transport you can assume to add a few hours each day on travel.

Five-day tours
- Asmara (2 nights); Massawa (2 nights); Keren (1 night)
- Asmara (2 nights); Massawa (2 nights); Dahlak Island (1 night)
- Asmara (2 nights); Keren (2 nights); Agordat (1 night)
- Asmara (2 nights); Senafe (1 night for Metera); Adi Keih (1 night for Qohaito); Decemhare (1 night)

Eight-day tours
- Asmara (3 nights, with option of day trip to either Decemhare, Segeneiti, Mendefera, Adi Qala, Debre Bizen Monastery or Filfil); Massawa (3 nights, with option of day trip to the islands); Keren (2 nights)
- Asmara (3 nights); Keren (2 nights); Nacfa (2 nights); Agordat (1 night)
- Asmara (3 nights); Massawa (3 nights); Assab (2 nights)
- Asmara (3 nights); Massawa (3 nights); Dahlak Island (2 nights)

Ten-day (or more) tour
Such a trip would depend on your mode of transport and your interests. Travelling by public transport requires a lot of time, energy and patience, but it is infinitely cheaper than hiring your own four-wheel drive. However, hiring your own vehicle can be very rewarding if you fancy doing a bit of your own exploring or you like to have the opportunity to stop along the way.

- Asmara (3 nights); Keren (2 nights); Agordat (1 night); Barentu (1 night); Tessenei (2 nights)
- Asmara (3 nights); Keren (2 nights); Nacfa (3 nights)
- Asmara (2 nights); Massawa via Filfil (3 nights); Thio (1 night); Assab (2 nights)
- Asmara (2 nights); Keren (1 night); Barentu via Agordat (2 nights); Mendefera (1 night); Senafe (2 nights)

Special-interest tours
Owing to Eritrea's size and diversity, there are a great deal of excursions that can fulfil special interests. These could include:

- **Archaeology** Including Qohaito, Metera, Adulis, Adi Keih and Belew Kelew.
- **Birdwatching** Includes camping in the Filfil region.
- **Architecture** Includes tours of the famous Italian and Turkish-style buildings of Asmara, Massawa and Keren.
- **Railway** Take a trip on the newly restored steam railway from Ghinda to Massawa. The line is soon to open from Asmara to Massawa.
- **Scuba diving** The Red Sea coast offers some of the world's best diving.

TOURIST INFORMATION AND SERVICES
The address of the Ministry of Tourism is PO Box 1010, Asmara; tel: 120073/123941/126997; fax: 126949; Keren; tel: 401649 (both open Monday to Friday 07.00-12.00 and 14.00-1800). The office is on the third floor of the

building in Liberty Avenue, where downstairs is the Eritrean Shipping Lines (one block west of Impero Cinema). For details of tourist agencies in Eritrea, see pages 96–7.

Besides the obvious damage wrought by war, the tourist industry is one area that has suffered considerably from the effects of the recent conflict. The total number of visitors to Eritrea more than doubled between 1994 and 1996, peaking at over half a million, but was halved again by 1999. However, this does not necessarily mean that your stay here should be unreasonably hindered. In fact the opposite could be said to be true. With so few tourists visiting Eritrea over recent years those in the tourist industry are keen to help you. The welcome you receive from the people in Eritrea will more than make up for any loss in organisation.

RED TAPE
Visas
Visas are required by all visitors and should be obtained in advance from an Eritrean Embassy or Consulate. Tourist visas are normally issued for one month, and cost £30 sterling in the UK. They take 24 hours to be issued. You will be required to show a return air ticket (or proof of onward travel), your passport and a photograph. A yellow fever vaccination certificate and US$40 (or its equivalent) per day of your stay must also be shown. If it is inconvenient to go personally to the consulate they will return all these and your visa by registered mail for a fee of £5.

Visa procedures are renowned for changing often, so for current details on the procedure send a sae to your embassy/consulate.

Visa extensions can be obtained from the Ministry of Immigration (next to Capitol Cinema on Revolution Avenue) if you wish to stay longer in Eritrea. Exit visas are not required unless you have been a resident in Eritrea for work purposes.

A number of publications for background reading are usually available from embassies, such as *Eritrea Profile*, the government-run English language weekly newspaper; *Horizons* magazine (though now stalled), provided by the Ministry of Tourism, which also provides various other fact sheets.

Bureaucracy
Unfortunately Eritrea is no longer a land devoid of bureaucracy. Papers, forms, stamps and signatures now rule the roost and one's plans can be quite severely curtailed without the necessary documentation. There is a wide range of situations for which you might need the right papers, but many of these have been implemented since the border conflict. For example, visiting archaeological sites requires the necessary pass from the National Museum (Nfa30); visiting areas west of Barentu (including Barentu itself) requires a pass from the Ministry of Internal Affairs (or Ministry of Information if you are conducting official business); visiting areas in the Temporary Security Zone (TSZ) such as Senafe, Adi Qala, Tacombia and Om Hajer will require a pass from the Eritrean Commission to the United Nations Mission to Ethiopia and Eritrea

(ECUNMEE) and to obtain this you may need a letter from the Ministry of Tourism; opening a bank account might require a letter from a 'sponsor'; permits from the Orthodox Headquarters in Asmara are required to visit the monasteries; and a permit is required to visit the islands off Massawa (except Green Island).

Obtaining these papers can be a time consuming and often trying process, but besides being rude it is also futile to lose your patience when following the necessary processes. Once you have the appropriate papers all doors are open to you and there should be no cause for problems. It is certainly worth investing in a little time at the start of your trip obtaining the necessary papers to save lot of time later on if you are caught without them. These papers will also be invaluable when confronted by 'security' personnel if they have a problem with you being in a sensitive area (near army barracks, government buildings, check points, etc) or particularly when taking photos that might be deemed to be a 'threat to national security'. For the tourist, one obvious negative effect of the recent war is the considerable increase in internal security, which on occasions can seem farcically paranoid, especially when self-appointed 'local heroes' decide to question your motives. Thankfully, this remains rare, though if it should occur, a bit of calm explanation and, preferably, some official papers will usually solve any dispute.

Before you travel to particularly remote areas it is worth contacting the Ministry of Tourism to check your itinerary. There are a number of reasons why certain areas may be off limits at any moment in time. Some areas near or in the Temporary Security Zone are still mined; flooding during the rainy seasons can cause damage to roads and bridges; army road blocks (or *blokos*) can frequently change and may ask for papers unexpectedly. If you are travelling to archaeological sites or the monasteries, it is worth checking with the National Museum or the Orthodox Headquarters in Asmara respectively as to whether the places are open. This can be done when applying for the permit. The National Museum is in Menelik II Avenue and the Orthodox Headquarters is in the large white building near the Lufthansa building (airport road, Tiravolo) on the opposite side of the road.

You should always carry your passport with you when travelling outside Asmara. Army checkpoints are now frequent along all major roads since the recent war. Although they are designed to ensure tighter internal security there may be occasions when you are asked to provide identification. When staying at any hotel it is necessary to sign a register on arrival, and passport details are usually required.

Bribery

Bribery is still not yet a feature in Eritrea, and if you think that any official is asking you for one, you have most likely misunderstood. In the unlikely event of a bribe being asked for, ask for a receipt. If this fails to deter, you can try politely suggesting that it may be an idea to confer with another official. This would put an end to the discussion given the government's rather rigorous moral code. I haven't yet heard of a bribe being given or asked for in Eritrea but it would be naive to suggest that this will always be the case.

Eritrean embassies and consulates overseas

China Ta Yuan Building, 1–4–2, No 4 South Liang Maho Rd, Chao Yang District, Beijing; tel: +86 1 65326534/65326535; fax: +86 1 65326532

Djibouti Tel: +25 3 358606; fax: +25 3 250212; email: erythree@intnet.dj

Egypt PO Box 2624, 13 Mohamed Shafick Str, Muhandessin, Cairo; tel: +20 2 3030517/3447093/3441955; fax: +20 2 3030516

EU 15-17 Av de Woluendael 1180, Brussels, Belgium; tel: +32 2 3744434/3744500; fax: +32 2 3720730

France 31-33, Rue Lecourbe, 75015, Paris; tel: +33 1 43061446/43061556/43061557; fax: +33 1 43060751

Germany Stavangerstrasse 18, 10439, Berlin; tel: +49 30 4467460; fax: +49 30 44674621

Italy Via Ferrucio 44/2, 00185 Rome; tel: +39 6 70497908/06 70497924; fax: +39 6 70497940

Kenya New Rehena House, 2nd Floor, Rhapta Road, Westlands, 38651, Nairobi; tel: +254 2443163; fax: +254 2443165

Kuwait Tel: +965 5339624; fax: +965 5317429

Libya PO Box 91279, Tripoli; tel: +218 21 4773568; fax: +218 21 478152

Norway Tel: +47 22 421781; fax: +47 22 421791

Netherlands Seelinckplein 9, 2517 GK, The Hague; tel: +31 70 4276812; fax: +31 70 4411578

Russian Federation Meshanskaya St 1, Moscow 129090; tel: +7 95 9710620; fax: +7 95 9713749

Saudi Arabia Al Siteen, Prince Fahad St 21421, PO Box 770, Jeddah; tel: +966 2 6740592; fax: +966 2 6762235

Sudan PO Box 8129, Khartoum; tel: +249 11 73165/74175; fax: +249 11 45 22 56

Sweden Ostermalmsgatan 34, Box 26068, 100 41 Stockholm; tel: +46 8 20 14 70; fax: +46 8 20 66 06

Switzerland Rue de Vermont 9, CH-1202 Geneva, PO Box 85; tel: +41 22 7402840; fax: +41 22 7404949

UAE PO Box 2597, Abu Dhabi; tel: +971 2 331838/2 326355; +971 2 346451

UK 96 White Lion St, London N1 9PF; tel: +44 20 7713 0096; fax: +44 20 7713 0161

USA 1708 New Hampshire Av NW, Washington DC 20009; tel: +1 202 319 1991; fax: +1 202 319 1304

Yemen Algeria Street Building No 68, Sana'a, PO Box 11040; tel: +967 1 209422; fax: +967 1 214088

Immigration and customs

As required when you obtain your visa, it is important to have a return ticket or proof of your next destination. If travelling overland, it is always useful to have a visa for a future date for another country, if you plan to travel on through Africa or to the Middle East. Overland travel into Eritrea has been somewhat curtailed by the recent border conflict with Ethiopia. The border with Ethiopia is most definitely off limits. The border with Sudan is now open and that with Djibouti is, theoretically, open, but crossing via this route is troublesome and should only be considered after you have checked the latest information with the Ministry of Immigration in Revolution Avenue (next to Capitol Cinema) before leaving Asmara.

You should also be in possession of 'sufficient funds', as defined when applying for your visa. Currency declaration forms are no longer issued on arrival in Eritrea.

On arrival personal computers, video cameras and other major electronic items that could be sold for profit in Eritrea are required to be registered at Customs (and are signed off on departure). When using such items make sure you have ascertained whether the socket is 110 or 220 volts to avoid disaster.

On departure you will be required to pay a US$15 airport tax. This must be paid in cash in US$.

GETTING TO AND FROM ERITREA
By air
Eritrea has concentrated on developing its aviation network and has recently completed an international airport in Massawa. Flights to Massawa have not yet started, but it has been suggested Massawa might eventually become the major airport in Eritrea over Asmara. However, in the short term it will at least provide a convenient access point for visitors from the Middle East coming for short stays. For the time being Asmara and Assab are the only two international airports. Flying from Europe there are a growing number of airlines that offer services to Asmara. They are: Lufthansa; Saudi Airlines; Regional Air (with British Airways); Egypt Air; Yemenia; Eritrean Airlines; and Sudan Airways. The private airline, Daallo, flies to Djibouti and Dubai.

It is impossible to list all the fares and flight information accurately as they are subject to frequent change and various conditions such as duration of ticket, seat class, stopovers, etc. However, unless stated, prices quoted here are for return fares to the stated destination and are valid for the shortest period of time (usually two to four months).

Lufthansa Lufthansa Building, Airport Road, Tirovolo, Asmara; tel: 182707 (European office +49 1803803803). Lufthansa fly to Asmara via Frankfurt six days a week; the fare from London is US$886; from Frankfurt US$861; and New York US$1717. Flights leave Asmara around midnight.

Egypt Air September 1 (Meskel) Sq, Asmara; tel: 125501/125500. (London office: 29 Piccadilly; tel: 44 (0)20 7437 6309; reservations: 44 (0)20 7734 2395). Egypt Air fly to and from Asmara once a week; the fare is US$474 with a stopover in Cairo. Flights leave Asmara at 04.45 on Fridays. If flying to or from London, Egypt Air have a six-hour stopover in Cairo.

Saudi Airlines 100–101 Liberty Av, Asmara; tel: 120166/120153. Flights to Jeddah are on Wednesdays and Saturdays (dep 12.00, arr 13.15) and cost US$360 return. Jeddah to London flights operate daily except Thursday. A return trip via Jeddah to London from Asmara costs US$1208. Asmara to Riyadh flights leave Asmara on Saturdays, with connections to London on Thursday, Friday and Saturday. A return trip via Riyadh to London from Asmara costs US$1263.

Sudan Airways Martyrs Av, Asmara (near Roma Cinema); tel: 120483/125313; fax: 120438. Sudan Airways fly to Khartoum twice a week on Wednesdays and Sundays; the fare is US$272. Flights leave Asmara at 09.10 and 06.00 respectively. Flights to London connect with the Sunday departure and cost US$721, which is non-refundable. If you wish to stop in Khartoum you will need a visa (Nfa540) from the Sudanese Embassy.

Yemenia 89 Liberty Av, Asmara; tel: 120199; fax: 120107. Operates flights between Eritrea and Yemen and Europe. Return flights are approximately: Sanaa: US$245; London: US$781; Frankfurt: US$736

Eritrean Airlines Liberty Av; tel: 125500/1 is principally a booking agent for other operators. Their office, situated one block west of the central cathedral, is a very useful place to obtain flight information on all the different carriers. They also have an office at the airport (tel: 181891).

Passenger plane arrival and departure information can be obtained from the airport (tel: 182817).

Overland

Border crossings between Eritrea and its neighbours have faced considerable changes since independence. Up until the border conflict with Ethiopia there was no problem crossing between the two countries. Now, with the Temporary Security Zone in place and 4,000 UN soldiers and over 200,000 soldiers from Ethiopia and Eritrea on the border, it is definitely *not* possible. It is impossible to say when this might change, but when it does it will most certainly be common knowledge as it is a vital trade route for many Ethiopians and Eritreans alike.

If and when the border reopens, the most common route is via Senafe or Ghundet, the border posts on the two main roads from Ethiopia to the Eritrean highlands. A handful of vehicles used to enter Eritrea via Assab, and then drive north through Denkalia – a stunning journey, but one for which you have to be well equipped (see *Through Denkalia*, page 141).

The borders into Sudan are currently open, the most common being via Tessenei and Ali Ghedir and Telta'sher to Kassala. Make sure you obtain a valid Sudanese visa from their embassy in Asmara. In 1995 the border was closed as Eritrea cut off diplomatic relations with the Sudanese regime on account of the latter's encouragement of Muslim fundamentalists. This has now changed and diplomatic relations with Sudan are currently good. Check before you plan your journey as this situation can readily change. The Foreign Office in the UK can provide current information as to whether the borders are open or closed. A second route to Sudan is via Karora in the north, but this is much a harder journey than through Tessenei.

Theoretically, the border with Djibouti is open, but the practicalities of crossing overland hardly make this option worthwhile. It is probably easier to catch a boat from Assab to the port of Djibouti. If you wish to consider these options it is vital that you first check the latest information from the Ministry of Immigration in Asmara.

By sea

If you would like to try your hand at getting a berth out of Massawa, for example to Egypt, Saudi Arabia or Yemen, the best place to ask is Eritrean Shipping Lines. They have an office in Asmara on Liberty Avenue (by Cinema Impero) and in Massawa next to the ruined Imperial Palace. A passenger ship used to connect Massawa with Saudi, where you could get a connection to Egypt, but it appears to have stopped operating now. However, it is always worth enquiring at the port in Massawa, as there might be some ships in the port that are willing to take passengers. If this is the case you should be ready to travel and therefore have the necessary visas for your onward journey.

Assab is an almost deserted port since the war, though ships do travel to and from Djibouti and Yemen. This makes it feasible to leave Eritrea from Assab, but the practicalities are somewhat limiting. You would need to have obtained the necessary visas from Asmara and be prepared for a potentially long wait for a ship that is willing to take you on from Assab.

HEALTH

Dr Jane Howarth Wilson and Dr Felicity Nicholson, with additions by the author

With some sensible precautions your chances of catching any serious disease are small. Most travellers who spend time in Africa experience some form of illness at some point, but this is most likely to be simple traveller's diarrhoea or a cold. Before you travel be sure to arrange the necessary immunisations and seek advice on which malaria tablets are sensible. More importantly, you should consider how you would prevent mosquitoes from biting you (see below).

Travel insurance

Don't even think about arriving in Eritrea without travel insurance. Make sure you take out a policy that will fly you back home, or to the nearest place with comprehensive medical facilities, in an emergency. Medical facilities in Eritrea are still pretty basic. The ISIS policy available in Britain through STA (tel: 020 7361 6262) is inexpensive and has a good reputation. Your bank might also offer a travel insurance policy.

Whatever policy you opt for, ensure that you have as extensive a repatriation policy as possible: if you are seriously ill it would be sensible, if possible, to return home.

Immunisations

The wisest approach to preparing for a trip to Eritrea is to visit a travel clinic (see below) or your local GP.

You should have immunisations against yellow fever, polio, typhoid, meningitis and tetanus, and take malaria prophylaxis. Hepatitis A immunisation with Havrix Monodose or Avaxim is also advisable as the disease could debilitate you for months. One dose gives you protection for one year and can be boosted at the end of this time for ten years' protection. It can be used up to the day before travel, but is best given at least two weeks before travel. If you are travelling far from medical facilities, consider being immunised against rabies; this can also be done at a travel clinic. Other vaccinations recommended for trips longer than six weeks include diphtheria, BCG and hepatitis B. Hepatitis B and rabies injections comprise three injections given over a four-week period, so you are advised to go to a doctor well in advance of your trip.

Travel clinics
UK
Berkeley Travel Clinic 32 Berkeley St, London W1X 5FA (near green Park tube station); tel: 020 7629 6233; email: shanetini@btinternet.com.
British Airways Clinics There are now only three BA clinics, all in London: 156 Regent St, W1B 5LB (no appointments); 101Cheapside, EC2V 6DT (tel: 020 7606 2977); and 115 Buckingham Palace Rd, Sw1W 9SJ (Victoria Station; tel: 020 7233 6661); see also www.britishairways.com/travelclinics. Apart from providing inoculations, they sell a variety of health-related goods.
MASTA (Medical Advisory Service for Travellers Abroad) Keppel St, London WC1 7HT; tel: 09068 224100. This is a premium-line number, charged at 50p/minute.
Nomad Travel Pharmacy and Vaccination Centre 3–4, Wellington Terrace, Turnpike Lane, London N8 0PX; tel: 020 8889 7014.
Thames Medical 157 Waterloo Rd, London SE1 8US; tel: 020 7902 9000. Competitively priced, one-stop travel health service. All profits go to their affiliated company InterHealth, providing health care for overseas workers on Christian projects.
Trailfinders Immunisation Centre 194 Kensington High St, London W8 7RG; tel: 020 7938 3999. Also 254–284 Sauchiehall St, Glasgow G2 3EH; tel: 0141 353 0066.

USA
Centers for Disease Control The Atlanta-based organisation is the central source of travel information in the USA with a touch-tone phone line and fax service: Traveler's Hot Line, (404) 332 4559. Each summer they publish the invaluable *Health Information for International Travel* which is available from Center for Prevention Services, Division of Quarantine, Atlanta, GA 30333.
Connaught Laboratories PO Box 187, Swiftwater, PA 18370; tel: 800 822 2463. They will send a free list of specialist tropical-medicine physicians in your state.
IAMAT (International Association for Medical Assistance to Travelers) 736 Center St, Lewiston, NY 14092. A non-profit organisation which provides lists of English-speaking doctors abroad.

Australia
TMVC Tel: 1300 65 88 44; website: www.tmvc.com.au. TMVC has 20 clinics in Australia, New Zealand and Thailand, including:
Brisbane Dr Deborah Mills, Qantas Domestic Building, 6th floor, 247 Adelaide St, Brisbane, QLD 4000; tel: 7 3221 9066; fax: 7 3321 7076
Melbourne Dr Sonny Lau, 393 Little Bourke St, 2nd floor, Melbourne, VIC 3000; tel: 3 9602 5788; fax: 3 9670 8394.

LONG-HAUL FLIGHTS

There is growing evidence, albeit circumstantial, that long-haul air travel increases the risk of developing deep vein thrombosis. This condition is potentially life threatening, but it should be stressed that the danger to the average traveller is slight.

Certain risk factors specific to air travel have been identified. These include immobility, compression of the veins at the back of the knee by the edge of the seat, the decreased air pressure and slightly reduced oxygen in the cabin, and dehydration. Consuming alcohol may exacerbate the situation by increasing fluid loss and encouraging immobility.

In theory everyone is at risk, but those at highest risk are shown below:

- Passengers on journeys of longer than eight hours duration
- People over 40
- People with heart disease
- People with cancer
- People with clotting disorders
- People who have had recent surgery, especially on the legs
- Women who are pregnant, or on the pill or other oestrogen therapy
- People who are very tall (over 6ft/1.8m) or short (under 5ft/1.5m)

A deep vein thrombosis (DVT) is a clot of blood that forms in the leg veins. Symptoms include swelling and pain in the calf or thigh. The skin may feel hot to touch and becomes discoloured (light blue-red). A DVT is not dangerous in itself, but if a clot breaks down then it may travel to the lungs (pulmonary embolus). Symptoms of a pulmonary embolus (PE)

Sydney Dr Mandy Hu, Dymocks Building, 7th floor, 428 George St, Sydney, NSW 2000; tel: 2 221 7133; fax: 2 221 8401.

Canada

IAMAT (International Association for Medical Assistance to Travellers) Suite 1, 1287 St Clair Av West, Toronto, Ontario M6E 1B8; tel: 416 652 0137; web: www.sentex.net/~iamat.

TMVC (Travel Doctors Group) Sulphur Springs Rd, Ancaster, Ontario; tel: 905 648 1112; web: www.tmvc.com.au

Irish Republic

Tropical Medicine Bureau This Irish-run organisation has a useful website relating to tropical destinations: www.tmb.ie

South Africa

There are four **British Airways travel clinics** in South Africa:
Johannesburg, tel: (011) 807 3132.
Cape Town, tel: (021) 419 3172.

include chest pain, shortness of breath and coughing up small amounts of blood.

Symptoms of a DVT rarely occur during the flight, and typically occur within three days of arrival, although symptoms of a DVT or PE have been reported up to two weeks later.

Anyone who suspects that they have these symptoms should see a doctor immediately as anticoagulation (blood thinning) treatment can be given.

Prevention of DVT
General measures to reduce the risk of thrombosis are shown below. This advice also applies to long train or bus journeys.

- Whilst waiting to board the plane, try to walk around rather than sit.
- During the flight drink plenty of water (at least two small glasses every hour).
- Avoid excessive tea, coffee and alcohol.
- Perform leg-stretching exercises, such as pointing the toes up and down.
- Move around the cabin when practicable.

If you fit into the high-risk category (see above) ask your doctor if it is safe to travel. Additional protective measures such as graded compression stockings, aspirin or low molecular weight heparin can be given. No matter how tall you are, where possible request a seat with extra legroom.

Knysna, tel: (044) 382 6366.
East London, tel: (0431) 43 2359.

Medical kit
Many travellers make the mistake of believing that if their stay is not a long one then they are less likely to become ill. This can be a dangerous assumption. It is often said amongst travellers that they experience food poisoning more often in Asmara than in rural areas, so a short stop-over in Asmara does not guarantee a trouble-free visit. However, rural healthcare facilities are basic, so it is as well to carry as comprehensive a medical kit as possible. Leaving aside individuals' specific ailments, the following list of medical requirements draws upon the experience of many travellers in Africa:

- basic sterile medical and dental kits
- malaria prophylaxis (plus quinine and Fansidar for treatment of malaria)
- painkillers (soluble aspirin or paracetamol)
- bandages and plasters
- potassium permanganate crystals (antiseptic)

- Cicatrin (antiseptic)
- cup filter
- insect repellent and net
- Clarytin (antihistamine)
- ciprofloxacin for dysentery
- Rehidrat (oral rehydration solution)
- treatment for eye, ear and throat infections
- multivitamins
- hydrocortisone cream for skin infections
- Tinidazole for giardia
- condoms/femidoms

Medical facilities in Eritrea

There are a number of government and private hospitals in Asmara, as well as a growing number of smaller private clinics. The largest hospital is **Mekane Hiwot** (tel: 127762) at the foot of Forto, not far from the museum. Another is **Halibet** (tel: 185400/134) on the southern ring road and a third is **Edaga Hamus** (tel: 123801). These are government-run and offer basic facilities with often very helpful staff. The smaller clinics are perhaps more efficient and hygienic. The most popular is **Sembel Polyclinic** at Sembel Complex; tel: 150175/150230 (buses Nos 1, 9 or 12). Another one worth recommending is **Selam Polyclinic**, behind Odeon Cinema, just next to Bristol Pension. Pharmacies are well stocked and you will be able to find most medicines for common ailments at any of the major outlets. The following are some of the best: **Asmara Pharmacy** on Liberty Avenue near Bar Royal; **Central Pharmacy** opposite the former Keren Hotel; and **Number One Pharmacy** behind the central post office. One word of warning, however: do not count on buying malaria prophylactics after arrival. Nevertheless, wherever you are, local standards of diagnosis are excellent, even if they are short of the preferred curative. This is particularly true of malaria.

For an ambulance, tel: 122244.

Health problems
Altitude sickness

A common complaint amongst travellers to Eritrea is that of altitude sickness on arrival. Asmara is at an altitude of nearly 2,500m and so presents the real possibility of feeling slightly nauseous, faint or experiencing headaches. You may also experience it when returning from the lowlands after prolonged periods. This will not last for very long so you needn't worry. Getting plenty of sleep and rest is the best way to overcome this mild problem.

Traveller's diarrhoea

Diarrhoea afflicts at least half of those who travel in the tropics. The best treatment is to stop eating solid foods, avoid alcohol, and take only clear fluids. Only take blockers (such as Imodium, Lomotil or codeine phosphate) if you do not have access to sanitation, for example if you are travelling.

The abdominal pains that are often associated with diarrhoea are caused by the bowel trying to expel bad food. If the bacteria that produce the poisons causing these symptoms are deprived of food they will die out within 36 hours. Taking blockers will generally keep the poisons in your system and you will feel bad for longer. Blockers are useful if bowel cramps continue for more than 48 hours, as they may do in the case of salmonella food poisoning, for example. It is dangerous to take blockers if you have dysentery (evidenced by blood, slime or fever with the diarrhoea). You should seek medical advice as soon as possible if you have these symptoms.

It is important to drink a lot if you have diarrhoea. Paediatric rehydration fluids such as Dioralyte and Rehidrat are excellent, and you can make your own salt and sugar oral rehydration solution (see box, page 62). If you are vomiting you can still absorb fluids. Drink slowly and in sips. Avoid drinks that are very hot or very cold; they will stimulate the bowel to open and may cause colic (belly ache). Drink a glass of rehydration solution, or any other liquid, each time your bowels open.

If you are vomiting, do not worry about the quantity you produce: the volume is never as much as it looks and provided you keep sipping slowly you will be replacing sufficient lost fluids (even if you have cholera). Dehydration is the only serious complication of diarrhoea and vomiting and you will avoid this by drinking. In a temperate climate, if you are not eating, you need to drink about three litres per day to maintain the body's fluid balance. If is hot, or you have a fever or diarrhoea, or you are at high altitude, you need to drink more than this.

Adults with stomach upsets associated with the production of a lot of sulphurous gas at both ends of the alimentary canal, and with abdominal distension, probably have giardia. Take a course of tinidazole (four x 500mg tablets in one go repeated one week later if symptoms persist. Abstain from alcohol when you take this or you will feel sick. This drug can only be obtained on prescription in the UK.

If you have diarrhoea with blood or you have a fever, it is sensible to organise a stool test and see a doctor. Provided that you take plenty of fluids, you need not be in a great rush to do this. In most cases no treatment will be required.

How to avoid diarrhoea

There are a great many myths about how diarrhoea is acquired, but most travellers become sick from contaminated food. Salads, especially lettuce, are always a likely source. Foods that are freshly cooked or thoroughly reheated should be safe, but such foods are often few and far between. Sizzling hot street foods are invariably safer than those served at buffets in expensive hotels. Ice cream is generally unsafe: it is an ideal medium for bacterial growth and is often not kept adequately frozen due to power cuts. Ice may have been made with unboiled water and could have been deposited at the roadside on its journey from the ice factory. Tap water is generally unsafe to drink, even when hotels claim it is drinkable. Bringing water to the boil kills 95% of bugs; boiling it for a further two minutes kills 99% of bugs. Boiling water renders it

HOW TO MAKE ORAL REHYDRATION FLUID

People with diarrhoea or who are vomiting regularly need to take in more fluids or they will become dehydrated. When the intestine is upset absorption of fluids is less efficient. All solids, especially if they are greasy, are poorly tolerated and may cause colic. The ideal solution is a mixture of two heaped teaspoons of glucose and a three-finger pinch (less than a quarter of a teaspoon) of salt in a glass of cooled boiled water. Drink a glass of this at least every time your bowels open; more often if you want. If you feel nauseous or are actually vomiting, sip the drink very slowly. If glucose is unavailable, sugar, palm syrup or honey are good substitutes. If none of these, or boiled water, are available put a pinch of salt in any flattened, sweet soft drink such as cola.

Any clear solution is OK to drink: from sweet black tea, a staple in Eritrea, to drinks made from Marmite and Bovril and clear thin soup. The secret is to drink a combination of salt and sugar, so add a little salt to sweet drinks, or sugar to salty drinks. The solution should taste no saltier than tears. Quantity is more important than constituents.

much safer than using iodine, which in turn renders it safer than using water purification tablets.

Sun and heat

The sun becomes more vicious the closer you are to the equator. It is difficult completely to avoid direct sunlight, but there is also no need to feel you must expose yourself: tanning ages your skin and can cause skin cancer. If you don't let your skin get used to the sun gradually, you will end up with sunburn. If you carry things too far, sunstroke – a potentially fatal condition – is a possibility and does occur in the coastal regions if precautions are not taken. Use sunscreen and build up your exposure slowly. Avoid exposing yourself for more than two hours in one day and stay out of the sun between noon and 15.00.

Be particularly careful when swimming or snorkelling. An old T-shirt will protect your back and shoulders, and shorts will take care of another vulnerable area, the back of your thighs.

Many visitors find they sweat a lot in Africa. You should drink more than usual to counter water loss, particularly in the summer months. In coastal areas there is often a breeze which, because it dries the sweat quickly, may make you unaware of the rate at which you are losing water. Use extra salt on your food as well if you are sweating a lot. Prickly heat, a rash caused by sweat trapped under the skin, is a common symptom when you first arrive. It's harmless but it is nonetheless unpleasant. Wearing 100% cotton clothes will help, as will sloshing yourself regularly with cold water and avoiding excessive use of soap. People tend to sweat most at the coast; if you are suffering badly you could always head to a higher altitude or find air conditioning for a few days.

Always wear clothes made from natural fabrics such as cotton. These help prevent fungal infections and other rashes. Athlete's foot is common: wear sandals or flip-flops in communal washing rooms. Small cuts are inclined to go septic in the tropics, especially those from scrapes on coral. If you cut yourself, clean the wound by dabbing with a dilute solution of potassium permanganate 2–3 times daily. Antiseptic creams are generally not suitable for the tropics: wounds need to be kept dry and covered.

Malaria

Malaria kills about a million Africans every year, and of the travellers who return to Britain with malaria, 92% have caught it in Africa. You are 100 times more likely to catch it in Africa than in Asia. It is impossible to say exactly where and when malaria occurs in Eritrea, but there are some general rules you can apply. Any area above 2,000m (including Asmara) is unlikely to be a problem. The most infected areas are the coastal regions and, particularly, the western lowlands. After the rains (August–December and Feb-April) is the worst time for malaria, as the mosquito larvae have plenty of places to spawn. You should take all reasonable precautions against being bitten by mosquitoes and take malaria tablets meticulously. To do otherwise is foolhardy. The situation regarding which tablets to take is constantly changing and a GP may not have current information. You should seek advice from a travel clinic or phone 020 7636 7921 for recorded information.

The *anopheles* mosquitoes that transmit malaria emerge at dusk and tend to hunt at ground level. It is therefore advisable to wear long trousers and socks in the evening and to cover any exposed parts of your body with insect repellent, preferably a DEET-based preparation such as Repel. Mosquitoes can bite through thin socks, so it is worth putting some repellent on your ankles, even if they are covered. DEET-impregnated ankle bands (marketed by MASTA at the London School of Hygiene and Tropical Medicine; tel: 0207 631 4408) are quite effective, though they may get you some puzzled looks. If you are sitting in one place for some time, light a mosquito coil between your feet.

Like many insects, mosquitoes are drawn to direct light. If you are camping, never put a lamp near the opening of your tent: you will have a swarm of mosquitoes and other insects waiting outside when you retire. If you are staying in a hotel room, especially one that is poorly screened, be aware that the longer you leave your light on, the greater will be the number of mosquitoes that gather in the room. Spraying your room with insecticide such as that marketed by Mobil (and available in Eritrea) can also help, as do mosquito nets which are often provided, but certainly not guaranteed. It is definitely worth carrying your own. Mosquito coils reduce the biting rate and, even though strains of mosquito that are skilled at flying in turbulent air have evolved, it's worth switching on a fan if your room has one. Sleeping in a screened tent will protect, provided that no mosquitoes get in while the flaps are open. Few Eritrean hotels have screened windows. However, on the coast and in the western lowlands it is so hot in the summer that sleeping indoors is often too uncomfortable. In this case you will need a mosquito net.

Even if you take your malaria tablets meticulously and take care to avoid being bitten, you might contract a strain of malaria that is resistant to prophylaxis. If you experience headaches and fevers, or even a general sense of disorientation and flu-like aches and pains, you may have malaria. It is vital that you seek medical advice immediately. The hospitals in Asmara are well equipped to deal with malaria as local doctors see malaria victims the whole time; they will recognise it in all its various guises and know the best treatment for local patterns of resistance. Untreated, malaria is likely to be fatal; but even drug-resistant strains normally respond well to one or other treatment, provided you do not leave it too late. If it is not possible to get to a doctor, take two quinine sulphate tablets three times a day. If after three days you still have not received medical help then take three tablets of Fansidar at the same time. Self-treatment is no substitute for professional medical help, but can still be life saving!

Malaria normally takes a few weeks to incubate, and for this reason you are advised to continue with prophylaxis for at least four weeks after you leave Eritrea. It is all too easy to forget to take your pills once you are back in the everyday routine of life at home, but you should make every effort to remember. If you display symptoms, which could possibly be malarial, even up to a year after you leave Eritrea, get to a doctor and ensure that they are aware you have been exposed to malaria; he/she may not think of it otherwise.

Dengue fever

If you suspect that you have dengue fever, which is quite common in coastal areas of Eritrea, it is imperative that you have a malaria test as soon as possible. Once you have ascertained that it is dengue fever that you have there is little else to do but go to bed and take painkillers until the fever passes.

The virus is spread by day-biting, clean-water-breeding Aedes mosquitoes. The more dangerous form, dengue haemorrhagic fever, does not occur in Africa. The incubation period is two to seven days. In classical dengue the worst part of the illness is unpleasant, with severe muscle pains (hence its other name, 'breakbone' fever), high fever (40°C) of abrupt onset and a characteristic measles-like rash, but it is short-lived, lasting for no more than a week, and is seldom fatal.

Bilharzia or schistosomiasis

In general water has been rather scarce in Eritrea so there isn't quite the same opportunity to face the temptation to swim in every river that looks half-clean. Nevertheless you should be as wary of bilharzia here as anywhere. It is caused by worms that spend part of their life inside freshwater snails and infect people when they swim or paddle in still or slowly moving, well-oxygenated, well-vegetated water. The first symptom of infection is an itchy patch where the worm entered, then perhaps a fortnight later, fever and malaise and much later, blood in the urine or motions if you have a heavy infestation. Although there is a very good cure for bilharzia, drug resistance is emerging. It is wise to avoid infection.

Bilharzia is endemic in most of Africa. Do not be lulled into a false sense of security by stories that if vegetation is scarce or the water rough you are 100% safe to swim. Nevertheless, it's reasonable to assume that a fast-flowing mountain stream is very low risk, while a sluggish river or any lake is high risk.

If you dry off promptly after spending ten minutes or less in the water, the parasite does not have sufficient time to penetrate your skin and so does not infect you.

AIDS and venereal diseases

Both AIDS and venereal diseases are prevalent in Eritrea although official figures would suggest otherwise. There is an increasing awareness of AIDS in the country and an extensive programme underway to tackle the issue of AIDS, which might do something to curb a similar tragedy befalling Eritrea as has occurred in other African countries. With up to 350,000 Eritrean soldiers on the frontline at the peak of the recent war, there remains a frightening potential for the transmission of sexually transmitted diseases. In a hospital you would be extremely unlikely to be given an injection with an unsterilised needle, but it is never worth the risk: it is worth carrying your own needles and even one of the small dental kits available from outward bound shops.

It barely needs saying that the risks involved in sleeping around, especially with prostitutes, are the same as anywhere in the world, only more intensified. If you cannot stick to a policy of celibacy, then carry condoms or femidoms. Condoms are widely available in Asmara and to a lesser extent, in other towns. Using spermicide creams or pessaries will also help reduce the risk of infection.

Meningitis

This is a particularly nasty disease as it can kill within hours of the first symptoms appearing. The telltale symptom is a combination of a blinding headache and a stiff neck, and usually feverishness. A vaccination (Mengivac A and C) protects against the common and serious bacterial form in Africa, but not against all of the many kinds of meningitis. If you show symptoms, get to a doctor immediately.

Rabies

Rabies is carried by all mammals – the domestic dog being the most common agent - and is passed on to man through a bite, or a lick of an open wound. Stray dogs in Eritrean cities are unusual, as there is a strictly enforced law against this, but it does not guarantee your safety. So you must always assume any animal is rabid (unless personally known to you) and seek medical help as soon as possible. In the interim, scrub the wound with soap and bottled/boiled water then pour on a strong iodine or alcohol solution. This helps stop the rabies virus entering the body and will guard against wound infections, including tetanus. If you intend to have contact with animals and/or are likely to be more than 24 hours away from medical help, then vaccination is advised. Ideally three pre-exposure doses should be taken over four weeks. If you are bitten by any animal, treatment should be given as soon as possible, but it is never too late to seek help as the incubation period for rabies can be very long. Tell the doctors if you have had pre-exposure vaccine. Remember if you contract rabies, mortality is 100% and death from rabies is probably one of the worst ways to go!

Tetanus
Tetanus is carried through deep, dirty wounds and bites. Ensure that any wounds are carefully cleaned. Immunisation gives good protection for ten years, provided you do not have an overwhelming load of tetanus bacteria on board. Keep immunised and be sensible about first aid.

Swimming and boating
Swimming in the Red Sea is generally safe. It is advisable to wear hard-soled swimming shoes if you intend to snorkel over coral. If you are unfortunate enough to step on Didema urchins (long black spikes), iodine or wine and vinegar will dissolve the spikes. One other piece of advice: given the perennial stories of holiday boat accidents around the world, do ensure, if hiring a boat, that the operator has lifejackets.

SAFETY
Theft
Stories of theft are extremely rare in Eritrea, as are instances of any sort of crime, though the recent war and its resulting poverty have created an environment where incidents have increased. The state of civil order instigated after independence has much to do with the remarkable absence of crime. Muggings are unheard of. That said, it is necessary to list a few simple precautions because Eritrea remains an extremely poor country; tourists invariably arrive with a certain amount of wealth and it would be naive to suggest that the infrequence of theft will last forever.

Should you need police assistance during your stay call Asmara Police Station; tel: 127799, fax: 115555. For the Fire Department in Asmara; tel: 117777

Documentation
The best insurance against a major disaster it to keep things well documented. Carry a photocopy of the main page of your passport and your visa. In addition, keep details of your bank, credit cards, travel insurance policy and camera equipment.

Keep copies of your travellers' cheque numbers and a record of the ones you have cashed, as well as the international refund assistance telephone number.

Make sure that you report any theft to the police immediately, if you wish to claim on insurance; try to get a copy of their official report.

One last thought
If you are robbed, do not be tempted to give chase. Firstly the person who robbed you is likely to be particularly desperate to have committed the crime;

secondly, if the crime was witnessed, it is very likely that other Eritreans will take care of the matter for you and it is best not to get involved in the meting out of street justice.

Women travellers

Eritrea is famously safe compared to many other African countries, or any other country for that matter. In this respect it is a country that should represent few problems for women travellers. Asmara is often said to be safe enough to walk the streets any time of day or night and this is largely true. Crime in Eritrea is rare and violent crime is practically unheard of, but this should not be a cause for being too blasé. Common sense and respect go a long way and with a bit of both you will not encounter problems. Remember that Eritrea has both a Muslim and a conservative Christian culture, so respect must be given when considering what to wear. Wearing tight, short clothes, especially in smaller towns or villages, will usually attract attention, but not of the positive kind (unless where appropriate, such as on the beach in Massawa). Smoking and drinking by women is also frowned upon, so if you need to do either of these it is best not to flaunt it. Go to a suitable bar or hotel. Generally though, and partially due to the EPLF's policy of sexual equality, there is a growing movement amongst women to drive the equality issue hard and as such, women's rights are heard louder here than in most African countries. The National Union of Eritrean Women (NUEW) is an umbrella organisation upholding the rights of women. They have a central office near the US embassy and a craft shop supplied and run by local women on Emperor Yohannes Steet, which is worth a visit if you want some souvenirs to take home with you.

WHAT TO TAKE

If you are planning to use public transport then a backpack or kitbag are the ideal way to carry your luggage. An internal frame is more flexible than an external one. Carrying a day sack is also a good idea, although you are rarely parted from your luggage on the buses. Some sort of body wallet is also a good way of carrying those things without which you would find yourself in serious difficulties: money, airline ticket and passport (or a photocopy of it – though the real thing is usually required at checkpoints).

There are no official campsites in Eritrea but if you are hiking or even wishing to camp on the coast there is nothing to deter you, so bring a lightweight tent (with mosquito netting). A sleeping bag and mat are useful, whatever your chosen means of transport, if you intend travelling outside the major cities: it can be cold in the highlands at night, you have the benefit of not having to worry about bedbugs, and you are insured against never quite knowing where you might be staying (it could be someone's hut).

Clothes

There is no need to travel with too many clothes; they take up a lot of room and there is often somewhere where you can have them washed cheaply or wash them yourself. If you are in the highlands in winter it is advisable to bring at least one set of warm clothes. Otherwise two pairs of trousers are enough: lightweight cotton for walking, and for wearing in the evening. Despite their limited resources Eritreans are always smartly dressed and even during sandstorms they seem to be able to remain incredibly pristine. Considering conditions when travelling in the countryside, I found this to be a minor miracle, and one that was difficult to match; you should however try to be as clean as possible – looking like a vagrant does not improve your chances of getting help in any situation. A sunhat is essential on the coast and in the west, as too are a good pair of sunglasses to reduce eyestrain, which can be quite severe in certain areas.

Other clothes should be comfortable, light and preferably made of cotton. A few T-shirts, two pairs of shorts/skirts and a few pairs of socks and underpants are adequate. Sports shirts, with collars, are often a good idea because although they are essentially T-shirts they look smarter, and more suitable if you are staying in a top hotel or just going to eat or drink at one.

Good walking shoes or boots are essential if you are travelling anywhere other than the major cities. Trainers, flip-flops or sandals are all useful,

HOW TO AVOID CASUAL THEFT

The bulk of theft in Africa is casual snatching or pick pocketing. This is not particularly aimed at tourists but you are fair game. The key to not being pick pocketed is not having anything valuable in your pocket; the key to avoiding having things snatched is to avoid having valuables in a place where they are snatchable. Most of the following points will be obvious to experienced travellers, but they are worth making:

- Most casual thieves hang around bus stations, markets and in large public gatherings. Keep a close watch on your belongings in these places and avoid having loose valuables in your pocket or daypack.
- Keep all your valuables (passport, travellers' cheques, etc) in a money belt. One you can hide under your clothes has obvious advantages over one that is worn externally.
- Don't carry your spending money in your money belt. A normal wallet is fine provided it only contains a moderate sum of money. Better still is a wallet you can hang around your neck. In a high risk area, wearing shorts with your money in them under your trousers is another solution. Try to avoid producing large sums of money for all to see, wherever you are.
- Distribute your money through your luggage.
- Many people prefer to carry their valuables on their person. Your hotel room, or better still a hotel safe if available, is generally safer.
- Do not bring jewellery of a high monetary or sentimental value.
- Be sure to lock your hotel room when you are out. Some lower-budget hotels have poorly secured rooms. If this is the case ask for a better room or find a different hotel.

depending on the purpose of your stay. Many Eritreans wear the black plastic sandals ('shida' or 'congo') that were standard issue during the struggle and are now immortalised by the sculpture halfway along Martyrs Av. They are remarkably cheap though the comfort they provide varies depending on whom you ask. Nonetheless, their almost comprehensive use says something for the practicality of sandals in the terrain.

Eritrea has a large Muslim population and women should dress with this in mind, not exposing the knees or shoulders. This will avoid a lot of trouble. Shorts are not generally worn, by men or women, in Asmara or other towns, with the exception of the coast, but obviously if you are travelling in Denkalia or other out of the way areas they are practical. As a general rule, Eritreans dress modestly and you should do the same: dental-floss bikinis are not the order of the day on the coast, nor are the tight shorts that some UN peacekeepers appear in from time to time in Asmara.

Other odds and ends

Some things which come in very handy and which may be difficult to obtain in parts of Eritrea include a torch, batteries (although common sizes are available in Asmara), a towel and camping equipment if you need it. Small gas cylinders of the type used in camping stoves are not easily available (but building a fire is usually just as easy an option).

A wide range of cosmetics are available in the larger towns and cities, but they are almost all exclusively imported and therefore expensive. If you like to have your usual home comforts it is probably best to bring them from home, otherwise local equivalents will more than suffice. Sun cream is a must, especially on the coast and the west. There are no contact lens' fluids available, though wearing lenses can be more of an irritation when travelling any distance from Asmara because the roads are invariably dirt-tracks and eye irritations are easy to pick up. Take glasses as well as lenses. Sanitary towels are often of Eritrean manufacture; if this is a concern bring your own. Tampons are available in Asmara. A basic first aid kit is always advisable.

Insect repellent is very useful to bring, although there is a particularly effective spray made by Mobil that is available (for spraying rooms though, not yourself). Mosquito nets are often provided where mosquitoes are particularly prevalent, but it is always advisable to take your own just in case – it often saves you against those sleepless nights where mosquitoes appear to be nesting in your ears.

A snorkel and goggles for the coast enable you to enjoy the underwater sights to the full; hard-soled swimming shoes also protect against sea urchins or cuts from the coral. Coral cuts can take an inordinately long time to heal.

Outside the upper range hotels you are unlikely to find loo paper. It is widely available, as are 'softies' (tissues); if travelling in the countryside take a good supply.

A collapsible umbrella is useful both in the sun and the rain. A one-cup capacity water filter such as Pentapure (made by Lifesystems) is especially good for peace of mind and averts the need to carry bottled water everywhere you go. It is available from outdoor shops such as any YHA Adventure Shop. A water bottle is useful for carrying your own water if you are likely to be away from towns for any length of time.

A travel alarm clock helps with early starts. Take all reading material with you – books, besides Eritrean history, in any European language are few and far between. If you are taking any gadgetry that needs mains power, such as a radio or video camera, carry a universal travel adaptor. A short-wave radio can be very welcome if staying in Eritrea for any length of time, given that news is difficult to come by through local sources once outside of the larger cities or towns. BBC World Service is the most reliable and often received information service, so much so, it is rare to see a group of soldiers without at least one soldier grasping a radio tightly to his ear and listening to the latest broadcast.

You are often likely to experience the kindness of Eritreans; while something in return is seldom expected, if you have room to carry some small gifts it is a very good idea to do so; anything from T-shirts to key-rings from your country will help cement friendships. If you are a keen photographer then a Polaroid camera is a guaranteed winner of friends and will draw much favour with potential subjects (see also *Photography*, page 82–3).

MONEY

The unit of currency is the nakfa (Nfa), named after the town in the Sahel mountains (spelt Nacfa) that provided a home to the liberation movement throughout much of the 30-year struggle and from where they launched their ultimately successful assault to liberate the country. The nakfa was introduced in 1998 to replace the Ethiopian birr, which signified a symbolic end to colonial rule and, as some say, contributed to tensions with their neighbour that eventually led to war.

The nakfa is divided into 100 cents. Denominations of notes are 100, 50, 20, 10, 5 and 1. Denominations of coins are 50, 25, 10 and 5. The government has recently floated the nakfa after it was tightly controlled at a rate of 10Nfa to US$1. Now the exchange rate is open to greater fluctuations but currently sits around 15Nfa to US$1, reflecting a truer market value. Fluctuations may be as much as between 10 and 20Nfa to the US$1, though it is likely that if stability remains in the region the nakfa will stabilise.

Foreign exchange

Money can be exchanged at any of the banks in all major towns and in the foreign exchange bureaus in Asmara. Exchange bureaus tend to be much faster and have better rates. Another advantage of exchange bureaus over banks is their opening hours. Banks are generally open from 07.00–11.00 and 14.00–16.00. Exchange bureaus tend to be open from around 08.00–18.00. There are about seven different exchange bureaus to choose from if you are just changing money, but Himbol provides the widest range of services, including money transfers. They also have three branches in Asmara. It is also usually possible to change money at government hotels where bills are payable in US dollars as well.

There are unofficial money-changers (particularly evident in Asmara around the central post office), but to change money outside a bank or authorised dealership is *not* legal and you do so entirely at your own risk.

Although there are banks in most major towns some have yet to open and others have been sacked by the Ethiopian Army (Barentu and Tessenei). It is advisable therefore to only change money in Asmara, Massawa, Assab and Keren. Elsewhere, although it is possible, it may take time. Decemhare, Adi Keih, Mendefera, Adi Qala, Afabet and Agordat all have banks. Barentu's is near completion and should be open by the time this book is published.

The best foreign currency to carry in Eritrea is US dollars. It is worth having some cash, but bring the bulk of your money in travellers' cheques as they are easier to replace if stolen. Unlike some African countries you will mostly use local currency, except when paying in some hotels, or buying a permit to visit the Dahlak Islands, or paying the airport tax. Try to bring various denominations: some of the smaller hotels that require bills to paid in US dollars may not have dollars to give you as change.

It is not a requirement to keep receipts, although if you find you have too much local currency when nearing the end of your trip you can change nakfa back to the original currency if you do have the official receipts. The central Commercial Bank provides this service, but the process is typically very long. Himbol is a much better option. Another reason for keeping receipts is that some hotels only allow room payment in nakfa if you can provide official receipts. This usually only applies in some government hotels where there is an official policy to clamp down on the booming black market trade in currency trading.

In an emergency, funds can be transferred to the Commercial Bank using Western Union Money Transfer, though the charges are quite severe. Himbol also provides a money transfer service and will help you contact your family or friends to get money transferred as efficiently as possible.

Credit cards
Credit cards are still relatively conspicuous by their absence, although a number of institutions do now accept them. These include most banks, travel agencies, airlines, major hotels and some foreign exchange bureaus. It is not advisable to rely wholly on credit cards, however, especially if you are spending time out of Asmara.

Budgeting
Eritrea is a cheap country to visit with the exception of some of the top hotels, car hire and visiting the islands. If you budget separately for these then making an estimate for other things is relatively easy. As a rough guide to day-to-day spending, soft drinks cost Nfa2–3; beer is about Nfa4. A snack or breakfast will usually cost around Nfa6–8. An evening meal in a local restaurant serving Eritrean food will cost Nfa15–25; at a hotel restaurant or one serving Italian food prices for each dish are around Nfa30.

Rooms in Asmara will cost anything from Nfa40–120 for most reasonable budget hotels and pensions, whilst more luxurious hotels are around

Nfa400–2,000. Budget pensions go as low as Nfa20, but you tend to get what you pay for. Conversely, if you prefer to spend over US$1,000 a night you can book the Presidential Suite in The Inter-Continental Hotel! It is impossible to generalise about hotels outside Asmara, but Massawa and Keren are about 10–20% cheaper, with few options for the luxurious, and other towns up to 75% cheaper, but the facilities tend to be more basic.

Car hire is relatively expensive, especially now due to the huge influx of NGOs. A Land Cruiser costs Nfa850–1,000/day, plus mileage over 80km of Nfa2 per km per day. Such a vehicle is not necessary if you are only visiting Keren, Massawa, the south down to Senafe or Adi Qala, or the west up to Barentu; beyond this circle the condition of the roads can be poor. For travel within this region you can safely hire a saloon car for around than Nfa400. However, sometimes it is good to have the option of going 'off road' if you wish, so plan your itinerary beforehand.

If you intend to visit the **islands** expect to pay Nfa2,300–4,300 per day for a boat, which will take up to eight people. In addition a permit is required which costs US$20 per person.

Travel on the **buses** is cheap. A fare from Asmara to Massawa is Nfa11.50; Asmara to Keren is Nfa9. If you were to travel all the way from Asmara to Tessenei the fare would be Nfa47.

In summary, if two of you are travelling by bus, staying in reasonably cheap hotels and eating and drinking what you want, US$25 each per day is certainly adequate.

GETTING AROUND
By air
The only internal flight available is from Asmara to Assab. Fares are bookable at Eritrean Airlines, 89 Liberty Avenue, Asmara (tel: 125500). It is possible that flights to Massawa will resume once the new airport is operating. As Nacfa has a new airstrip (2,000m long), that may also become a viable destination.

By rail
The railway in Eritrea currently offers trips for organised tours from Ghinda to Massawa. Enquire at the railway office (tel: 123365/123633; fax: 291 1 201785) for travelling on the railway. Once the line is complete between Asmara and Massawa (estimated for 2002), it is scheduled to provide frequent trips for tourists. The route of the railway, from the highland plateau to the Red Sea coast, will undoubtedly provide one of the world's best railway journeys.

By bus
Buses are certainly affordable and reasonably comfortable, though they do tend to vary in quality considerably. For a quicker and normally more comfortable ride it is worth taking a minibus. These follow the same routes as the shorter distance buses and cost the same. The only problem is if you are travelling with limited time there is no set timetable on either buses or

minibuses. You pay your fare and then just wait until the bus is full, when it will depart. Wherever you are starting from buses tend to start leaving for destinations around 06.00. If you are travelling long distances there might be just one or two buses a day and these will leave early. For shorter distances, such as Asmara to Keren, buses operate until mid-afternoon about once every half hour. Don't leave it too late in the day, though, as buses tend not to travel after dark. If you are travelling from Asmara all buses leave from around the main bus station. See box below for some typical prices and times. These fares, though correct at the time of writing, are bound to alter, and are stated here just as an approximation.

By sea
Boats do travel between Massawa and Assab and between the islands. To find out the various prices and lengths of journeys you can enquire at Eritrean Shipping Lines (Massawa: tel: 552475; fax: 552391; Asmara: tel: 120402; fax: 120331).

Hitchhiking
Due to the relatively low rate of car ownership and crime in Eritrea, hitch-hiking is a much more attractive and common means of travelling than it is in most countries. On the edge of most towns and villages, there will be many individuals or groups of people waving down any vehicle that is willing to carry them to their destination. This can often provide the most interesting journeys, as it is a good way of meeting people and sometimes seeing parts of the country you might not see if travelling by public transport. In addition to this, it is invariably much quicker than public transport. Of course, it would be foolish to suggest that there are no risks involved in hitch-hiking, but provided you take the usual precautions, you shouldn't have a problem.

SOME TYPICAL BUS JOURNEYS

Asmara to Massawa	3 hours	Nfa11.5
Asmara to Decemhare	1 hour	Nfa4
Asmara to Adi Keih	3 hours	Nfa12
Asmara to Senafe	4 hours	Nfa13.5
Asmara to Mendefera	2 hours	Nfa6
Asmara to Adi Qala	3 hours	Nfa9
Asmara to Keren	3 hours	Nfa9
Keren to Afabet	4 hours	Nfa12
Afabet to Nacfa	4 hours	Nfa16
Keren to Agordat	2 hours	Nfa8
Agordat to Barentu	3 hours	Nfa7
Barentu to Tessenei	4 hours	Nfa16
Asmara to Tessenei	12 hours	Nfa47
Asmara to Assab	2 days	Nfa120

ERITREA'S REVITALISED RAILWAY

Eritrea's railway is a remarkable tale of achievement on the one hand and maltreatment on the other. Construction started shortly after the Italians arrived in Eritrea to provide supply routes to the advance army positions, which were moving inland at the time. The railway reached Ghinda (alt 888m, 49km from Massawa) by 1904 and Nefasit (alt 1,672m, 93km from Massawa) by 1910. The stretch between Nefasit and Asmara is the most remarkable; with over 20 tunnels, 65 bridges and viaducts and an incline of 1:30, this section is testament to some astonishing feats of engineering. The line eventually reached Asmara (alt 2,330m, 119km from Massawa) by 1911. The average incline between the coast and the capital is a staggering 2%. Further north and west from Asmara, the going was much easier, but work was slowed significantly due to World War I. Keren (alt 1,392m, 222km from Massawa) was not reached until 1922, then finally Agordat (alt 606m, 306km from Massawa) in 1928. It was designed principally to assist in trade and exporting of goods to the Middle East (and Sudan and Ethiopia if the project had been completed), as well as the transportation of raw materials intended to be mined in Eritrea. Other uses included the supply of raw materials to construction sites and the armed forces, as well as providing passenger transport from the coast. After World War II however, it was in much less demand and used predominantly to shuttle passengers between Asmara and the coast. Then during the struggle it faced neglect and eventually ceased operating from 1962. Since this time until liberation it was gradually destroyed or dismantled. The materials were used in the war effort and rolling stock laid to waste or used for storage.

However, after its mixed history, it looks certain that the railway will soon be carrying tourists from Asmara to Massawa on a resurrected system rebuilt over about seven years by a committed workforce, many of whom were

Driving in Eritrea

Eritrea's roads are in pretty good condition and compared to most other African countries they are excellent. All the roads connecting major towns are sealed except the roads from Keren to Nacfa via Afabet and the road from Barentu to Tessenei. Both these stretches are still pretty rough and take some time by bus. The most impressive developments with the roads are the links from Massawa to Assab, Massawa to Afabet and Mendefera to Barentu. Though they are not yet fully completed they will provide huge savings in time and provide a much more comfortable journey, as well as opening up vast areas of the country to potential development.

Driving is on the right-hand side of the road. It is not advisable to drive at night, especially on mountain roads with their precipitous edges. In some of the far-flung areas driving at night may actually be prohibited; if this is the case then you will be prevented from leaving the town you are in close to nightfall. In other words it is not a mistake that you will make accidentally. If in any among those that used to run the railway in its prime in the 1950s. Most workers have come out of retirement to lovingly restore the locomotives with the care and attention of impassioned craftsmen. Some are well over 80 years old and are not ashamed to admit that this railway was and will always be their life. It is a delight to visit the workshops in Asmara, running pretty much as they were in the 1920s, and see these men at work.

Despite the Eritrean railway stopping short at Agordat (although during the 1930s it did extend several kilometres beyond the town), the system had originally been planned to link up to the rail networks in Ethiopia and Sudan. Similarly high ambitions are being aired today in Eritrea and perhaps, one day, there will be a connection with Sudan providing valuable transportation to the agricultural areas of the western lowlands. To see the passion and commitment of the workforce one dare not doubt the viability of their ambitions. For the time-being, however, the goal is Asmara and although the recent war drained valuable manpower there are droves of volunteers, national servicemen and formerly retired workers returning to complete the project. The track has been laid from Massawa up to Embatkala and is now being worked from Asmara down towards Nefasit. The two projects should connect before the end of 2002. It would be difficult to doubt the dedication of the workers on this railway. They have reconstructed the line, bridges, tunnels and locomotives by hand with little or no help from outsiders. The result might have meant that the deadline for the railway's inauguration has slipped a little, but it is a wholly Eritrean project for which the country can be extremely proud. To ride on this railway is one of the finest travelling pleasures and the incredible scenery must make it one of the most beautiful railway journeys in the world. If it is open during your visit to Eritrea it should be one of the priorities on your itinerary; you will not be disappointed.

doubt check with the local administration. As the volume of traffic increases so will the danger factor on the roads. Drive with extreme care – on some roads there is hardly enough room for a car and a lorry to pass each other. International driving licences are valid in Eritrea; those of one's home country should also be carried. Third party insurance is mandatory. Fuel, both diesel and petrol, is easily obtainable everywhere, bar Denkalia and Sahal.

ACCOMMODATION

Accommodation is generally good, though it can be limited in the smaller towns. Asmara has a number of good hotels. Keren has a couple of good hotels and a further one currently being constructed, while Massawa and Assab have two each. Otherwise there is always plenty of budget accommodation ranging from Nfa10 for a bed to Nfa100 for a room with shower. At government hotels prices are payable in US dollars. Sometimes the 5–10% sales tax and 10% service charge is included, sometimes not. Check when you book in.

Most private hotels can be paid for in Nfa, though some demand US$. The budget accommodation outside the major cities (Asmara, Assab, Massawa and Keren) is basic. Washing facilities are shared and depending on the time of the year there may be no running water. Outside Asmara, loos are usually of the squatting variety, but are generally fairly clean. Often rooms are communal and contain two to six beds. If you want privacy, you can pay for the whole room. In the hotter regions there is always an option to sleep outside, which is not only rather romantic, but often a lot more comfortable.

Theft has not hitherto been a problem: stories of theft from hotel rooms are virtually unheard of, though this doesn't mean you shouldn't take the usual precautions. Locking your room when you are out and putting valuables in the hotel safe are two obvious measures to minimise risk.

Camping

There are no official campsites in Eritrea but nobody seems to have had any problems pitching a tent on the coast, for example. If you are hiking in the highlands and wish to camp, there are some areas of the country that used to have campsites during the Italian occupation. Now, though, they are unused, but it is unlikely that anybody would have objections to you pitching a tent for the evening. It is always worth asking someone if you are near a village or settlement, just in case.

ERITREAN CUISINE

The staple is *injera*, a spongy pancake made from teff, wheat or sorghum. The grains are ground up, made into a watery dough and then left to ferment for a couple of days before being fried or baked. *Injera* is eaten with stew made from meat, fish, vegetables, or any combination of these. Meat or fish stews are called *zigini*. When it is served, several *injera* are usually put on a tray and the stew poured into the middle. You eat with your hands by breaking off bits of *injera* and scooping up the stew. People eat together, sharing the food. In practice the choice of food is often limited when you are in the countryside. The following are some of the more common dishes available:

zigini	meat stew
zigna assa	fish stew
dorho zigni	chicken stew
tibzi	fried meat
spris	mixed dish, served with spicy sauce
ful	stewed beans with onion and tomato, normally eaten for breakfast or dinner
ful massala	*ful* served with egg and cheese
kitcha fitfit	pieces of *kitcha* (similar to unleavened bread) served with yogurt and butter
shiro	chick pea purée
ades	lentils
capretto	goat, usually served like a rack of lamb

frittata	scrambled eggs with onion, peppers, etc
arrosto	roast meat, usually beef
nai-tsom	fasting food (vegetarian combination)

Drinks

Eritreans drink a lot of locally made drinks served only in private homes, though occasionally you might be able to find the following drinks in some restaurants or local bars. The names and strengths vary enormously around the country, but the most common are *siwa*, similar to home-brewed beer; *mes*, like a type of mead; *daga* in Barentu; *caticala*, a very strong spirit from the western lowlands; and *abake*, a non-alcoholic alternative produced by the Eritrean Muslims.

'Official' drinks that can be found almost everywhere in Eritrea are Asmara beer, and a wide range of liquors produced by Asmara Brewery, founded by the Melotti family in 1939 (tel: 120028). The most popular of these is *Ariki*, an aniseed flavoured spirit that packs a mean punch. Coca-Cola, Sprite and Fanta are also widely available.

Tea (*shahi*), coffee (*bune, machiato* and *cappuchino*) and milk (*tsaba*) are very popular in Eritrea. The one significant difference you may find is the quantity of sugar Eritreans have in their hot drinks. This is said to derive from the struggle when hot drinks were the only way soldiers could get their necessary daily requirement of energy. If you prefer a more savoury flavour, just ask for *bezzai shuquer* (without sugar).

Water is not regarded as particularly safe to drink, so mineral waters tend to be the desired option for most travellers. Until recently the only two options, besides boiling all your water, were the local *mai gas*, which is a carbonated mineral water sourced on the route to Massawa and cost Nfa2–3 for a 75cl bottle; and imported mineral waters from Italy or the Middle East, which tend to cost in excess of Nfa10 for 1.5 litres. This made drinking quite an expensive business. However, in 2001 a local brand of mineral water has been introduced, which sells its water in a number of different sized containers. If you are here for some time, it is worth buying the 10 litre bottles, which cost Nfa27, Nfa20 of which is a deposit.

Coffee ceremony

Coffee is something of a delicacy in areas outside the major cities and to be asked to take coffee is an invitation not to be refused. Popcorn is often eaten at the same time and incense burned. The coffee is always made by a woman, who washes the green beans and roasts them in a pan called a *menkeshkesh*. The little burner is called a *fumello*. When the beans are dark enough they are ground and put on a small rush mat (*mishrafat*), which is used as a funnel to pour the coffee into its pot (*jebena*). Water is added and the coffee brought to the boil. It is shameful to let the coffee boil over. When all is ready sugar is put in the small cups (*fenjal*) and the coffee is strained into them. If you have accepted an invitation for coffee be prepared to wait an hour for it to be completed – it is rude to leave early. Standard practice is that you must have three cups, after which you are able to leave whenever you wish.

PUBLIC HOLIDAYS

The pattern of public holidays is still being established but the major ones include:

New Year	January 1
Orthodox Christmas	January 7
Timket (baptism of Christ)	January 19
Eid el-Fitr	Winter (date determined by lunar calendar)
International Women's Day	March 8
Eid el-Adha	Summer
Good Friday	Spring (determined by Easter)
Easter (Fasika)	Spring
International Labour Day	May 1
Independence	May 24
Martyrs' Day	June 20
Eid Mawleed el-Nabi (Prophet's birthday)	Autumn
Start of the Armed Struggle	September 1
Orthodox New Year	September 11
Meskel/Festival of Timket (Finding of the True Cross)	September 27
Christmas	December 25

There are a seemingly large number of festivals, because to a greater or lesser extent those of all three major faiths are observed. The Muslim festivals are especially hard to list since their calendar is lunar. Weddings are particularly numerous in January and February.

SHOPPING

Things are improving rapidly in Asmara but Eritrea is still no place for the avid shopper. Souvenirs are available, ranging from rather uninteresting African souvenirs which you might find in any duty-free shop on the continent, to some much more interesting gold and silver jewellery, and religious artefacts such as prayer scrolls, old decorated Bibles and crosses and incense-burners. Keren is the best place to hunt for jewellery. Elsewhere in the country, in the west for example, you can find pottery, swords, daggers, traditional haircombs, baskets and other items in the marketplaces.

While many of the textiles worn by Eritreans are attractive you may be disappointed to discover that most of the material is imported from the Far East. The Tigrinya shawl (*netsela*) you will see everywhere in the highlands is the most authentic cloth you can buy in Eritrea, but since the war it has soared in price, as most were imported from Ethiopia. Eritreans are slowly developing a manufacturing industry of their own (see the *Segeneiti section*, page 190). With this and the ever-wishful hope that economic trade will soon begin again between these two countries, the prices should fall. This also goes for many foodstuffs, including coffee beans.

The marketplaces are always good to wander around; a wide variety of fresh vegetables, fruit, spices and pulses are available in the central market in Eritrea Square in Asmara. There is also a more craft-oriented market behind the main mosque that sells a wide range of wicker and pottery goods. Although you may find these items for a much cheaper price outside Asmara, this is certainly the most practical place to buy such things.

In Asmara there are also a number of Italian-style grocery shops where you can buy anything from mineral water to chocolate to Chianti. A wide range of wines, spirits and imported beers can also be bought in these shops. The only place to buy such items outside Asmara is in Assab.

Bargaining

It is not common to be overcharged as a tourist, whether you are buying vegetables from the market or taking a taxi, but there are signs that this is changing. Although prices do tend to be genuinely fixed (not the perceived norm in many parts of Africa), you might often find that being an obvious source of money might encourage a certain entrepreneurial tendency in some people. If you know that you are being charged over the odds do not be afraid to point this out. Bargaining does not usually apply when purchasing foodstuffs such as vegetables, fruits and spices.

If taking a taxi from your hotel ask at reception how much your fare should be. Bear in mind that the new fleet of yellow Opel taxis understandably charge more than the older taxis. If you are buying large amounts of silver try negotiating a discount for bulk. Sometimes this works, sometimes it doesn't.

Prices do vary a bit around the country: the transport costs of getting a soft drink to Tio, in Denkalia, are obviously rather higher than if the destination is Asmara, although this doesn't hold true for Nacfa, where you can find the cheapest bottled beer in the country. Accommodation and food tends to be much cheaper once you are outside Asmara.

Tipping

Tipping is common in cities and is sometimes included in the bill. At the more expensive hotels and restaurants a 10% service charge will already apply, though how much of that goes to the staff that serve you is unknown. Otherwise a tip of Nfa2–5 for a meal amongst friends would certainly be appropriate. Most of the waiting staff are on very low wages and work extremely long hours, so giving even a small tip makes a lot of difference. In the more rural areas, or smaller towns, tipping is not so common, but it differs from place to place, so use your discretion.

ARTS AND ENTERTAINMENT

The arts are being revitalised in Eritrea, after years of neglect during the Ethiopian occupation. Drama, art, music and dance are all culturally very important. Dance in particular plays a major role in traditional culture, varying considerably from one ethnic group to another. Besides enjoyment, it is a very important means of storytelling. If you are in Asmara between May 20–24 you will experience many public dances in the streets to celebrtate the liberation of the country.

Theatre is harder to come by, though the Theatro Asmara, in Asmara often has some intresting plays that are greatly appreciated by the local audiences.

Music is something you will probably have to get used to in Eritrea. The familiar beat of Eritrean music and the repetition of the most popular songs can become a little wearing, as there are few places in which it is not played at a high volume. To experience locally played music, however, is a different matter altogether and well worth it if you can find a venue. Some of the nightclubs in Asmara have live music, otherwise being invited to a wedding or other major ceremony should guarantee the opportunity. Eritrean music has a distinct beat created by the *koboro* (drum) accompanied by a range of different instruments like the *krar* (guitar), *wata* (violin), *shambuko* (flute), *embilta* (wind instrument) and *melekhet* (traditional saxophone).

Art is becoming more popular in Eritrea and there are a growing number of budding artists having their works displayed on the international circuit. The most famous of these, and a student of the renowned EPLF's Revolutionary School, is probably Michael Adonai, who recently had his work on display at the UN headquarters in New York. Appreciation for art in Eritrea is definitely on the rise and the central Art College in Asmara produces many fine young artists. Modern works tend to display cultural symbolism and be of an abstract style using bright, vivid colour.

A good opportunity to experience different cultural shows, including dancing, live music, drama and singing, is during the 'Festival', at the end of July and beginning of August. This is held in Eritrean communities all over the world, but in Asmara, the festivities take place in Expo, on the airport road.

Entertainment in Eritrea is sometimes deemed as limited. This might be partially true outside Asmara, though many larger towns have cinemas and many lively bars. In Asmara there are four cinemas, one theatre, many different nightclubs, literally hundreds of bars and restaurants, some with billiards, and even a bowling alley.

MEDIA AND COMMUNICATIONS

One of the cornerstones of the democratisation process in Eritrea was meant to be the establishment of an unrestricted media. This extended only as far as newspapers, with radio, TV and other printed journals still being solely a government domain. The Eritrean people have a long history of enjoying diversity in news. After World War II there were many different newspapers available in English, Arabic and Tigrinya. During the Ethiopian occupation this ceased, but was taken up again with relish after independence. Sadly, due to 'the interests of national security', the independent newspapers have recently been 'temporarily' closed. How long this will last remains to be seen. Therefore there is at the moment only one weekly newspaper in English, *Eritrea Profile,* and a daily newspaper in Tigrinya and Arabic. All are widely available and cost Nfa1. Many stationers in Asmara sell *Time, Newsweek* and the *Economist,* and foreign newspapers are available in the British Council Library, Alliance Française and sometimes at the top hotels in Asmara.

EriTV, the government TV channel, operates every evening from 18.30, except at weekends, when it starts at 14.00. The English language news is on at 21.30. CNN and BBC are also widely available in hotels. The British Council shows BBC World every evening from around 17.00.

Internet

The internet has enjoyed a boom in Eritrea since early 2001, with well over a quadrupling of outlets in the first six months of 2001. However, such is the Eritrean thirst for information that demand still easily outstrips supply. It is very easy to find access to email and the internet, but because of the high demand you might have to queue in some places. The connection is fastest early in the morning and after 19.00 in the evening, when offices have closed. For internet locations in Asmara, see page 110–11.

For details of general websites on Eritrea, see *Appendix 2*, *Further Information*, page 206.

Post

The post office is very efficient but seemingly random customs checks can result in your post being kept on a bureaucrat's desk for at least a couple of weeks. This is not as rare as it should be, but no convincing answers were forthcoming from any officials. The postal workers are always very helpful and willing to assist if you have an enquiry. Standard mail should not be a problem; it is usually only the thicker or bulky packets that raise attention. Poste restante is a reliable way of receiving mail. Mail should be addressed as follows:

SMITH, John
Poste Restante
Post Office
Asmara
Eritrea

Telephone services

Telephone rates are quite expensive, and if you use a hotel telephone the cost is likely to be as much as 25% extra. One way round this is to make calls from the telecommunications building in whichever town you are in, which are open 08.00–22.00 daily. You pay a deposit of Nfa200 for an **international call**, and pay/collect the difference when you have finished. Rates per minute vary, but should be between Nfa17 for the US and Nfa22 for Europe, Asia and Africa.

If you pick a quiet time, making an international call from Asmara is a speedy and straightforward process. **Faxes** can also be sent and received. Prices are charged per minute and vary between Nfa23 for UK and Nfa29 for America, Europe, Asia and Africa. Incoming faxes can also be received; the fax number in the Asmara telecommunications building is 291-1-122904 and faxes should be marked 'for collection'.

MAKING THE BEST OF YOUR TRAVEL PHOTOGRAPHS
Subject, composition and lighting
If it doesn't look good through the viewfinder, it will never look good as a picture. Don't take photographs for the sake of taking them; film is far too expensive. Be patient and wait until the image looks right.

People
There's nothing like a wonderful face to stimulate interest. Travelling to remote corners of the world provides the opportunity for exotic photographs of colourful people and intriguing lifestyles which capture the very essence of a culture. A superb photograph should be capable of saying more than a thousand words.

Photographing people is never easy and more often than not it requires a fair share of luck plus sharp instinct, a conditioned photographic eye and the ability to handle light both aesthetically and technically.
* If you want to take a portrait shot, always ask first. Often the offer to send a copy of the photograph to the subject will break the ice – but do remember to send it!
* Focus on the eyes of your subject.
* The best portraits are obtained in early morning and late evening light. In harsh light, photograph without flash in the shadows.
* Respect people's wishes and customs. Remember that, in some countries, infringement can lead to serious trouble.
* Never photograph military subjects unless you have definite permission.
* Be prepared for the unexpected.

Wildlife
There is no mystique to good wildlife photography. The secret is getting into the right place at the right time and then knowing what to do when you are there. Look for striking poses, aspects of behaviour and distinctive features. Try to illustrate the species within the context of its environment. Alternatively, focus in close on a characteristic which can be emphasised.
* The eyes are all-important. Make sure they are sharp and try to ensure they contain a highlight.
* Get the surroundings right – there is nothing worse than a distracting twig or highlighted leaf lurking in the background.
* A powerful flashgun can transform a dreary picture by lifting the subject out of its surroundings and putting the all-important highlights into the eyes. Artificial light is no substitute for natural light, so use judiciously.
* Getting close to the subject correspondingly reduces the depth of field; for distances of less than a metre, apertures between f16 and f32 are necessary. This means using flash to provide enough light – build your own bracket and use one or two small flashguns to illuminate the subject from the side.

Landscapes
Landscapes are forever changing; good landscape photography is all about light and mood. Generally the first and last two hours of daylight are best, or when peculiar climatic conditions add drama or emphasise distinctive features.
* Never place the horizon in the centre – in your mind's eye divide the frame into thirds and exaggerate either the land or the sky.

Cameras
Keep things simple: light, reliable and simple cameras will reduce hassle. High humidity in tropical places can play havoc with electronics.
* For keen photographers, a single-lens reflex (SLR) camera should be at the heart of your outfit. Look for a model with the option of a range of different lenses and other accessories.
* Totally mechanical cameras which do not rely on batteries work even under extreme conditions. Combined with an exposure meter which doesn't require batteries, you have the perfect match. One of the best and most indestructible cameras available is the FM2 Nikon.

- Compact cameras are generally excellent, but because of restricted focal ranges they have severe limitations for wildlife.
- Automatic cameras are often noisy when winding on, and loading film.
- Flashy camera bags can draw unwelcome attention to your kit.

Lenses

The lens is the most important part of the camera, with the greatest influence on the final result. Choose the best you can afford – the type will be dictated by the subject and type of photograph you wish to take.

For people

- The lens should ideally should have a focal length of 90 or 105mm.
- If you are not intimidated by getting in close, buy one with a macro facility which will allow close focusing. For candid photographs, a 70–210 zoom lens is ideal.
- A fast lens (with a maximum aperture of around f2.8) will allow faster shutter speeds which will mean sharper photographs. Distracting backgrounds will be thrown out of focus, improving the images' aesthetic appeal.

For wildlife

- Choose a lens of at least 300mm for a reasonable image size.
- For birds, lenses of 400mm or 500mm may be needed. They should be held on a tripod, or a beanbag if shooting from a vehicle.
- Macro lenses of 55mm and 105mm cover most subjects, creating images up to half life size. To enlarge further, extension tubes are required.
- In low light, lenses with very fast apertures help.

For landscapes

- Wide-angle lenses (35mm or less) are ideal for tight habitat shots (eg: forests) and are an excellent alternative for close ups, as you can shoot the subject within the context of its environment.
- For other landscapes, use a medium telephoto lens (100–300mm) to pick out interesting aspects of a vista and compress the perspective.

Film

Two types of film are available: prints (negatives) and transparencies (colour reversal). Prints are instantly accessible, ideal for showing to friends and putting into albums. However, if you want to share your experiences with a wider audience, through lectures or in publication, then the extra quality offered by transparency film is necessary.

Film speed (ISO number) indicates the sensitivity of the film to light. The lower the number, the less sensitive the film, but the better quality the final image. For general print film and if you are using transparencies just for lectures, ISO 100 or 200 are ideal. However, if you want to get your work published, the superior quality of ISO 25 to 100 film is best.

- Film bought in developing countries may be outdated or badly stored.
- Try to keep your film cool. Never leave it in direct sunlight.
- Do not allow fast film (ISO 800 or more) to pass through X-ray machines.
- Under weak light conditions use a faster film (ISO 200 or 400).
- For accurate people shots use Kodachrome 64 for its warmth, mellowness and gentle gradation of contrast. Reliable skin tones can also be recorded with Fuji Astia 100.
- To jazz up your portraits, use Fuji Velvia (50 ISO) or Provia (100 ISO).
- If cost is your priority, use process-paid Fuji films such as Sensia 11.
- For black-and-white people shots take Kodax T Max or Fuji Neopan.
- For natural subjects, where greens are a feature, use Fujicolour Reala (prints) and Fujichrome Velvia and Provia (transparencies).

Nick Garbutt is a professional photographer, writer, artist and expedition leader, specialising in natural history. He is co-author of 'Madagascar Wildlife' (Bradt Publications), and a winner in the BBC Wildlife Photographer of the Year Competition. John R Jones is a professional travel photographer specialising in minority people, and author of the Bradt guides to 'Vietnam' and 'Laos and Cambodia'.

Public telephones cost Nfa0.40 for a local call and are usually easy to find, though it is common that they be out of order. This can be partially avoided if you use telephone cards, which are available from the telecommunications building. These are only used for local calls.

Mobile phones are just being introduced in Eritrea and will no doubt become as popular as anywhere else in the world.

Useful telephone numbers
Local operator 99
Directory enquiries internal 97; external 98

ELECTRICITY
220 volts, 50Hz (110 volts, 60Hz is very rare, but does occur in some areas). Power surges occur frequently, so an uninterrupted power supply (UPS) is vital to protect valuable electronic equipment. These are available locally. Plugs are the southern European style, ie two round pins.

BUSINESS
Business is generally quite problematical in Eritrea relative to what you may be used to in the US, Europe or Asia. This is, essentially, due to the level of bureaucracy that prevails in the system. Business stamps are a necessity for every piece of paper that leaves or enters an office, making business slow and often unnecessarily complicated. Paperwork and its needless creation can often be tiresome, but it must always be remembered that this is a system still struggling to get to grips with a fast and technologically advanced world into which it was forced to engage almost overnight. Lack of facilities, equipment and manpower compound the problem. Typewriters and handwritten receipts are often the norm and will remain so until more technologically advanced systems can be implemented, or more importantly, afforded. On occasions, this makes certain practical issues difficult to manage, such as faxing, emailing, printing, etc.

In general, insist on signing a contract which includes an advance payment before you start doing any work, for it could be many weeks or months before the necessary paperwork is created that will allow you to receive full payment. This unfortunate inefficiency is certainly not likely to be caused through any desire to swindle. Eritreans are unreservedly honest to their word; it's simply that the system struggles to operate efficiently at the best of times.

Tax is paid on a sliding scale, but works out at around 30%.

A FINAL WORD ON DOS AND DON'TS
Eritreans are a proud, perceptive and dignified people. Your behaviour is always a reflection of your own culture and will undoubtedly make an impression on those that interact with you on your visit. It is vital therefore that this interaction be a positive, two-way experience rather than one taking advantage of another. It is not uncommon to see visitors behaving inappropriately, either through ignorance or by accident, but seldom through

Above left Coptic priests
celebrating Meskel Festival

Above right Coptic priest with
traditional ceremonial cross

Left A traditional church
painting from the Highlands

Next page Agordat mosque
at sunset

malice. It is important, therefore, that we understand how best to behave when visiting other countries. Here are a few pointers to help prevent the more obvious problems from occuring in Eritrea. Dress can be a cause for ill-feeling. Gregarious behaviour is also not particularly welcomed. You will seldom find an Eritrean behaving in an unreserved manner. Smoking and drinking are largely private pastimes and you should confine these to the appropriate places. Public drinking is not acceptable. Heavy petting or overly amorous behaviour in public is also inappropriate. If you are invited for food or coffee at someone's home it is polite to remark on its excellent taste and in the case of coffee ceremonies, wait for at least three rounds before leaving.

A tradition amongst Asmarinos when invited to another house is to take a selection of pastries or cakes, which can be wrapped up to take-away from any pastry shop. Learning some Tigrinya also makes a world of difference, even if it is the very basics. A short greeting or conversation in Tigrinya is sure to gain much respect and gratitude. Traditional greetings consist of shaking hands or, amongst locals, the shoulder greeting, which you will see on many occasions. This looks like two people engaging in a scuffle, but is actually a symbol of friendship. As with shaking hands, this greeting may take some time, so do not be disconcerted by this. Gifts and, as is mentioned under photography, Polaroid cameras are an easy way of making friends or saying thank you. If you can leave a memento it makes a lot of difference, especially to children.

Be aware also of the fragile environment in Eritrea. Environmental awareness is not as prevalent in Eritrea as it now is in parts of America, Europe and Asia, so you may not be warned of the damage you might be causing. Be aware of the environment and try at all times to minimise your impact on local ecosystems. Amongst other things, this applies to driving off-road, walking and climbing (don't damage the terraces or step on tree saplings), disposing of rubbish, camping (when disposing of human waste, make sure you are sufficiently far from watercourses), purchasing rare or endangered species, and swimming, snorkelling or diving. It was a great sadness that on one trip to Dahlak Island a number of Eritreans visiting from overseas took considerable delight in taking floral coral from the sea to decorate their homes back in the US. Inevitably, the corals barely survived the boat journey back to the mainland, let alone the journey across continents.

As visitors, whether on holiday, on business or visiting friends or relatives, it is of utmost importance that we try and remain as culturally aware and as socially and environmentally sensitive as possible to the people in whose country we are welcomed guests. It only takes a little to make a big impression. As has already been said, common sense and respect go a long way.

Part Two

The Guide

Asmara 4

Asmara (2,347m), sitting atop the Eritrean highlands on the eastern edge of the vast escarpment, has an air of being a city above the clouds. Asmara has to rank amongst the most remarkable cities in the world. It was largely constructed in the 1930s and so Italian Modernist architecture abounded in Asmara, alongside a fascinating assortment of other styles from the period. Turkish styles fuse with Classical styles, which in some cases embrace more vernacular styles. The result of this extraordinary mix is a most unique and visually interesting city. To wander the streets of Asmara simply for the pleasure of relishing this aesthetic feast and participating in the innately pleasurable experience of being a subject in Asmara is one of the most enjoyable experiences to savour in Eritrea. Asmarinos love their city and it shows, and there are few visitors who visit Asmara and do not also fall giddily in love with it. Testament to this is the large number of visitors who return time and time again just to revel in an urban culture that is uniquely safe, calm and so alluring.

Asmara's central boulevard is Liberty Avenue, running from east to west and dominated by the central Catholic Cathedral. Liberty Avenue resembles a southern Italian town with its attractive palm trees, broad pavements, bars, cafés, pastry shops and barbers. To experience the evening's '*passeggiata*' along Liberty Avenue is to witness one of the great triumphs of urban planning. The streets of Asmara are its parading ground, where people love to be seen, to mingle and to discuss the day's events. Its back streets are no less interesting either, with their boutique shops, balconies bedecked with laundry, and quaint doorways and ornate gates. Bougainvillaea and jacarandas abound. Unlike many other Eritrean towns, Asmara was relatively undamaged during the struggle due to the Ethiopian forces fleeing the city at the end of the war. Time and poverty have been more damaging to the physical fabric of the city, though it is with every hope that this might change as peace in the region is maintained. Already, there are several bars, offices and residential buildings under extensive refurbishment or restoration, guided under the watchful eye of the newly established Cultural Assets Rehabilitation Programme, one of whose enviable mandates is preserving architectural heritage in Eritrea.

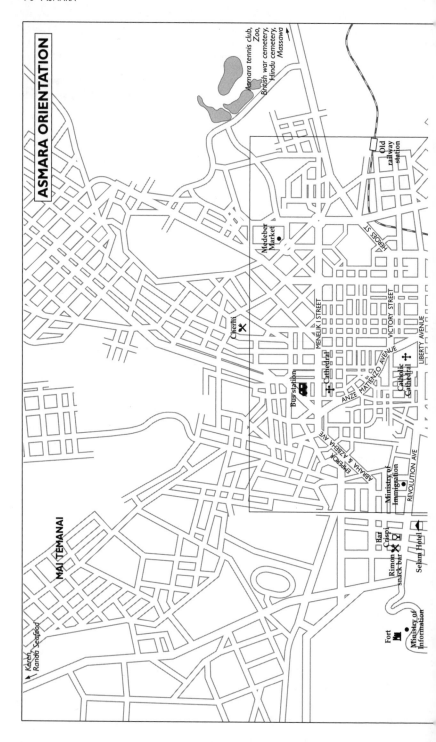

ASMARA ORIENTATION

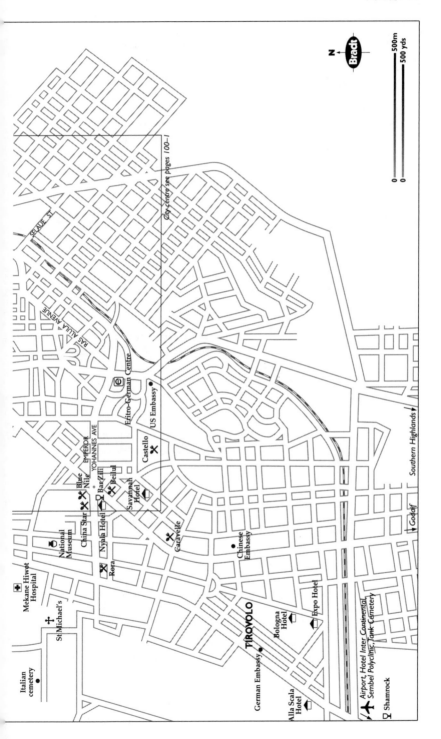

Italian cemetery

Mekane Hiwot Hospital

St Michael's

National Museum

Blue Nile

China Star

Rora

Nyala Hotel

Bar Zilli

Beirut

Savannah Hotel

Castello

EMPEROR YOHANNES AVE

Caravelle

Eritro-German Centre

US Embassy

RAS ALULA AVENUE

SELADE ST

City centre see pages 100–1

N

Bradt

0   500m
0   500yds

German Embassy

TIROVOLO

Alla Scala Hotel

Bologna Hotel

Expo Hotel

Chinese Embassy

Airport, Hotel Inter-Continental, Sembel Polyclinic, Tank Cemetery

Godaif   Southern Highlands

Shamrock

HISTORY OF THE STREET NAMES OF ASMARA
Mebrahtu Abraham, Cultural Assets Rehabilitation Programme

In 1899 the Italians moved their colonial capital from Massawa to Asmara. During the 1890s, 1920s and 1930s Italian town planners were busy carrying out massive projects to develop Asmara. With the significant expansion and development of the master plan of the town, it was obvious for the town planners to adorn Asmara with well-planned and perfectly laid out streets, avenues and squares.

Street name-plates, made from a quadrangle Lamiera (a piece of iron sheet) were for the first time posted on walls to identify street names. Of course, the name on the plate was written in Italian. Streets, avenues and squares could assume their designated names according to their broadness and narrowness. The Italian words – Strada, Via, Viale, Corso, Piazza – describe these differences. All street names during the Italian colonial period obviously reflected Italian history from different angles. Some were names of great leaders and heroes; others were names of army officers, explorers and great writers; and in some, names of Italian localities, towns, mountains, rivers etc...

By April and May 1941, the Italians had lost their East African Empire and the British became the new masters of Eritrea. During the British period several street names related with Italian Fascism were changed. Viale Benito Mussolini changed to Corso Italia. Viale Generale De Bono and its extension Viale Conte Galezzo Ciano changed to Viale Roma e Milano.

In 1952 Eritrea was federated with Ethiopia. The last months of 1952 witnessed the name changing of four main avenues of Asmara. These were:

Corso Italia to Avenue Haile Selassie I
Viale Roma e Milano to Addis Ababa Avenue
Viale Badoglio e Azzi to Edwardo Anse Matienso Avenue
Corso Del Re to Empress Menen Avenue

In 1953, the Federal Government of Eritrea set up a commission to study and rename the streets, avenues and squares of Asmara. Therefore, after 1953, the process of changing street names continued apace, right up to

Asmara is a living city in every sense of the term. It is evolving, as all cities should and, like all cities, it has its faults. The original design of the city had its strict quarters, in which 'natives' could, or definitely could not, be seen. The area to the south of Liberty Avenue is the old European quarter and boasts some of the finest villas and buildings in Asmara. To the north of Liberty Avenue, especially north of the main market in Eritrea Square, is the old 'native' quarter where the houses, to this day, are considerably more modest in their construction and size. It is equally worth visiting these areas to see the 'real' heart of Asmara beating as it is to enjoy the aesthetic of the old European quarter. The population density of these old 'native' quarters is evident by the sheer number of people you see walking around compared to the leafy

1982. The plates of street signs, which were posted on walls, were made from snow-white marble quadrangles. Transcribed on them was the name in three languages: Ge'ez, Arabic and English.

The Ethiopian authorities were busy in rooting out not only the remains of Italian colonialism and its traces but also in introducing their culture and history to their Eritrean subjects.

On May 24 1991 Eritrea was liberated by the EPLF. Following liberation, two avenues were renamed for the glory of victory and the fallen heroes and heroines. There were:

National Avenue, which became Harnet Avenue
Queen Elizabeth II Avenue, which became Semaetat Avenue

Since they were first laid down, the above two avenues changed their names five times in different historical events. Here follows the years of change of Harnet Avenue:

Viale Benito Mussolini (1925–April 1941)
Corso Italia (1941–October 1952)
Avenue Haile Selassie I (1952–1974)
National Avenue (1974–May 1991)
Harnet Avenue (After May 1991)

And the history of Semaetat Avenue is:

01 – Viale De Bono and Viale Conte Galeazzo Ciano (1930s–April 1941)
02 – Viale Roma e Milano (1941–October 1952)
03 – Addis Ababa Avenue (1952–February 1965)
04 – Queen Elizabeth II Avenue (1965–May 1991)
05 – Semaetat Avenue (After May 1991)

Now it is time to replace all the old street names, most of which refer to old Ethiopian nobles and place names. By the year 2002 all Asmara's streets will have new names.

quietness to the south of Liberty Avenue. It is no less functional and enjoyed by its residents than the more comfortable areas to the south, but the necessary development of Asmara's poorer residential quarters will be an enormous challenge in the future development of Asmara.

Asmara is the starting point for travel to any other part of the country as all buses (except to Nacfa, which leaves from Keren) depart from Asmara and, due to its geographical location, it does constitute the centre of the country. Legend has it that in this region the Queen of Sheba gave birth to the son of Solomon, Menelik I. Asmara means the 'forest of flowers'. While there are still trees at Bet Gergish to the east, the surrounding countryside is not as forested as it once was.

At the western end of Liberty Avenue are City Park and the former Imperial Palace, which is currently undergoing restoration; at the eastern end is the almost alluringly monstrous September I Square, so-called to commemorate the beginning of the armed struggle. It is one of very few structures built by the communist Derg regime and is a clear legacy of such an ideologically charged administration. Although there are calls to pull this down, it would seem inappropriate to deny this legacy, as well as any other in Asmara, for without the legacies of colonial powers, Asmara might not exist. Much can be said for the Eritrean ability to shrug off the shackles of the past and to use the facilities left behind by others. So this arena stands as a monolithic tribute to yet another oppressive regime from which Eritreans emerged ultimate successors and is now used most effectively for national celebrations, such as Independence Day on May 24, or religious holidays, such as the Festival of Timket on September 27, when the stadium is full to capacity. Midway along Liberty Avenue stands the elegant Catholic Cathedral, which provides as a very good landmark if you find yourself a little lost or disorientated wandering around the city.

Everywhere is spotlessly clean thanks to armies of blue-coated street cleaners who start work just after dawn. Traffic has increased considerably over recent years, despite early government initiatives to reduce car usage. However, despite an influx of new vehicles (especially four-wheel drives) there still remain a large number of old Fiat Cinquecentos and other cars from the sixties. In this respect Asmara is a working museum of classic cars. Horse-drawn *gharis* are also plentiful, although they tend to be used functionally rather than as transport for tourists. The city is remarkably safe and you can wander around both day and night without being hassled, which makes a welcome change from the majority of African capital cities; this even applies in the bustling market area in Eritrea Square, to the north of Liberty Avenue.

Although the village of Asmara was known to Venetian travellers as early as the 14th century, the history of the modern city began in the last century when Ras Alula, Abyssinian governor of Hamasien province, developed it as an administrative centre and fortress in the 1880s. The original village is now contained within the northeast part of the city. It was made the capital city in preference to Massawa by Governor Martini in 1897 and today is by far the largest city in Eritrea with a population of some 400,000. The period of most rapid development was in 1935–36, during the Italo-Ethiopian war; the population literally exploded with immigrants and workers from Italy and Eritrea taking part in the build-up to the establishment and consolidation of the Italian East African Empire. By 1940 Asmara had more than 100,000 inhabitants. Asmara's very diverse cultural heritage is obvious: three of the most prominent landmarks in the city are the Catholic Cathedral, Al Qurafi al Rashidin Mosque, and the Coptic Cathedral. While most of the city is Italianate there is substantial Islamic influence in the northern parts of the city. The result is a very comfortable mix of Italian café culture around Liberty Avenue and the eastern-influenced market and mosque area just to the north.

THE ASMARA–MASSAWA CABLEWAY

Sadly this is one of the Italian engineering feats that did not survive as it was dismantled and removed by the British, along with much of Eritrea's industrial capability. It was the longest cableway in the world and was used to transport supplies direct from the port in Massawa to Asmara city centre. At 71.8km, its total length was rather less than the road. Work commenced in 1935 and took two years to complete. It had 1,620 trolleys, each 100m apart and able to carry 300kg, and moved at 9km/h. The usefulness of the cableway is illustrated by the fact that it could carry 730 tonnes of goods in a day. Interestingly it did take passengers as well (for 6 lira from Massawa to Asmara, the uphill leg, and 2 lira from Asmara to Massawa). The total weight of the cables, pylons and other material was 3,900 tonnes. Leaving Massawa from the Campo di Marte, just inland from the salt flats, or from the old munitions site 3km away at Moncullo, the cables met and joined at a place called Zaga, 6km from the Campo di Marte. It was powered by eight generating stations on the journey. Whether it was actually electrified before being dismantled is not known. It is interesting that the possibility of reconstructing a similar line has been raised as and when the volume of traffic from Massawa to Asmara increases.

The relaxed and welcoming atmosphere is enhanced by the climate. The annual mean temperature is about 17°C, the coolest months being between November and January, and the warmest April to June which see top temperatures of about 26°C. 'Little' rains are in April and May; 'big' rains in July and August. Total annual rainfall is supposed to be about 500mm. Even in winter the days are invariably characterised by clear blue skies, and it is warm enough to wear short-sleeved shirts. Except during the big rains, when it can reach 70%, humidity is rarely above 50%.

Asmara is, by any standards, a very safe, picturesque and relaxed capital.

GETTING THERE

Asmara is the usual starting point of any visit to Eritrea, having the only International Airport in Eritrea (bar Assab). There are many direct flights each week from Europe and the Middle East. Once you have cleared customs and immigration at the airport you have two choices of transport to get you to town. If you are not in a hurry, the cheapest option is the Number 1 bus, which costs Nfa0.50 and goes right through the centre of town, or the more comfortable option is a taxi, which costs around Nfa40–60 for rides to town. One thing to be said for the bus, despite the price if you are on a tight budget, is that the airport is the terminus, so it will be empty when you get on (although most certainly not when you get off). The bus runs from around 06.30–21.00 and at half-hourly intervals. Taxis are available 24 hours.

Foreign embassies and diplomatic missions in Eritrea

The following countries currently have embassies in Eritrea:

Belgium (consulate) Tel/fax: 126695
Canada Tel: 181940/1; fax: 184241
China Tel: 185274; fax: 185275
Denmark Tel: 124346/8; fax: 124343
Egypt Tel: 123603; fax: 123294
France Tel: 126599; fax: 121036
Germany Tel: 182670; fax: 182900
Greece Tel: 121979; fax: 122017
Israel Tel: 185626/185521; fax: 185550
Italy Tel: 120774; fax: 121115
Norway (consulate) Tel: 201291; fax: 126571
Russia Tel: 127172 fax: 127164
Saudi Arabia Tel: 120979; fax: 120893
Sudan Tel: 120672; fax: 200760
Sweden (consulate) Tel: 122301; fax: 126571
Switzerland (consulate) Tel: 181701
UK (consulate, to become an embassy in 2002) Tel: 120145; fax: 120104
USA Tel: 120004; fax: 127584
Yemen Tel: 184892; fax: 181183

Others
European Union Tel: 126566; fax: 126578
Libyan Arab Brotherhood Bureau Tel: 126055; fax: 125578
Liaison Office of Rwanda Tel: 123423; fax: 123422

GETTING AROUND

Taxis are plentiful. The old Fiat variety are cheaper than the new Opel imports. Fares vary considerably and having white skin doesn't help either; a trip to the outskirts of town from the centre will cost Nfa40–60; to Tiravolo Nfa20–30; in the centre everywhere is within easy walking distance. If you have a bicycle this is perhaps the most efficient means of transport. Buses are also an easy way of getting around and the cheapest. Each journey costs Nfa0.50, regardless of distance. The most useful are: No1: The Airport to Biet Girgish; No2: Gezamanda to Mai Temanai (via Cathedral); No4: The Market to Godaif (Decemhare Road); No9: Sembel to The Market (via University); No11: The Market to Mai Temanai; No12: The Market to Sembel. The minibuses follow the same routes as the buses but are a little faster, though much more congested. A single fare is Nfa0.75.

Travel agencies

Unfortunately the once excellent Eritrean Tour Service (ETS) no longer operates, but there are still a number of other firms providing good services and tours. Of these I would highly recommend **Travel House International** whose service, experience and range of tours are excellent. They also provide an extensive ticketing service if you need flights from Eritrea. Other popular companies include **Ghidei**, **Gulf** and **Falcon**.

There are over 20 registered travel agencies in Asmara. These are some of the other travel agents that offer similar services, but depending on demand and availability there might be restrictions to advertised itineraries and services:

Alpha Travel and Tour Agency Behind September 1 Sq and Inter-Continental; tel: 201355/151970; fax: 201355

Falcon International PO Box 3659; tel: 126467/120238; fax: 120801; email: falcon@cts.com.er

Gulf Travel 13 Liberty Avenue; tel: 120397/124848; fax: 120443

Ghidei Travel 1st Floor, 55 Liberty Av; tel: 120303/123838; fax: 200501; email: ghideit@yahoo.com

Heron Travel PO Box 5216, Asmara; tel/fax: 122130; email: heron@gemel.com.er

Hico Aviation Tel: 127378

Jasser Travel Agency Tessenei St; tel: 202535

Keckia Travel 75 Semaeat St; tel: 120483

RTB Travel and Tour Services, Menelik Street, next to the National Museum; tel: 123257

Travel House International, PO Box 5579; tel: 201881/2; fax: 120751; email: thi@eol.com.er

Car hire

There are over 20 car hire firms operating in the city, though reservations often need to be made well in advance due to the demand from NGOs. Prices fluctuate depending on demand and the quality of the vehicle. Four-wheel drives vary considerably in this regard and you should check which vehicle you will be given before paying any deposit. There are often stories of people paying high prices to be stuck at the side of a road for hours or even days.

Car hire companies include:

Africa Car Rental Tel: 121755

Alfa Behind September 1 Square; tel: 201355/123595; or in Hotel Intercontinental; tel: 151970

Amico Rent Cars Tel: 122349/116105

Dina Car Hire Next to British Consulate, Emperor Yohannes St; tel: 116124

Fontana Garage 66 Ras Beyene Beraki St; tel: 120052; fax: 127905

Garage Odeon Tel: 121668; fax: 122052

International Car Rental Ras Alula St; tel: 120120

Khartoum Car Hire tel: 184221

Leo Rent a Car Ras Desta Damtew St No 6, PO Box 4578; tel: 202307; fax: 202306

Luna Car Hire Tel: 201016

Rematco Tel: 121439

Star Car Rental Tel: 126849; fax: 123056

Travel House International Tel: 120208; fax: 120064

MAPS

Maps are still hard to come by and as yet no sufficient tourists maps have been drawn up. Some stationery shops stock rather poor city and country maps. The most common map that is used is produced by the tourist office and costs around Nfa10. It is poster-sized so not ideal for walking around with, but as a reference it does the job. You can find this in most good stationers and certainly at Awghet Bookshop in September 1 Square. If you are trying to find something before entering Eritrea, try Stanfords in London (tel: 020 7836 1321) or other specialist map shops. The current Michelin map of East Africa is a non-starter. International Travel Maps (530 West Broadway, Vancouver BC, V5Y 1E9, Canada; tel: +1 604 879 3621; fax: +1 604 879 4521; web: www.itmb.com) publish a good map of Eritrea which has been used to produce some of the maps in this guide.

WHERE TO STAY

There is a wide range of accommodation in Asmara, catering for all budgets. At certain times of the year it might be difficult to find a bed in the price-range you want, especially during the June–September holidays when Eritreans from overseas visit in considerable numbers, but generally there is seldom a problem. You will only be able to book from overseas in the upper-range hotels. Although the government has sold off a number of hotels, a few still remain under state ownership. Typically, these lack much in the way of maintenance and can appear shabby. The privately owned hotels are a safer bet, with many of the independent 'pensions' also being more than adequate. The lower-range pensions often double as brothels and you tend to get what you pay for – very little.

Water and electricity supplies in recent months have proven to be somewhat of a problem depending on where you are staying in the city and what time of year. There has been no public statement explaining the shortages but excuses range from too many visitors showering too often to internal wrangling between the service providers. Despite the obvious inconvenience caused, the problems tend not to last for too long. Some of the better hotels have their own generators and large water storage, so you are unlikely to be affected if staying at one of these.

Prices below are given in nakfa per night, unless US dollars are the only method of payment. If you are in Asmara on business, and are therefore expecting phone calls and visitors, it is strongly recommended that you make friends with the staff at the hotel. American-style service is not yet the order of the day but people will make every effort to help, particularly if they know you. Dealing with tourists is still a new experience for most Eritreans.

Unfortunately, since telephone numbers and fax numbers are in the process of changing it is very difficult to guarantee that the numbers listed will remain correct for very long. If you have any problems finding the correct number it is worth phoning Directory Enquiries on tel: 97.

Upper range

Hotel Inter-Continental Deb. Mie. 04 Expo Area, PO Box 5455, Asmara; tel: 291 1 150400; fax: 291 1 150401; email: intercon@eol.com.er; web: www.interconti.com.

170 rooms between US$175 for deluxe singles and US$1,350 for the Presidential Suite. A deluxe double costs US$200, with special rates as low as US$130. Family doubles cost US$250 and executive doubles cost US$650, with 20% discount for special rates. However, all prices are subject to 10% service charge and 10% sales tax. The newly opened Hotel Inter-Continental is undoubtedly Eritrea's most luxurious hotel. With 3 restaurants; 2 bars; 1 café; 2 heated swimming pools (one indoor, one outdoor); 2 squash courts; 2 tennis courts; gymnasium; Turkish baths; children's playroom; and 420-seat conference centre, this hotel has just about everything anyone requires for a stay, whether for business or tourism.

Hamasien Dej. Hailu Kebebe St; tel: 123411; fax: 122595. 29 rooms: Nfa235–374 single/double/suite plus 10% service charge and 10% sales tax. The Hamasien is one of the few remaining government hotels and is suffering a bit from under-investment. It is twinned with the Ambasoira Hotel just next door. The building is a particularly interesting 'Swiss style' Italian colonial building and certainly makes for a hotel of character. It still offers a degree of comfort, with very spacious rooms. Restaurant facilities are next door in Ambasoira Hotel.

Alla Scala Airport Rd, PO Box 2481, Asmara, Eritrea; tel: 151610/151540; fax: 151541. Nfa330–649 single/double plus 10% service charge and 10% sales tax. One of the newest additions in Asmara's growing hotel population. Rather typical, modern high-rise with sterile interior. The restaurant is not exceptional, with dishes around Nfa30–50 for pizza or pasta. On the airport side of the Tiravolo district, it is about 3km from the town centre.

Ambasoira Dej. Hailu Kebebe St; tel: 123222; fax: 122595. 50 rooms: Nfa235–374 single/double/suite plus 10% service charge and 10% sales tax. Next door to the Hamasien and well positioned 300m from Liberation Avenue. This is a very popular hotel, and something of a meeting place in the early evening for all sorts of visitors whether tourists, aid workers or business people. As with Hamasien next door, rooms can only be paid for in nakfa if you can provide official foreign exchange receipts, otherwise you will have to pay in US$.

Nyala Martyrs Av; tel: 123111/123756. 67 rooms: Nfa150–330 single/double/suite plus 10% service charge and 10% sales tax. High-rise hotel some 800m from the centre of town. Its restaurant serves both Eritrean and Italian food at a reasonable price. The Nyala is still a government hotel and therefore in need of a little care and attention. Rooms can be paid for in nakfa and US$.

Ambassador Liberty Av No 38; tel: 126544; fax: 126365. 36 rooms: Nfa300–520 single/double. Excellent location right opposite the cathedral with views up and down Liberty Avenue from the roadside rooms. Although on the main street, noise at night is not a problem as traffic stops early. Now in private hands it should benefit from improvements and refurbishment in due course. Availability of water has been known to be a little unreliable. The bar downstairs is a popular drinking hole and meeting place for many foreign visitors.

Sunshine Emperor Yohannes St No 76; tel: 127880; fax: 127866. 26 rooms: US$67–85 single/double plus 10% service charge and 10% sales tax. This is a popular hotel with NGO staff and those visiting Asmara on business. It has a popular restaurant and bar serving the usual sorts of Italian and local foods at inflated prices, but it is a place where foreigners (especially women) can go and relax and have a

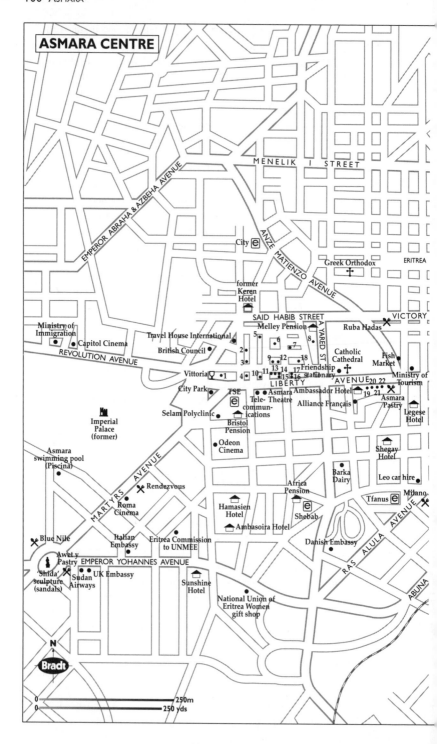

ASMARA CENTRE

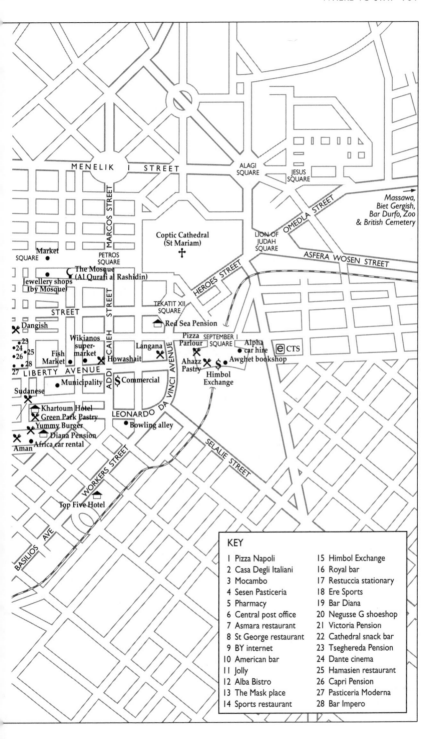

KEY

1 Pizza Napoli	15 Himbol Exchange
2 Casa Degli Italiani	16 Royal bar
3 Mocambo	17 Restuccia stationary
4 Sesen Pasticeria	18 Ere Sports
5 Pharmacy	19 Bar Diana
6 Central post office	20 Negusse G shoeshop
7 Asmara restaurant	21 Victoria Pension
8 St George restaurant	22 Cathedral snack bar
9 BY internet	23 Tseghereda Pension
10 American bar	24 Dante cinema
11 Jolly	25 Hamasien restaurant
12 Alba Bistro	26 Capri Pension
13 The Mask place	27 Pasticeria Moderna
14 Sports restaurant	28 Bar Impero

Map labels:

MENELIK I STREET
ALAGI SQUARE
JESUS SQUARE
MARCOS STREET
Massawa, Biet Gergish, Bar Durfo, Zoo & British Cemetery
OMEDLA STREET
Coptic Cathedral (St Mariam)
LION OF JUDAH SQUARE
Market SQUARE
PETROS SQUARE
ASFERA WOSEN STREET
The Mosque (Al Qurafi al Rashidin)
Jewellery shops (by Mosque)
HEROES STREET
STREET
TEKATIT XII SQUARE
Dangish
Red Sea Pension
Pizza Parlour
SEPTEMBER I SQUARE
Alpha car hire
CTS
Wikianos super-market
Langana
Howashait
Ahazz Pastry
Awghet bookshop
Fish Market
Himbol Exchange
LIBERTY AVENUE
Municipality
Commercial
Sudanese
LEONARDO DA VINCI AVENUE
ADDI CAIEH STREET
Khartoum Hotel
Green Park Pastry
Yummy Burger
Diana Pension
Bowling alley
Aman
Africa car rental
SELALIE STREET
WORKERS STREET
Top Five Hotel
BASILIOS AVE

drink without raising eyebrows. The garden out the back is a pleasant place to have a drink without being disturbed. They only accept US$ for payment of rooms, but the prices do include breakfast.

Savannah Christopher Da Gamma St No 9; tel: 202144/116185; fax: 202146. 58 rooms: US$24–80 single/double/suite plus 10% service charge and 10% sales tax. About 1km from downtown, this hotel is in a quiet part of the city but not very convenient for shops and entertainment. You may pay in local currency at the prevailing exchange rate that they provide.

Mid range

Expo Hotel Addis Ababa Av; tel: 184242/181967; fax: 182714. 65 rooms: Nfa240–516. Expo is a five-minute taxi ride from the town centre in the Tiravolo district. Taxis should not cost more than Nfa20. The Nos 1, 9 and 12 buses are cheaper alternatives at 50c each way. It is a private hotel with a good Italian restaurant, and a sauna. The rooms are small but spotlessly clean. Even the showers are rather more reliable than most hotels.

Bologna Addis Ababa Av; tel: 181360; fax: 182686. 34 rooms: US$48 first class, US$36/60 single/double. Tiravolo district. A very comfortable, new, private hotel near Expo, with larger rooms than the neighbouring Expo Hotel. Offstreet parking, en suite bathrooms, and an excellent restaurant.

Selam Menelik II Av; tel: 127244; fax: 120662. 47 rooms: Nfa150–300 single/double/suite plus 10% service charge and 10% sales tax. Extra bed costs Nfa50. Large, business hotel refurbished in 1993 to a high standard; though still in government hands it is in the process of being privatised. The hotel is a classic example of Art Deco architecture and interior design. The restaurant remains largely as it was when first built and is a 'must see' for Art Deco admirers. It has conference facilities.

Khartoum Ali Osman Buri St No 35; tel: 128008//119348; fax: 121427. 14 rooms: Nfa70–120 single/double. Centrally located in a side street opposite the Impero Cinema in Liberty Avenue, this is another relatively new, private hotel. It is no surprise that it has a distinct Sudanese feel to it and the restaurant serves good food. It is ideally located in the town centre with Green Park Pastry downstairs serving excellent cakes and coffee and the Sudanese Restaurant across the road serving good local Sudanese food. The hotel also has a car-hire business.

Shegay Desta W/Yesus St No 6; tel: 126544/62. 12 rooms: Nfa88–110 single/double. Private bathrooms; and good views of the city centre from the roof terrace. Can be a bit noisy being near to several local bars.

Top Five Sehtegnatat St No 8; tel: 124919/22; fax: 124931. 13 rooms: Nfa120–333 single/double. This new hotel is in a quiet residential area east of the town centre. It is very clean and the restaurant serves good, albeit limited, food.

Keren Hotel This was a much-loved hotel with something of a colonial feel, but it is currently under extensive restoration and it seems unlikely that its original character will be preserved. It is due to open sometime in late 2002.

Budget

Africa Tel: 121436. 11 rooms: Nfa60–80 single/double. Probably the best in the budget range and set in a beautiful garden. Home to many 'long-term' residents as it has a family atmosphere and very big bright rooms, though the rooms downstairs can be very noisy. The building itself is another fine example of Italian Modernist architecture, though now far from the proud condition it would have been when it was the city Mayor's residence. Water supply (especially hot water) can be unreliable.

Bristol Tel: 121688. Nfa70–100 single/double plus 10% sales tax. Another pension that attracts long-term guests owing to its central but quiet location and refurbished, clean rooms. The building is yet another fine example of 1930s architecture and the polished floor made from sea shells is worth a look in itself. Located behind Cinema Odeon, by the Asmara Art School.

Red Sea Nfa35–60 single/double. This excellent pension has a Muslim owner and they operate a strict policy that requires couples sharing double rooms to be married. The rooms are very clean and quiet, facing into a peaceful internal courtyard.

Victoria Tel: 121648. 16 rooms, Nfa60–90 single/double. Situated right in the centre of town on Liberty Av, this pension is ideally located for those wishing to be in amongst the life of the city. The rooms vary but if you choose the right one they can be excellent for the price.

Diana Tel: 121529. US$5/8 single/double. Just around the corner from the Legese, in Ras Welye Behil Street. Clean, large rooms but bathrooms are shared. Very friendly owners, although their English is limited.

Capri 18 rooms: Nfa50–70 single/double. Centrally located with large clean rooms and shared bathrooms. Excellent views of the Cathedral from the west-facing rooms and from the roof terrace. The juice bar downstairs serves the best juices in town.

The list of accommodation in this category is almost endless and if nothing on this list should be available a short walk around any block in town is likely to provide a handful of reasonable alternatives. All of the above have been checked, as have these (if you still can't find a room!): **Melley Pension** behind the cathedral and **Tseghereda Pension** (tel: 123864) behind Impero Cinema.

WHERE TO EAT

The choice of types of food (see *Eritrean cuisine*, page 76–7) is not wide, but most restaurants offer good value for money. Menus are usually in Tigrinya with an English translation. More exotic cuisine such as Chinese, Indian and Thai restaurants are appearing, though their authenticity remains questionable due to the limited resources and availability of rare ingredients in Eritrea. Nonetheless, such restaurants provide a welcome change if you happen to be in Asmara for any considerable length of time. The restaurants in the Inter-Continental are probably the only ones to overcome this problem by flying all their ingredients in from overseas on a daily basis.

Most upper- and mid-range hotels have their own restaurants, but the quality does vary. The buffets at the Hotel Inter-Continental (every day, Nfa99) and China Star (Thursday afternoon) restaurants provide excellent 'all you can eat' deals for those wishing to spoil themselves. One of the things that will hopefully change is the limited variety of dishes available in restaurants. This is partly due to a dearth of culinary expertise and partly due to the rather unimaginative purchasing policies of most restaurants. If you are ever asked to eat at someone's house seize the opportunity – all the really memorable meals are those taken in friends' homes. That said, there is an increasing number of private restaurants opening up in Asmara and it should not be long before a more varied cuisine is commonly available around the city.

Eating out in local restaurants in Asmara can require patience and understanding. Finding most options on the menu 'finished' or having your choice of meal decided for you independently by the chef is a common and often trying surprise. The most logical explanation I have heard for this scenario is that the concept of a restaurant, as a place you go to enjoy and pay for food and service, is a relatively new concept in Eritrea. Instead, the culture of going to a friend's or family home to eat in the company of others just to enjoy the communal atmosphere (as well as have a very fine feed at the same time) is much more deeply ingrained. In going to someone's home to eat, you eat what you are given and are doubtlessly grateful for the opportunity, as it is sure to be better than most restaurants you are likely to visit. In a restaurant you normally expect a degree of service and choice, which runs slightly against the grain of traditional communal eating in Eritrea.

Vegetarians can find it difficult to get a variety of options in many restaurants. Eritreans are very fond of meat and tend to go to restaurants on special occasions and will invariably choose meat dishes, therefore restaurants tend not to cater for a vegetarian diet. However, there are a number of restaurants that can reliably provide 'fasting food' or other vegetarian options. These are mentioned below in the specific restaurant details.

Another word of advice is to eat earlier rather than later. Eritreans tend to eat early and therefore if you go to eat out after 20.00 or 21.00 expecting a full range of options from the menu, you are likely to be sorely disappointed. Sundays can also be quite limited due to the markets being closed.

Prices and menus are virtually uniform at local restaurants and will vary in the hotels depending on the grade of hotel. Expect mid–upper range hotels to cost between 50–100% more than local restaurants. These prices will include a 10–20% service charge and/or sales tax. Snacks or breakfast will cost between Nfa4–10 for *frittata* (scrambled egg with tomatoes and pepper), *ful* (stewed beans with onions and pepper), or a cheese sandwich. A first course of pasta, tagliatelle, cannelloni, lasagne or soup will cost Nfa9–15 and a main courses of fish, *arrosto* (roast meat), *capretto* (goat), lamb cutlets, chicken or steak between Nfa15–25. Thus a meal for two in the main restaurants will cost Nfa40–60 without drinks. Local Asmara beer, which is very drinkable, is Nfa4 a bottle. Italian wine at around Nfa100 a bottle is available in many restaurants. Soft drinks are usually around Nfa2.50.

Alba Bistro This is a fashionable, newly refurbished establishment that is centrally located amongst Asmara's emerging trendy nightlife district. It has a bar and café, as well as restaurant upstairs. The food is varied and of a good quality – especially the superb soups. Prices are a little on the high side.

Asmara Restaurant This is always packed at lunchtime being in about as central a location as is possible, next to the post office. Very good local food, and if you want to try *zigini* (Eritrean stew) for the first time (or the hundredth) this is as good as any of the larger restaurants. Vegetarian foods are reliably available, as are most options on the menu. Prices vary between Nfa13–30.

Beilul Opposite the Nyala Hotel; well known for its traditional food.

Blue Nile Located around the corner from China Star restaurant, opposite the new 'Shida' sculpture on Martyrs Av. This is one of the most popular restaurants in Asmara and serves excellent local dishes, as well as a fine range of international foods, including a delicious Thai coconut curry. It is always very busy and reservations are not available, so queuing is sometimes necessary, but worth it. The prices are high at around Nfa25–50 per dish plus service charge, but the food is a cut above the rest. They also do good pizza.

Bologna Attached to the eponymous hotel in Tiravolo district. This is tastefully decorated, service is excellent and the food is enterprising (fish in ginger sauce, prawn cocktail, etc).

Caravelle Dimly lit and very curiously decorated with everything from fish bowls to an old ship's bowsprit. The first half is a bar which is very popular and worth visiting in its own right; the second half is the restaurant. Good spaghetti carbonara and pizzas.

Castello This is one of the best restaurants for Italian food, though not ideally located on a hill behind Sunshine and Savannah hotels. The cannelloni is a speciality. Here you are likely to be given the day's choice verbally rather than on a menu. It has quite a history: when Princess Anne dined here on a visit in 1994, the waiter took great delight in announcing that he hadn't served royalty since King George VI.

Cherhi Restaurant Built in 1983, this curious building atop a hill, ten minutes' walk to the north of Liberty Av, resembles an air traffic control tower, though at night looks like it has just arrived from outer space, and is thus easy to find. It was one of Asmara's two Chinese restaurants, but now is reported to serve mainly Thai cuisine owing to the new Thai owner. The prices are fairly high at around Nfa30–40 per head for a main course. If you don't feel uncomfortable eating your meal whilst looking out over Asmara's worst slum it is a worthy option for a change.

China Star The only remaining Chinese restaurant in Asmara and very popular with NGO and UN staff. The menu is as long as those in Chinese restaurants in Europe, but the quality is variable and, if you order extensively (as in Europe) you will find the bill topping anything else in the city. Since the Chinese chef left, the authenticity is not exactly true, but it isn't at all bad. The service can be appallingly slow, and you certainly shouldn't expect an apology for this because you won't get one.

Dangish This is one of Asmara's newest local restaurants and appears to be one of the most reliable. The menu is fairly standard but always available. It is by far the best place to get local fish dishes at such a reasonable price. The *spris* fish is particularly excellent at Nfa15. Very friendly owner and staff.

Expo Hotel Even if you are not staying here the restaurant is worth trying and is very popular in the evening. Pizzas are the speciality. Be warned though, that for some reason, which is not the price of potatoes, french fries count as a main dish here and elsewhere; they are not a budget snack.

Hamasien Turn right off Liberty Av after Impero Cinema and Hamasien is a few metres down on the right-hand side. It has quite a large range of local and Italian food. The food and prices are quite reasonable at around Nfa15–25 for a wide range of dishes including salads, fish, goat, beef, etc.

Hotel Inter-Continental The hotel has 3 restaurants serving a wide variety of food. The main restaurant, La Fontana, offers a different type of cuisine each evening. This includes Thai, Lebanese, Italian and American, and costs Nfa140. The all-you-can-eat buffet is Nfa99, which includes pastas, local foods, salads and dessert. Pizzas cost between Nfa35–50. The food is better and more varied than most restaurants in town as most ingredients are imported. The prices are subject to 20% charges and do fluctuate considerably due to special deals and the unstable exchange rate.

Langana At the east end of Liberty Av, just before you reach September 1 Square. A clean and simple restaurant with the standard range of local and Italian foods including a good beef steak and traditional dishes between Nfa17–25. The adjoining bar is also very popular.

Legese Hotel A short distance down Ras Beyene Baraki St (off Liberty Av opposite the Ministry of Tourism). A good restaurant with slightly more innovation than most others. A lot of effort has also gone into the decoration and other design features, reflecting the owner's years spent abroad. The restaurant is all that is left of the hotel, as the accommodation side of the business has been closed since the recent war.

Pizza Napoli Four doors east of Bar Vittoria and serving the most authentic pizzas in town, Napoli is a very popular place for locals and foreigners alike with a big selection of different pizzas, which cost Nfa18–28.

Pizza Power Behind September 1 Square, Pizza Power serves a wide range of reasonably priced pizzas.

Howashait Tucked in a side street, Adi Keih St, just off Liberty Avenue opposite the High Court, Howashait is a pleasantly decorated restaurant with a reasonable selection of food. The new owners have injected some life into the place and the menu is quite reliable. They do good vegetable dishes and also serve a range of pizza. Dishes are around Nfa15–25.

Randa On the Keren Rd, near the Coca Cola factory, Randa is a reliable place to get a decent seafood meal. The prices are quite reasonable and it is a welcome change from the restaurants in the centre of town.

Rendezvous New restaurant on Martyrs Av near Cinema Roma. The food is good and they provide a tasty starter with every meal. The pasta dishes are delicious. The prices are very reasonable at around Nfa20–30 per meal.

Restaurant Milano Opposite the Shell petrol station at 76/78 Ras Alula St. This restaurant is in two halves: the front is standard Eritreo-Italian fare with pizzas, chicken, veal, fish, etc; the back is one of the best traditional Eritrean restaurants in town with excellent local fare, including a superb range of fasting food. Dishes are Nfa22–35 each.

Rora Restaurant Opposite the transport police station just west of the giant sandals (*shida*) sculpture on Martyrs Av. This is Asmara's only 'Indian' restaurant. It once had an Indian chef, but the menu remains reasonably authentic and the servings are a very good size.

Ruba Hadas Just south of Victory Rd not far from Dante Cinema. This local restaurant serves excellent Eritrean food, especially lamb and chicken dishes. Options are often limited but the food is generally of good quality and value.

Sports Restaurant Just off Liberty Av opposite the Ministry of Education (huge pink building at the west end of Liberty Av). This is ostensibly a Sudanese restaurant, though they do a limited range of Eritrean dishes as well. The owner is friendly and efficient and will do her best to get you what you want, though the options on the menu are not always reliable. If you fancy a change to *injera* then they do serve a lot of rice dishes and even chapatti. The food is generally very good.

St George Once a popular restaurant if not for the food then for the interior décor. However, things have changed and it is far from what it once was. The food on the menu is seldom available and often of poor quality.

Sudanese Restaurant Opposite the Khartoum Hotel on Ali Osman Buri St, this authentic and simple restaurant serves a good fish dish, as well as other Sudanese fare, such as *bamyia* (okra and meat), *molo keeya* (glutinous stew made from okra), and *ful*.

Undecismo Embarderho If you have transport try this restaurant 11km from Asmara on the Keren road. Excellent traditional cooking – for the best results try to order in advance. Unfortunately this means an extra trip, as Undecismo is not on the phone.

Cafés, bars and snack bars

There is a subtle difference between cafés, bars and snack bars, which are all very common around the city. Cafés tend to serve hot drinks and a wide variety of cakes and pastries, while snack bars tend to offer simple dishes such as sandwiches and *frittata* (scrambled egg with tomatoes, onions and green peppers) or *ful* (pronounced 'fool') – a bean dish served with onions, peppers and sometimes egg and cheese. Bars are there to serve beer and spirits, though some serve a limited range of snack foods or fruit juices.

Café life is very much alive and kicking in Asmara and is one of the real joys of the city. The choice is vast and all offer fast, efficient and friendly service (often not to be found in hotels). Prices are very good value and many have a mouth-watering selection of pastries, *pizzete* (mini-pizzas), ice cream and other delicacies to plug a gap at any time of day. Tea (*shahi*), one of the national staples, will cost between 50 cents and Nfa1 (don't be alarmed by the quantity of sugar Eritreans put in their tea, it is standard practice); cappuccino Nfa2–3; machiato Nfa1–2; snacks from Nfa1–3 for a *pizzete* or pastry to a Nfa6 for *frittata*. Soft drinks are available everywhere as is bottled Eritrean mineral water (*mai gas*), which is very drinkable, and about Nfa2.5 a bottle. In many cafés it is necessary to pay first at the counter for whatever you want and then hand your ticket to the waiter. This is not uniform practice though so just see what everyone else is doing when you arrive. Among the most popular or best located are the following:

Aman Restaurant On Ras Beyene Baraki St further down from Legese Hotel on the opposite side of the road. Though technically a restaurant, this newly opened establishment currently operates more as a bar. The American-Eritrean owner is a very friendly guy and has decorated the bar with images of Chicago. They provide good snack food and if the Tigrinya music in other bars is wearing a little thin then this provides a welcome change.

Ahazz Pastry In the centre of September 1 Square, Ahazz Pastry serves a good coffee and a wide selection of pastries.

American Bar At the west end of Liberty Av this bar is a little rough around the edges but it serves a decent coffee and is just one of three places where you can sit outside on Liberty Av.

Asmara Pastry Central and very popular. Great cakes and tea.

Awet y Pastry opposite the Blue Nile Restaurant by the giant sandals, offers a good range of creamy pastries.

Bar Crispi Towards the west end of Revolution Av, opposite the Ministry of Health, this bar boasts a fine original interior and is a good place for a drink at any time of day.

Bar Diana just opposite the cathedral, boasts one of the more formidable arrays of Johnnie Walker bottles behind the bar. The walls are covered with posters of chimpanzees, à la PG Tips, and pictures of fighters. Very local, a little grubby but buckets of atmosphere.

Bar Impero is the Royal Bar at the east end of Liberty Av and next to the eponymous cinema. Serves a range of pastries as well as a comprehensive range of drinks. One of only three places to sit outside on Liberty Av and watch the world go by, whilst it watches you.

Bar Zili Between Blue Nile and Awet y Pastry on Martyrs Av, this is one of a selection of bars that serves draught beer in pint-sized glasses for the ardent beer drinker.

Bar Vittoria In Itegue Zehaitu St at the intersection with Lorenzo Tazas St (British Council Library), this bar is one of the oldest cafés in the city with a fine selection of cakes and some ice creams. Interesting murals by Emmanuel Ghilazghi.

Capri The best place for juices in town is on the ground floor below Capri Pension. Depending on the season they serve superb mango, papaya, mandarin, guava and banana juices. They also serve good ice cream, which you can have dipped in the juice if you wish.

Casa Degli Italiani has a pool table, good snacks and is set to the side of an attractive courtyard. Very popular with foreign residents of Asmara and NGO staff for being secluded from the street. The gateposts, with their fascist symbolism, are an interesting reminder of Eritrea's darker history.

Cathedral Snack Bar has recently been refurbished and now looks somewhat sterile. Only seems to serve drinks (non-alcoholic).

City Park is the only place in the centre where you can sit outside without being choked by traffic fumes and is therefore always full. The café is one of Asmara's few places where you feel anything remotely like being in a park. Serves good fruit juices and some reasonable ice cream.

Green Park Pastry On the corner, next to Khartoum Hotel, this café serves excellent pastries and coffee.

The Mask Place Probably the newest and trendiest bar in town, The Mask has successfully captured the young and foreign market with its burger and chips menu and modern, faux-African interior. A must for those feeling a little craving for home comforts or wanting to meet other Westerners in town. The food is certainly quite good and the atmosphere lively.

Pasticeria Moderna A new addition to Liberty Av, styled to look like an Italian café. It has a gawdy interior, but also seating outside, and is popular with locals and visitors.

Rimon Snack Bar, just down the road from Bar Crispi (diagonally opposite the Ministry of Health), offers a good selection of snacks and light meals. Very clean and usually quiet.

Royal Bar Sadly, this bar no longer has seats on the pavement of Liberty Av, but it is still one of the main meeting places in town.

Sesen Pasticeria, just up the road from The Mask Place, is a delightful local haunt and serves the best value pastries at Nfa1 each, probably the last café in town to do so. The waitresses and owner are very friendly.

Yummy Burger Just next to Green Park Pastry, this small fast-food outlet makes a fine burger. The friendly Armenian owner is a keen fan of Eritrea and will willingly discuss the country with you at considerable length.

The choice is endless and one of the enjoyable things for any visitor will be finding their own favourites, whether on Liberty Avenue or in the side streets. In the evening some of the livelier bars are in the area around the Legese Hotel.

NIGHTLIFE

Discos are normally at weekends and are well-advertised in the streets. The most popular but seedy club is **Shamrock** in Expo. Since the UN arrived it has become an inevitable centre where prostitutes can reliably earn their salaries. A more local joint is **Warsa**, in the Godaif district, which has good live music at the weekend. There are also squash courts and billiards for those wanting more varied entertainment. Other reasonable clubs include: **Patamatas**; **Mata'a**; **Mocambo**; **Lagetto**; and **Sembel Huts**. Entrance fees vary from Nfa50-100. There are often bands playing for special occasions. **Casa Degli Italiani** also has functions or exhibitions put on by various groups or organisations such as Alliance Française and the British Council. There are also four **cinemas** to choose from for films (see page 114). All are well advertised in shops and hotels. Do not base your visit to Asmara on its potential nightlife; with the exception of the discos life shuts down by 11pm.

SHOPPING

There has not been much demand for souvenirs even since independence, the number of visitors still being very low. The one or two souvenir shops that are in business are often not the places to find anything authentic or interesting. A couple of the largest souvenir shops are on Liberty Avenue, but their selection is pretty dire and perhaps not all that ethical either. A leopard skin has sat in one for well over six months. One of the better outlets is **Jolly**, next to The Mask Place. This sells a wide range of higher quality craft items, albeit at higher prices. For cloth, ceramics, silver and gold and basketwork you are much better off going to the market and hunting around.

Jewellery shops are confined to two areas of the town; one being the street running west from the entrance of the main Mosque, the other running west from the side entrance of the cathedral (around The Mask Place). In the silver shops and stalls you will tend to find new products on display; it is always worth asking if they have any old pieces as these are often the real finds, though Keren is a better place for treasure-hunting, even if the selection of new jewellery is more limited. Silver is priced around Nfa10-20 per gram in Asmara (sometimes as low as half this price in Keren) depending on what quality you are buying, but if you are buying a number of pieces it is well worth bargaining. The same pieces are often to be found elsewhere and the quality of craftsmanship and design are not especially remarkable. Some interesting religious artefacts such as Coptic crosses and old Bibles and scrolls can be found in the market but may take some looking for. Do not buy anything that has obviously been removed from a religious institution. Unless you are a numismatist do not buy coins either; you are likely to be disappointed.

Eritrea has long been famed for the quality of its leather goods, which used to have a ready market in Italy. The industry is being rebuilt. There are a number of good leather shops around the city centre, on Liberty Avenue and near The Mask Place. The main items on sale are bags, shoes, jackets and smaller goods like belts and wallets. The range of locally made shoes on sale around the city is certainly one of Eritrea's best exports and the price is usually excellent for the quality. A good choice for a large selection of shoes is **Negusse G** opposite the Cathedral, at 86 Liberty Avenue.

For posters, cassettes and videos most good stationers will have a decent range. You can find a particularly good collection in the information centre at the September 1 Square end of Liberty Avenue on the north side, as well as T-shirts and other Eritrean memorabilia. Another good place for memorabilia is **Ere Sport** just west of the Cathedral.

There are good, Italian-style grocery shops opposite the Catholic Cathedral, in Fessahaie Kifle Street and at the corner of Ras Mangasha Yohannes and Itegue Zehaitu Streets. **Wikianos** is the most popular supermarket, opposite the Municipality building in Liberty Avenue and has a good range of foreign foods. **Barka Dairy** by the park behind Ambassador Hotel has by far the best range of dairy products including good cheeses and yoghurt, fresh daily.

Markets

The other obvious and most pleasurable shopping experience is to visit Asmara's markets. The largest market is in **Eritrea Square** and sells a vast array of beans, pulses, grains, fruits and vegetables. The mini-mills around the outside of the market are worth taking a look at as the workers separate, sieve and prepare the various grains to make flour, with remarkable efficiency. For local souvenirs such as wicker baskets, mats and pottery items, the market behind the central mosque is the best place to visit. There is a wide range of goods and the prices are reasonable, but only if you bargain hard! Another market worth going to just for the sake of browsing is **Medeber market** (from the Tigrinya word for 'together') in the northeast corner of town. This is a marvellous example of resource-management through recycling. Any piece of discarded material will be remanufactured here and made into something new. As the Eritrean phrase from the struggle attests: 'Everything has its use and then another use'. There is no better place to see this in action than at Medeber, where oil drums, truck engine parts and bicycle parts are transformed into anything from ovens to gravestones.

Books and newspapers

Bookshops in Asmara mainly stock textbooks and second-hand Italian books. Other types of book are usually in Tigrinya or Arabic, so bring a good supply of reading material. An English-language newspaper with the name *Eritrea Profile* is available on Saturdays. It is a government newspaper and the content as well as the style leaves much to be desired, although for Nfa1 it's still not a bad way of staying in touch with local events. A local daily in both Tigrinya and Arabic is also available for Nfa1. Foreign newspaper availability is limited to the top hotels and various other libraries such as The British Council Library and Alliance Française. Copies of publications such as *Time* and *Newsweek* are always available in most stationers. A number of reliable bookshops can be found around the Central Post Office. These include: **Restuccia Stationary** opposite Sports Restaurant; **Friendship Stationary and Store**, next to the Cathedral; and **Awghet Bookshop** (tel: 124190) in September 1 Square next to Himbol foreign exchange. As most books on Eritrea are published by Red Sea Press in Trenton, New Jersey, you will need to find a specialist bookshop with contacts with that publisher. In London all Red Sea titles, and any others on Eritrea, can be obtained from the Africa Book Centre, 38 King Street, WC2E 8JS (tel: 020 7240 6649).

COMMUNICATIONS
Post and courier services

If you are sending or receiving parcels you need to go to the parcel office, which is one block west of the post office – just ask for directions. The process of sending or receiving parcels is relatively simple. All incoming parcels are opened by the staff to ensure you don't need to pay tax on incoming items (such as electronic goods), and carry a Nfa1.50 charge.

The post office is open 07.00–18.00 Monday–Saturday. The parcel and EMS offices are open 08.00–noon and 14.00–18.00.

Courier services

TNT Express Worldwide; tel: 116914; fax: 120438
DHL Express Courier Service; tel: 120069; fax: 122882
EMS Eritrea Tel: 125029; fax: 120623; email: eps12@eol.com.er This is the Eritrean Postal Service's express service and operates worldwide. It is approximately twice the price of normal registered mail, but guarantees a 2–3-day registered delivery service.

Internet

The places listed below are some of the most popular places to log on and in some cases also provide other computing and printing services:

Alliance Française (behind the Ambassador Hotel)
British Council Lorenzo Tazaz St No 23. You need to become a member to use this. Membership is Nfa20 per year. Internet use is Nfa5 per hour, printing is Nfa1 per sheet.

City Internet Anse Matenzo St. Fast connection and good facilities. Not as busy as most other places. Nfa10 per hour.

CTS (east of September 1 Square) Nfa10 per hour.

Eritro-German Centre (near American Embassy) Free.

PCS (around the corner from Asmara Pastry) Expensive and crowded. Printing is Nfa2 per sheet.

Shebab Internet Café (next to Africa Pension). Very friendly staff and a spacious place, but usually very busy. The café serves coffee and soft drinks if you have to wait. Nfa7 per hour, printing is Nfa1 per sheet.

T-fanus (near Milano Restaurant) Nfa10 per hour, printing is Nfa1 per sheet.

TSE Internet (behind Telecommunications building) Nfa10 per hour, minimum half an hour, printing is Nfa1.25 per sheet.

WHAT TO SEE

One of the most enjoyable things to do is just to wander around Asmara sampling café life and dipping in and out of the large market area to the north of Liberty Avenue. To be able to do this safely and freely is one of the unusual qualities of Asmara as an African capital city. Here you can watch how the population really carries on its daily life among stalls selling fresh produce, spices, pulses, coffee and tea, pottery, silver, clothes, furniture, religious artefacts and household utensils. The main market area is north of Liberty Avenue; you can't miss it. The two fish markets are not, however, within the main market area: one can be found next to the cathedral in Anse Matenzo Street; the other set a little back from Liberty Avenue opposite the Municipality. A selection of tuna, bream, red snapper and other species are available fresh from Massawa. Prices are considerably cheaper than other types of meat.

The Roman Catholic Cathedral (The Church of Our Lady of the Rosary) stands about halfway along Liberty Avenue and is an unmistakable Italian inheritance built in 1923 by the architect Scanavini. Its tall Gothic bell-tower is visible from everywhere in the city and is a useful landmark if you ever lose your sense of direction. The view from the top of the 52m bell-tower is spectacular and can be enjoyed for just Nfa5 on any weekday. The eight bells in the tower were placed there in 1925. The bells, as well as the angel atop the cupola, are said to be made from the melted-down metal of Austrian field guns captured at the Battle of Carso. The cathedral, as well as the primary school, printing press, the monastery of the order of Capuchins and the nunnery, are all in the same compound and can be visited. Among the interesting sights in the cathedral is the plaque naming Mussolini as one of the benefactors.

St Mariam's Coptic Cathedral was built in 1917 and is a combination of Italian and Ethiopian religious styles. With its twin towers it is another useful landmark. The vast open area in front of it is usually packed for big festivals and has a traditional stone bell just to the left side. Inside the cathedral, as is common practice, the men sit on the left and the women sit on the right. The murals are interesting as period pieces.

ARCHAEOLOGICAL SITES IN ERITREA

The best information on these can be gleaned from the research section at the museum. The sites do not rank as highly as some of the great Ethiopian discoveries, but are nevertheless interesting. A huge amount of work needs to be done and it is hoped that UNESCO or some similar body will help in this process in time. Adulis, the Axumite port and arguably the most important site in the country, is probably still 90% underground. The following are the major sites in the country:

Place	Province	Nature of site
Karora	Northern Red Sea	Cave paintings
Rora Bakla	Anseba	Ruins, pottery, stelae
Orotta	Northern Red Sea	Pottery and inscriptions
Fode	Gash Barka	Pottery
Augaro	Gash Barka	Pottery
Mount Elit	Gash Barka	Pottery and ruins
Qohaito	Dubub	Pre-Axumite dam; Axumite ruins and graves
Metara	Dubub	Axumite ruins and stelae
Debre Bizen	Northern Red Sea	Religious artefacts including over 1,000 parchments in Ge'ez
Hamm Monastery	Dubub	Graves, mummies, religious artefacts
Hirgigo	Northern Red Sea	Mosque ruins
Adulis	Northern Red Sea	Axumite port
Adi Keih	Dubub	Rock paintings at 25 locations in the area
Beilul	Southern Red Sea	Pottery
Dahlak Kebir	Northern Red Sea	Necropolis

This is the museum's 'official list'. The major sites that can be visited comparatively easily by public transport are the rock paintings around Adi Keih, Debre Bizen (bus to Nefasit), and Metara (bus to Senafe). It is always best to have someone with you who knows where the places are, because there are no signposts or explanatory details when you arrive. Details of getting to Adulis and Hamm Monastery are included under the relevant geographical sections.

Al Qurafi al Rashidin Mosque ('Followers of the Right Path') was built in 1937 and replaced a smaller mosque. The lower part of the minaret is a fluted Roman column revealing the Italian influence on its construction. The side arches used to open and as part of the original city's Master Plan provided a walkway from the north of town right through to the area south of Liberty

Avenue.

St George's Greek Orthodox Church, established by the Helenic Community, is a haven of tranquillity in the area by the market. The old church is a small building, but recognisable by the small belltower that can be seen peeping above the trees and walls that surround the compound. It is a pretty church, with an elaborate interior full of paintings, ornate decorations and an interesting ceiling.

To the west of the city, above the main hospital (Mekane Hiwot), the Italian **Forto Baldissera** (home to the Ministry of Information) sits on raised ground and has good views over the city. Next to it is **St Michael's Church** and further to the west is **Kagnew Station**, built as an American military base and easily identified by the piles of military detritus behind it (generally known as the **tank cemetery**). The incredible **Italian Cemetery** is also beside St Michael's Church and well worth a visit for those interested in sculpture or Art Deco.

The **National Museum** was dealt a rum deal when the government allocated public buildings to the various institutions and ministries. Formerly in the Imperial Palace at the head of Liberty Avenue close to the government buildings, it has now been moved to an old convent further to the west of town not far from the Selam Hotel, where it sits in a rather sorry state, and most of the exhibition is closed. This is certainly no fault of the museum's. The building is not appropriate to house exhibitions and it remains to be seen whether a more suitable venue is agreed upon.

As a result, the museum as it is currently is hardly worth visiting, unless you are seeking permits to visit the various archaeological sites. Despite the rather disturbingly moth-eaten animals hanging from the walls that are testament to the wonderful array of wildlife that once roamed this part of the world before Western civilisation shot it all, there are some other interesting items. These include artefacts from the excavations of Adulis, the Axumite port; inscribed tombstones from the Dahlak Islands dating from the 9th-15th centuries; some Sabean material; and scrolls in Ge'ez, the ancient religious language. The fine collection of weaponry from the 19th century, including Menelik's sword and another sword given by Generale Baratieri to Bahta Hagos, as well as all sorts of artefacts from the struggle remain in the old museum building along with a number of other significant artefacts. It is still unknown as to the fate of these collections. The information on the archaeological section is not extensive, largely because most of the sites have not been properly excavated, but you will see as much of interest here in the museum as at most of the sites.

The former **Imperial Palace**, built by Ferdinando Martini, the first Italian civil governor of Eritrea, in 1897, is now being extensively refurbished behind closed walls. The building is at the far west end of Liberty Avenue, as it merges into Revolution Avenue, behind the rather pleasant park. You won't miss it due to its Classical façade and the enormous gardens that surround it. It has not yet been announced as to what will become of this grand building or what has happened to the fine interior fixtures and fittings. Having been put into public hands after liberation it would be a great loss to see it being closed again to the public.

One Italian legacy that has had a profound affect on Asmarino lifestyle besides the cafés is the array of **cinemas** in Asmara. Most cinemas were constructed in the 1930s and reflect this golden era of film-making. Although the range of films is somewhat limited (action films are a big hit in Eritrea) the cinemas are worth visiting just to see such fine buildings in their original state, albeit a little worn out. The best examples are **Impero**, on Liberty Avenue and **Odeon**, just opposite City Park, behind Bristol Pension. Both these cinemas have their original interiors and some interesting details such as the marble staircases, Art Deco lights and plaster mouldings. Seats cost around Nfa3–6 depending on whether you sit upstairs or down. **Dante Cinema** is smaller and has recently been refurbished. It is situated around the corner, behind Odeon and seats cost around Nfa10. The most expensive cinema is the newly refurbished **Cinema Roma** on Martyrs Avenue. Originally built in 1936, it has been renovated to how it looked during the 1940s. Seats are around Nfa15–40. Sadly the striking 'Capitol Cinema' on Revolution Avenue no longer shows films, but it is worth going to see it just for its imposing Rationalist style, synonymous, almost, with Normandy gun placements.

Another form of entertainment that is certainly worth trying at least once just for the experience is **bowling**. Built during Haile Selassie's reign, the alley is still in its original state, with manual re-loading of pins and balls. The small army of boys employed to operate this fine relic is always very helpful and will help you with the scoring if you are only a beginner. The building also houses a number of other smaller games such as **billiards** and **computer games**. Billiards can also be found in many local bars.

If you fancy a cooling down, there are now two places for **swimming** in Asmara. Until recently there was just the *'Asmara piscina'*, which is still operating, but it has a café inside and you have to put up with a certain amount of staring from those that line the poolside whilst having their coffee. The other more secluded, but more expensive option is at Hotel Inter-Continental, with its indoor and outdoor heated swimming pools. To swim here you need to be either a guest or a member. Membership can be bought for one-, three- or twelve-month periods. Other sports available at Hotel Intercontinental include **squash, tennis** and a **gymnasium**. **Tennis courts** are also available at Asmara Tennis Club near the zoo. This area is designated for a large complex including conference centre, hotel, sports club and golf course. Warsa nightclub in the Godaif district is another place where you can find **squash courts**.

The **zoo** and **British War Cemetery** are 4km outside Asmara on the Massawa road. The zoo is a rather tragic collection of tired old animals and is probably best avoided, although it is reported to have been recently renovated. The cemetery is worth visiting; it is very well kept and interesting for the diversity of different nationalities serving under the British flag during the conquest of 1941. Asmara was occupied on April 1 1941. Just before the cemetery on the left is the **Hindu** burial site of the Indian soldiers serving with the British. A little further out of town along this road is **Biet Gergish**, which sits on the edge of the escarpment with sweeping views of the mountains below. If you fancy an afternoon's peace and quiet, it is a perfect place to sit and marvel at the views. It is very possible you will be joined by the many **baboons** that live in the area. It is easy to get to and from, as it is the last stop eastwards on the Number 1 bus, though beware, if the wind is in the wrong direction Asmara's only rubbish dump may spoil the beauty somewhat.

The recently resurrected **railway** is definitely worth a visit if railway nostalgia interests you. The old workshops and goods yards just south of the Massawa Road are an astonishing step back in time. All the lathes and the vast, metalworking machinery are operated by belt drives as they were when first installed nearly a century ago. What is even more remarkable is that nearly all the workers are the same as when the railway last operated. Now out of retirement, these devoted men have rebuilt their railway literally from scratch by hand. As this book was being compiled they were laying the tracks from Asmara down to Nefasit – 83-year-old men hauling the newly shaped metal rails to their resting places. The steam engines have been completely stripped down to their bare components, cleaned and rebuilt ready to be used again when the track is in place. Their work is an inspiration. Taking a walk along the tracks towards Nefasit or chatting to the workers in their workshops will certainly provide a memorable experience.

The **Theatre** (also known as **Cinema Asmara** or the **Opera House)**, built by Cavagnari in 1918, is also worth a visit. It is located on Liberty Avenue next to the telecommunications building. The exterior is an eclectic mix of classical styles and the interior, with its painted ceiling, is also worth seeing.

Bar Durfo is a café on the left, 9km outside Asmara on the Massawa road and has stunning views of the first part of the descent to the coast. Sheer drops of some 250m to the valley floor on either side make this a very good place to go for a sundowner or to stop on your way to the coast.

Asmara to Massawa

THE DESCENT TO MASSAWA

The descent from Asmara to Massawa is almost 2,500m, a truly dramatic drive that takes about two hours by car or three and a half hours by bus. The distance is 115km. Leaving Asmara, you pass the Hindu cemetery on your left and the zoo and British cemetery on your right on the eastern outskirts of the city. Immediately afterwards the road begins its snake-like path down the escarpment. If you experience an appalling smell at this point it is the Asmara rubbish dump, which, people will almost proudly tell you, has been burning since the 1920s. Bar Durfo, 9km from Asmara, is a good place to stop and look at the superb views. With sweeping views of the valley floor it affords a good taste of things to come.

Often the hilltops are shrouded in thick white cloud, which swirls through the gaps in the peaks in vast plumes. Building this stretch of road from the coast, the Italian engineers were almost overwhelmed by the many seemingly insurmountable challenges. The area is now named '*Shegerunyi*', which means '*I am having a hard time*'. So hard was the task of finding a way to cut the road out of this last stretch of the mountainside that one engineer is reported to have committed suicide. The solution in the end was to build a bridge. Down to the right along this road you will see the new railway track that has recently been laid. This stretch of the Asmara to Massawa railway is the most densely tunnelled section with over 20 tunnels in 20km. Another good view is from Seidieci ('Three Seasons') restaurant, 16km from Asmara. After 20km a stretch of hairpin bends takes you down to the first town of Nefasit (1,648m). As you turn the last bend into the main street, a road to your right, heading south, will take you to Decemhare (40km away). In Nefasit, perched high above the town and often invisible due to the cloud cover, is the monastery of Debre Bizen. To visit **Debre Bizen**, make sure you obtain a permit from the Orthodox Headquarters in Asmara and take a bus to Nefasit. The snaking footpath to the monastery is easily visible from the road and takes between one-and-a-half and two hours to climb. It is well worth the climb as it affords stunning views and a good taste of ancient building techniques and religious history.

Maihabar is a village near Nefasit, on the road to Decemhare, where many disabled fighters have settled. Here they manufacture goods and learn craft skills, which then become a source of income. It is possible to visit the community.

DEBRE BIZEN (2,450M)

Debre Bizen was founded by Abuna Filipos; in legend he moved the Coptic religious community up the mountain from Nefasit because he preferred the roar of lions to the distraction of women's faces. The monastery began life in 1361 and by the time of Filipos' death it had risen to a position of significant power in the Coptic Church, with over 900 monks. There are currently 120 monks in service. Due to the strategic position it occupies, it is remarkable that Debre Bizen has managed to survive successive waves of invasion from that of Somali hordes of Ahmed Gragn to the Derg. There is a remarkable collection of over 1,000 manuscripts in Ge'ez, a large round church whose massive beams and pillars are testament to the huge forests once blanketing the region, Filipos' tomb, and various other interesting buildings such as the warehouse and kitchen. The views to the sea and Dahlak Islands, to the Buri Peninsula and the Gulf of Zula, and south to the mountains of Akele Guzai, are among the most impressive in Eritrea. Only males are allowed to make the two-hour climb to the monastery (provided you are reasonably fit), but to gain entry it is necessary to obtain permission from the Headquarters of the Coptic Church in Asmara.

Embatcala (1,340m) is 31km from Asmara, and considered by many to have the best climate in Eritrea. It is certainly in an attractive setting and the air is fresh. The town, dominated by a large church, is surrounded by green hillsides. Arguably even more attractive is **Ghinda** (905m), 45km from the capital; the town sits on a plain that, especially during the early part of the year, is a sharp contrast to the dryness on much of the high plateau. The road swings left into the main street, crossing a bridge in the process. It was always a favourite spot for Italian residents not least because the rain and fertile soil made it, and still do make it, a major growing area.

Ghinda is a popular place to stop on the journey and the buses usually do so for half an hour for a break. Ghinda is particularly famed for its climate and good agricultural land. Any of the restaurants opposite the bus stop are worth trying for refreshment. There are two places to stay in Ghinda, should you get stuck there on the way to or from the coast. One is the central **Red Sea Hotel** and the other is the **Semret Hotel** on the eastern outskirts of town. Both are fairly basic but perfectly adequate for an evening's stopover.

Dongollo (966m) is 60km from Asmara and therefore just over halfway to Massawa. The second half of the journey is considerably faster going. In Dongollo, famous for its mineral water, you can see the ruins of one of the factories: the side of the building advertises *Fonte Acqua Thermo Minerale*. Like Ghinda the town is usually green. Soon after it you can see one of the springs for Sabarguma mineral water a few kilometres to the north of the road. The Dongollo area used to be more heavily wooded and separates the plain of Sabarguma from the basin in which Ghinda lies.

After the road has reached the lowlands you arrive at a village called Ghatelai. It is here that the road from Filfil joins the main Asmara to Massawa road. The early part of the road to Filfil is one of the newest roads in Eritrea and will form the beginning of the road from Massawa to Afabet along the coast. When this is completed the trip to Sahel should be much quicker via this route than the current road via Keren. This road also takes you to the famous **Mai Wui** hot springs. There are a number of sites in this area, with Mai Wui and **Arafayale** being the only two currently operating. Over 700 people a day visit Mai Wui in the peak season. A third site, **Akwaar** (*aqua*), was developed by the Italians in 1938, but destroyed during the struggle. However, it is planned for redevelopment into a spa resort.

A large fort in the hills to your left after 86km marks **Sa'ati** (160m), first occupied by the Italians in September 1886; the fort was surrounded in the following year by Ras Alula, who massacred a relief battalion at Dogali. The Italians retreated to Massawa. Sa'ati was reoccupied in 1888 by Generale San Marzano who built a railroad to Massawa. When Emperor Yohannes led a force of some 80,000 men to dislodge the Italians once again he had to withdraw to fight the Dervish threat in the west. After this, Italian control of the coast was a foregone conclusion.

Another site of significance in the early years of Italian expansion is the bridge over the river at **Dogali**, 94km from Asmara. The bridge, which has three arches, is dedicated to Generale Menabrea and bears the inscription *Ca Custa Lon Ca Custa* ('whatever it takes'). Now on the coastal plains you pass the EPLF Martyrs' cemetery on your right, 7km outside Massawa, and, on the outskirts of Massawa, the Italian cemetery, also to your right. Just as you approach the city boundary there was, until the end of 1994, a corrugated iron enclosure to the left with a single tree protruding from the top. In the compound were the skeletons of some 800 Ethiopian officers who were rounded up by Ethiopian President Mengistu in 1989 after a failed coup attempt and shot. It is not known why they were brought here and why they were not interred, but one theory has it that Mengistu sought to demonstrate his ultimate power over the rebels by denying them even the ability to go to heaven. The compound has long since been removed and the bones laid to rest.

To the east the low, white, Turkish, Egyptian and Italian buildings of Massawa stretch out into the Red Sea, an impressive sight even amid the destruction, which is still evident. The mainland part of Massawa town has been extensively built since 1991, with the most obvious development being the Korean housing complex on the south side of the town, similar to the Sembel Complex in Asmara. Another recent development is the new bus station, where you will be dropped off if arriving by bus from Asmara. From here you will need to take a local minibus or taxi, which should cost no more than Nfa3 per person. Three kilometres before you reach the centre of Massawa the road forks – the left fork takes you past the Rashaida huts to the cement factory and then to **Gurgussum Beach** and the **Hamasien Hotel** (9km and 12km respectively from the turn-off); the right fork goes straight to the centre of Massawa. The beaches north of Gurgussum can really only be visited by boat because of the very soft sand and the lack of a road.

MASSAWA

Massawa was once the largest and safest port on the east coast of Africa but suffered terrible damage during the war, finally being liberated after intense fighting in February 1990. Despite the fact that almost no building remained undamaged the town still has a great charm, especially at night when the little alleyways between the Turko-Egyptian and Italian buildings come alive. The town is now the capital of the Northern Red Sea province.

The process of rebuilding and renovation is likely to be a long and costly one, but it is thankful that this option has been preferred to razing the ruins and erecting monstrosities in their place. This has enabled the city to retain much of its character. Every tourist comments that they hope that this process remains *simpatico*, but inevitably as Massawa attracts investment, and its old industries start to function again, some compromise will occur. Signs of this are already very evident on the neighbouring Taulud Island, where two pyramid-topped buildings have been erected which must constitute the most ugly buildings in the whole of Eritrea. Among the foremost attractions of Massawa, both day and night, are the bars and restaurants. As a result Massawa is Eritrea's major venue for tourists, not least because it is the departure point for trips to the islands. One is free to enjoy the sights with the minimum of hassle and maximum safety, no mean feat in a major African port.

Massawa appears like an oasis after the aridity of the coastal plains, which lie at the foot of the descent from Asmara. There is not much of interest in the mainland part of the town although this is where the majority of the population live. But crossing the first causeway, built by the Swiss adventurer Werner Munzinger in the 1870s, the atmosphere changes.

The first of the two islands is called **Taulud**. Of Massawa's two islands it has the more Italian feel with its neat rows of one- and two-storey villas and the **old railway station.** The **Orthodox Cathedral** (St Mariam's) and the Turko-Egyptian **Imperial Palace** are also found on Taulud, enhancing the impression of Massawa as a historical and cultural melting pot. The promontory of **Signora Melotti's** (of brewing fame) enormous villa is also a landmark beyond the landing stage, although access to this site is restricted. Also to your right is the **Red Sea Hotel**, which has been refurbished and now stands as one of the best hotels available in Massawa. At the end of the causeway is the unmistakable **tank monument** on which rest the three tanks that led the final assault on Massawa in 1990. Behind this monument is St Mariam's Cathedral. Proceeding along Taulud to the northeast the old train station is on the western shore. The formerly magnificent Imperial Palace to the north is still awaiting urgent restoration. The original furniture still sits inside, now blanketed under decades of dust. It is fascinating to wander around the building (you will not be allowed inside) and marvel at what dejected opulence now remains. It is hoped that the building will attract urgent investment in the near future and be restored as a museum of some

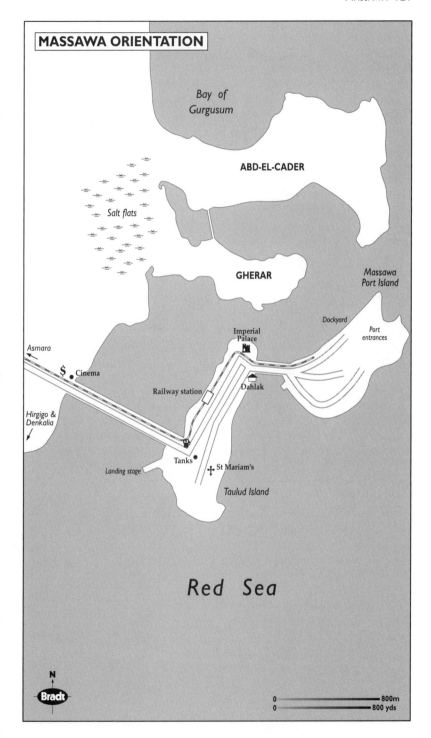

MASSAWA ORIENTATION

Bay of Gurgusum

ABD-EL-CADER

Salt flats

GHERAR

Massawa Port Island

Dockyard

Port entrances

Imperial Palace

Asmara

Cinema

Railway station

Dahlak

Hirgigo & Denkalia

Tanks

Landing stage

St Mariam's

Taulud Island

Red Sea

N

Bradt

0 — 800m
0 — 800 yds

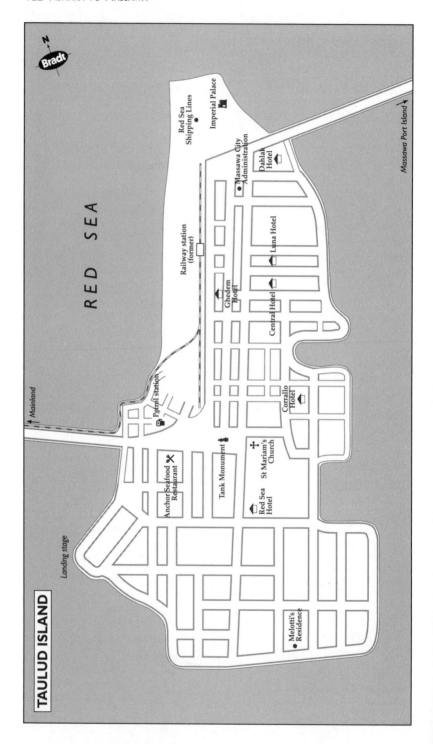

sort. Its foundations date from the 16th century, although the present building is more recent. The Lion of Judah gates are a reminder of Haile Selassie's reign. Just across the street from the palace is the **Dahlak Hotel**, looking out over Massawa's main island.

Crossing the second causeway you enter Massawa old town and the port area. This is a marvellous place to wander about, sampling the cafés and a very different way of life from that of Asmara. The port is Eritrea's main port, though smaller than the temporarily redundant Assab port. Intermingled with larger ships are numerous *houris* from Yemen and Saudi Arabia. This part of the town has a particularly Middle Eastern feel at night and the food is a welcome change to that which you find in the highlands. There are many interesting architectural features to be found which are evocative of Zanzibar's Stone Town or Kenya's Lamu. The ancient **Sheikh Hammali Mosque**, **Tomb of Sheikh Durbusc** and the decorative façade of the **House of Mammub Mohammed Nahari** are just some of the highlights, as well as many carved wooden doors, shutters and balconies. The **old covered market**, and the **former Italian Bank** by the entrance to the port, and many residential buildings in the northern quarter, make for a delightful, albeit very hot, wander. Many of these buildings are in a poor state after the struggle and are in need of urgent restoration. The construction is very often of coral block and therefore constitutes a rare method of building which should be preserved.

Climate
The climate on the coast is hot. The best time to visit is between November and April when temperatures range from 25°C to 35°C. From April onwards it increases steadily, regularly reaching the mid-40s in June to September. One of the disarming things is that there are no significant fluctuations between daytime and night-time temperatures except in the winter months. This makes air conditioning a must if you are not used to such extremes.

Where to stay
Upper range – Taulud Island
Red Sea Hotel Tel: 552839; fax: 552544. This hotel has recently been refurbished and is very comfortable and clean. There are 50 rooms costing between Nfa270–330, plus 20% service charge and tax. All are air-conditioned and are en-suite. The hotel has a swimming pool, tennis court and private access to the sea.

Dahlak Hotel Tel: 552818/552980; fax: 552782. 45 rooms. Nfa180/200/300 single/double/triple with en suite and air conditioning. This was the first hotel in Massawa to be refurbished and remains one of the best hotels in the country. It is currently being extended as another huge construction is being built next door which will house a casino and extra hotel space. This will make it one of the largest, and doubtless most popular, hotels in Eritrea. It has been leased to a friendly Italian-Eritrean lady named Luccia whose fine touch is evident. The kitchen is good and offers variety, with specials on the menu each day. The rooms are spacious, with powerful showers and silent air conditioning. The hotel even boasts a tennis court. A boat can be hired for Nfa250 to Green Island return, while more ambitious boat trips

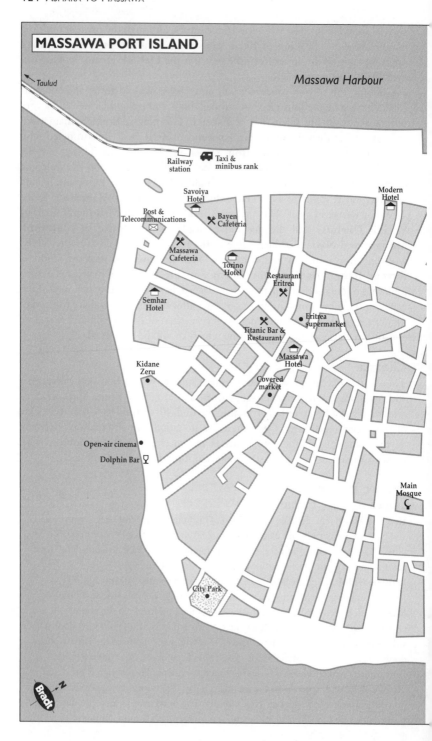

MASSAWA PORT ISLAND

Taulud

Massawa Harbour

Railway station

Taxi & minibus rank

Savoiya Hotel

Modern Hotel

Post & Telecommunications

Bayen Cafeteria

Massawa Cafeteria

Torino Hotel

Restaurant Eritrea

Semhar Hotel

Titanic Bar & Restaurant

Eritrea supermarket

Massawa Hotel

Kidane Zeru

Covered market

Open-air cinema

Dolphin Bar

Main Mosque

City Park

Brad N

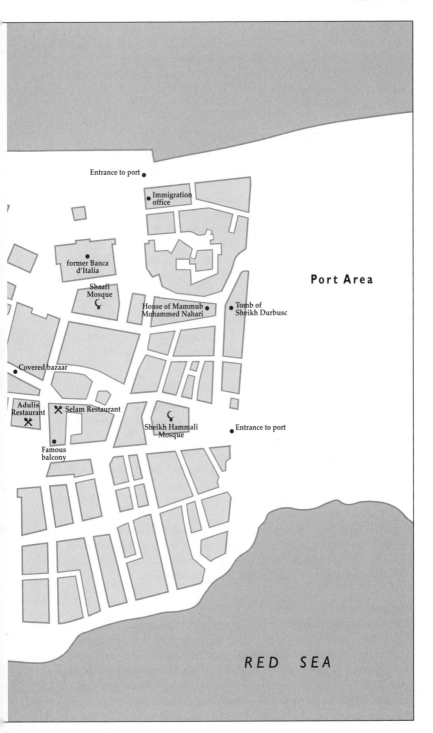

can also be arranged at the Dahlak booking office. Unfortunately, their luxury yacht, Nobile, was burnt and sunk during maintenance work a few years ago, but has been replaced by another yacht which now provides trips to the islands.

Central Hotel Tel: 552002. Positioned next to Luna Hotel, Central has 24 rooms with air conditioning ranging between Nfa180-240. It has recently been refurbished and has a good restaurant.

Upper range – Massawa Mainland

Gurgussum Beach Tel: 552911; fax: 291 1 552911/551902. 89 rooms. There are a number of different standards of room available at Gurgussum ranging from Nfa180–486, for a single/double/suite/family cottage. Gurgussum Beach Hotel is perhaps Massawa's most popular hotel, as it attracts all those seeking sun, sand and sea. The beach can get crowded at weekends and especially throughout the summer holidays from June to September, when thousands of Eritreans visit from overseas. The water is not as clean as it once was and certainly not as good as you'd find around the islands. However, the hotel is very pleasant and has clean rooms, a nice outside bar, and good food. There are plenty of deck chairs and umbrellas on the beach, which can be hired for Nfa10 per person.

Hamasien Tel: 552725. 31 rooms. This is another beach option further north of Gurgussum. It is quieter and the sea is often regarded as cleaner than at Gurgussum. The beach-view rooms upstairs are the best; although they have shared bathrooms, they are bigger and brighter than the first-class rooms on the ground floor. Nfa120–144 shared bathroom/en suite.

Note: If you don't have your own transport, taxis from town to Gurgussum/ Hamasien cost around Nfa30-40, or you can take a mini-bus for Nfa5. Minibuses leave from the rank outside Savoiya Hotel on Massawa Island

Mid-range – Taulud Island

Luna Hotel Tel: 552272. 15 rooms. Nfa 60-130 single with fan/double with air conditioning. Also recently refurbished, this offers a good and cheaper alternative to the Dahlak Hotel if you want to be in town as opposed to on the beach. All rooms have their own bathrooms.

Corrallo Tel: 552406. 26 rooms. Nfa60-150 fans/air conditioning. The Corrallo is slightly better than Luna, and just along the shore from it. It has a wide range of rooms to suit most budgets. Being right on the water it has views across to Sheik Said (Green) Island and to Mount Ghedem. The restaurant is also very good.

Budget

There are an increasing number of hotels in this category offering rooms for Nfa20–50. Don't expect much from this range other than a basic room and shared bathroom. Most come with fans. In no particular order they include the **Ghedem** (Taulud) which is a lovely old wooden building (although there have been reports of burglary from the rooms), **Savoiya** (tel: 552266), **Torino**, **Modern**, **Ghenet** and **Massawa** (all on port island). Bear in mind that, depending on the time of year when you visit, a ceiling fan or air conditioning may be a must, making it worth paying a little more. You may also find that some of these offer beds on the roof for around Nfa10, which, except for the noise, can be a better option than sleeping indoors. Massawa Island is generally noisy in the evenings owing to the numerous bars and clubs on the island, so if you are after a bit of peace and quiet, head for Taulud or the mainland.

Where to eat
The best thing about eating in Massawa is the range of seafood, which is hard to come by in the highlands and certainly won't be as fresh. Many different types of fish are always available, with the availability of other seafoods, such as prawn, crab and octopus being dependent on recent catches. There are a number of excellent restaurants open on Massawa Island, where you can choose your own fish. The most popular is **Selam**, just by the covered bazaar, but there are others such as **Adulis** around the corner, so don't be afraid to look around. **Restaurant Eritrea** nearer the centre of town is also excellent. The fish *zigini* (stew) is magnificent. All in all the food is better than at most restaurants in Asmara and it is a lively venue. A two-course meal for two people will cost less than Nfa40. Another recently-opened restaurant that serves excellent seafood is **Kidane Zeru** in the piazza near the open-air cinema. The fish kebab and mixed seafood are superb. **Anchor Sea Food** in the entrance to Taulud from the mainland is also quite reasonable. As far as the hotels are concerned the Dahlak Hotel and the Red Sea Hotel are the best for food, but you'll find it hard to beat a night at a local restaurant on Massawa Island.

Many of the cafés serve local food and the usual breakfast specialities such as *frittata* and *ful*. The **Beyan Cafeteria** and the **Massawa Cafeteria** opposite, by the post office, are both good for snacks or drinks. The **Savoiya** also does good basic food and you can sit outside in front of the port.

What to see
Massawa is a popular place for **nightclubbing** and Asmarinos tend to rely on it for getting out of the city and letting their hair down. One popular place is the Torino Hotel facing the entrance of the island, which has a bar and club on the roof terrace. Gurgussum also has a nightclub. There are many bars on Massawa Island where you can enjoy the atmosphere and the warm evenings. You don't have to look very far to find any of these, but be warned about the increasing prostitution on the Island. Kidane Zeru is a pleasant spot for a drink in the evening. The Dolphin Bar is also a nice venue overlooking the sea behind the cinema and has a small dance floor.

There are two **cinemas** in Massawa; one is on Massawa Island, the other on the mainland. The Sigalet Centre just to the left of the causeway as you head towards Taulud has a cinema upstairs and a popular bar downstairs, showing CNN most of the day. The cinema on Massawa Island is a better venue for the romantics who like to watch their movies under a warm star-lit sky. It is a little way along the ring road on the right hand side after entering Massawa Island.

Banking

The Commercial Bank is on the mainland just before the causeway leading to Taulud.

Post and telecommunications

The post and telecommunications building is to the right of the main square as you enter Massawa Island.

Shopping

There are still very few shops in Massawa. The **Eritrea Supermarket** is as good a place as any for yachtsmen to stock up, but several other places have opened up recently along the same street, offering a wide range of supplies. You can even get laundry done at the **Expo Laundry** if you've been out at sea for some time.

There are a couple of jeweller's/souvenir shops situated around the centre of Massawa Island, including one leading to the port entrance and another under the covered bazaar.

Dahlak Islands

See *Chapter* 7 (page 141) on how to get to the islands and what to see. Note that Sheikh Said (Green Island) is easily visited from the town.

The Islands

6

The opportunities for diving, birdwatching, seeing
dolphins and looking for turtle and dugong make
the islands the real jewel in Eritrea's crown.
Although still to be developed in even the most
basic sense, visiting the islands now affords a
good opportunity to see the virtually
undiscovered habitat before the crowds arrive. 'Undiscovered' may
be an exaggeration but accessibility has virtually been nil in recent
years, although many explorers such as Alvarez, Poncet, Bruce and Salt
travelled in the islands, as did tourists before war made this impossible.
This lack of human incursion has actually served to protect the rich
variety of submarine life.

The islands guard the approaches to the ancient Axumite port of Adulis as
well as to the more modern port of Massawa and have therefore always had an
important and interesting role in Eritrean and Ethiopian history. For many
centuries the domain of Arabs, Turks and Egyptians, they came under Italian
rule towards the end of the 19th century.

GEOGRAPHY
The coastline of Eritrea covers about 1,200km between 12° and 18° north. It
ends at the constriction of Bab el Mandab ('the Gate of Tears') and the Gulf
of Aden. The 209 Dahlak Islands are the closest islands to Massawa and, with
very few exceptions, have a maximum altitude of 15m. The inner islands are
moderately or poorly developed reefs while the outer islands are better
developed.

The larger offshore islands are of uplifted fossil coral deposited in the
Upper Pleistocene period and faulted more recently to produce the present
pattern of islands and troughs. The climate is arid and there is little fresh
water. The temperature is about 25–30°C between November and April, when
it starts to warm up, reaching temperatures of up to 45°C in June to
September. Tidal fluctuations are small, ranging between 50 and 120cm.

The marine resources of Eritrea are one of its most important assets and it
is heartening to see that the ministry charged with protecting these is one of
the most active. The process of developing both tourism on a limited scale and
the natural resources will take time. To begin with there wasn't even an
adequate survey of the islands. But good, and considered, progress is being

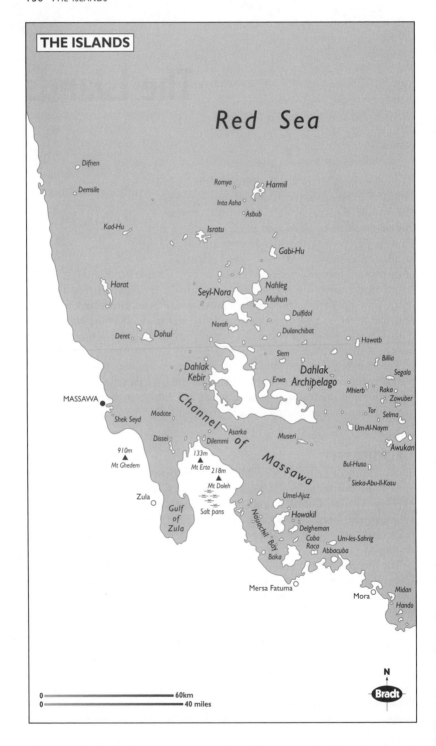

THE ISLANDS

Red Sea

Difnen

Demsile

Romya   Harmil

Inta Asha

Asbub

Kad-Hu

Isratu

Gabi-Hu

Harat

Nahleg

Seyl-Nora   Muhun

Dulfidol

Norah

Dulanchibat

Deret   Dohul

Hawatb

Siem

Billia

Dahlak
Kebir

Dahlak
Archipelago

Erwa

Segala

Mhierb   Raka

Zowuber

MASSAWA

Tor   Selma

Shek Seyd

Madote

Um-Al-Naym

Channel

Awukan

Dissei

Asarka

Dilemmi

Museri

of

910m
Mt Ghedem

133m
Mt Erta 218m

Mt Doleh

Massawa

Bul-Huso

Sieka-Abu-Il-Kosu

Zula

Gulf
of
Zula

Salt pans

Umel-Ajuz

Howakil

Delgheman

Coba
Raca

Um-les-Sahrig

Abbacuba

Baka

Mersa Fatuma

Mora

Midan

Hando

N

Bradt

0 ———————— 60km
0 ———————— 40 miles

made and the coast looks set to become an important part of Eritrea's economic development.

The importance of Eritrea's territorial waters to the country can be considered in proportion to its size, which at 60,000km^2 is about half the size of the land mass.

THE DAHLAK ISLANDS

As far as the tourist is concerned the Dahlak Islands are the easiest to visit, even if transport and accommodation are still in a rather nascent stage. The diving and birdlife are the major attractions.

An inventory of the islands

For the information on this and many other marine subjects I am greatly indebted to Dr J C Hillman of the Ministry of Marine Resources. While the information may be detailed, there are scant other sources available if you are visiting Eritrea and I have therefore chosen to err on the side of detail because of the potentially differing interests of visitors.

In a survey of the islands – the government, after 30 years of war, was starting with a largely blank sheet – an island was taken to be an area of land with over 50m in any one measure of extent, surrounded by the sea and appearing above water at all times. British Admiralty Charts were the main source for this information, supplemented by data from Ethiopian and Soviet records and field surveys.

It is evident that many of the islands are little more than small sand or rock banks close to the mainland coast or outlying the larger islands. There are also a number of shoals and submerged reefs which are not associated with any particular island and which never appear above water but are important in the overall ecology of the area. These are particularly plentiful in the north of the archipelago; divers have reported on the significance of two in particular – Fawn's Reef and Saunders' Reef. Of similar interest for their part in the ecosystem, but also not included in the island count as such, are the *secca* or areas of mud/sand/rock which appear above water at certain low tides. When looking at a map, there are a number of different words used for 'island': *isola* (Italian), *Gezirat* or *Jezirat* (Arabic), *Deset* (Tigrinya) and 'islet'.

One hundred and thirty-seven of the islands, or almost 40%, had no name at the time the survey was carried out in 1993, although only one of these fell within the top ten in terms of size. In addition many of the names used on charts have been superseded by more traditional local names. These will take longer to collate. I found it particularly confusing when looking at the islands off the Buri Peninsula, south of Massawa, to have them named in Arabic, Tigrinya and sometimes even Afar, according to who was providing the information.

There are, using the parameters above, a total of 354 islands and islets in the Eritrean Red Sea, the Dahlak Islands being the most numerous. These have a total land area of 1,334.7km^2 and total shoreline of 1,258.4km. In other words, the islands' coastlines double the 1,200km length of the shoreline of mainland Eritrea. The count includes:

- Small islands, less than 1km², totalling 276, or 78% of the total. They account for less than 1% of the area.
- Medium-sized islands, between 1 and 10km² in area, numbering 63, or 17.8% of the total. Their combined area is 223km².
- There are only 15 islands whose area is greater than 10km² and they account for 1,101km², 82.5% of the total area.

Certainly until there are more boats operating in the islands and offering the opportunity to travel further afield, tourists are likely to find it easier to visit the larger ones. The names of these are as follows:

Island	Size (km²)	Island	Size (km²)
Dahlak Kebir	643	Harat	20
Norah	103	Isratu	18
Halba	78	Adjuz	14
Baka	48	Unnamed	14
Howakil	41	Aucan	13
Erwa	34	Dohul	12
Nahaleg	31	Dar Dase	11
Harmil	22		

The majority of the islands lie off the province of Semhar (210), Denkalia (137) and a few in the north off the Sahel coast (7). They occur naturally in a number of clusters often associated with a major bay on the mainland coast:

Area	No of islands	Area	No of islands
North Coast	7	Arafale Bay	20
Arkiko Bay	1	Ed Bay	5
Dahlak Archipelago	209	Barra Isole Bay	13
Gulf of Zula	7	Beilul	13
Buri Peninsula	4	Assab Bay	30
Howakil Bay	44	Djibouti border	1
		Total	**354**

The average height of the islands is only 6m, although a few with old coral cliffs, such as Dahlak, have been lifted as much as 30m above sea level.

The inhabited islands

Due to a number of factors, principally the size of the islands, the lack of fresh water and disruptions to daily life and fishing patterns caused by the war with Ethiopia, only ten islands are inhabited: Dahlak Kebir, Norah, Dohul, Dissei, Arena, Baka, Dilemmi, Howakil, Adjuz and Abbaguba.

Only the first three of these lie in the Dahlak Archipelago proper. Although a census has yet to be carried out, surveys of the relevant provincial administrations would seem to indicate that there is only a total of some 2,500 inhabitants on these ten islands.

EXCHANGE & REMITTANCE SERVICES

We offer the widest range of financial services for travellers to Eritrea

Competitive Exchange Rates

Accept Personal Cheques and Credit Cards

Accept Travellers Cheques

No Commission on Cash and Cheques

Exchange between Foreign Currencies

International Money Transfer

Exchange Nakfa back to original Foreign Currency
(provided that you have a HIMBOL receipt)

Provides receipt for every transaction

HIMBOL

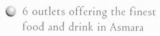
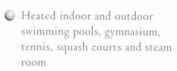

Marine characteristics of the Red Sea

The Red Sea has a number of attributes that are different to other seas. It is very narrow, covers a broad range of latitude and has at times been totally isolated for long periods from other water bodies. It is very saline (40–43 parts per 1,000 versus a more 'normal' 36 parts per thousand) and very warm.

Because of its isolation it has a very high level of endemism; latest studies show that 6% of corals are endemic, and 17% of the fish – although in some sub-groups this is as high as 90%. The Eritrean islands lie on a large continental shelf in the 0–200m depth range; the Dahlak Archipelago covers about 25% of this shelf. The shelf is widest (120km) at the latitude of the archipelago and narrowest in the north (15km) off the Sahel coast. In the south it also narrows to about 30km.

FLORA AND FAUNA
Birdlife

There remains an enormous amount of work to be done in researching this, but there are a large number of species of birds and fish for the visitor to see – even if only spending two or three days in the islands. The islands provide a natural habitat and breeding ground for birds, which must at least be partly linked to the very sparse human populations. As shown by the survey, many are extremely isolated.

The birds feed on migrations of sardines, anchovies and other fish passing north as far as Massawa during the latter part of the year. Recorded to date there are 109 bird species in 41 families on the islands, which should give some idea of the diversity. The main families and their species which have been recorded are as follows:

Family	Species	Family	Species
Phaethontidae	red-billed tropic bird	Anatidae	shoveller
		Accipitridae	black-shouldered kite
Sulidae	brown booby		black kite
Pelicanidae	pink-backed pelican	Accipitridae	Egyptian vulture
Ardeidae	green-backed heron		hooded vulture
	reef heron		white-headed vulture
	grey heron		marsh harrier
	black-headed heron		pallid harrier
	goliath heron		Montagu's harrier
	little egret	Pandionidae	shikra
		Pandionidae	osprey
Ciconiidae	yellow-billed stork	Sagittariidae	secretary bird
	saddle-billed stork	Falconidae	lesser kestrel
	Abdim's stork		fox kestrel
Phoeenicopteridae	greater flamingo		common kestrel

Family	Species	Family	Species
Falconidae	sooty falcon	Sternidae	white-cheeked
	lanner falcon		tern
Phasianidae	European quail		little tern
Numididae	tufted guinea		noddy
	fowl	Rynchopidae	skimmer
Rallidae	corn crake	Pterclididae	spotted
Otididae	Arabian bustard		sandgrouse
Haeatopodidae	oystercatcher	Columbidae	pink-headed
Recurvirostridae	black-winged stilt		dove
Dromdidae	crab plover		Namaqua dove
Burhinidae	spotted thicknee	Alcedinidae	white-collared
Glareolidae	cream-coloured		kingfisher
	courser	Meropidae	olive bee-eater
Charadriidae	little-ringed plover		European
	black-headed		bee-eater
	plover	Upupidae	hoopoe
	ringed plover	Alaudidae	white-fronted
	Kentish plover		sparrow-lark
	grey plover		hoopoe-lark
	Kittlitz's plover		short-toed lark
	great sand-plover		crested lark
Scolopacidae	sanderling	Hirundinidae	sand martin
	little stint		swallow
	curlew sandpiper	Motacillidae	tawny pipit
	common snipe		yellow wagtail
	bar-tailed godwit		white wagtail
	whimbrel	Turdidae	black bush-robin
	curlew		black-tailed
	redshank		rock-chat
	greenshank		Isabelline wheatear
	green sandpiper		pied wheatear
	wood sandpiper	Sylviidae	striped-back prinia
	terek sandpiper		Orphean warbler
	common		willow warbler
	sandpiper		whitethroat
Laridae	sooty gull		chiffchaff
	white-eyed gull	Nectariniidae	Nile valley sunbird
	black-headed gull	Oriolidae	golden oriole
	lesser black-backed	Corvidae	Indian house-crow
	gull		pied crow
Sternidae	Caspian tern		brown-necked
	swift tern		raven
	lesser-crested tern	Ploceidae	Ruppell's weaver
	common tern	*Emberizidae*	Cretzschmar's
	bridled tern		bunting

THE DUGONG

The dugong, *dugongo dugon*, is a sea-cow. It measures between 2.4m and 4.1m when adult and weighs anything from 360kg to 1,000kg. The young are pale cream turning to deep slate with maturity. Feeding is their main preoccupation and they use bristles on their lip-pads for grasping sea grasses, and the mouth plate for uplifting tubers and roots. It is the only herbivorous marine mammal and the elephant is believed to be its closest present-day non-Sirenian relative (Nishiwaki and Marsh, 1985). The only other surviving Sirenian species are three species of manatee. Their principal natural enemy, other than man, is the shark.

The dugong has been classified by IUCN as 'vulnerable to extinction'. The depletion in numbers is hard to counter, given that the dugong only reaches sexual maturity at about ten years old and then has just a single calf at intervals of 3–7 years. Nevertheless a survey by Anthony Preen for the Saudi Marine and Environmental Protection Administration in 1989 concluded it was possible that the Red Sea population was as high as 4,000, rather more than previous estimates. The survey was more extensive than any carried out before.

There are many interesting facts and legends surrounding the dugong. The Ark of the Covenant was covered in red dugong skin. They have been used by fishermen because of their uncanny foreknowledge of bad weather. A Lamu legend makes them the descendants of some women who were lost at sea in ancient times. To this day fishermen in Zanzibar have to swear they haven't interfered with their catch prior to landing: the exposed nature of the genitals and the two teats under the flippers appear always to have been the fuel for fishermen's imagination.

Mammalian wildlife

Mammalian wildlife has also yet to be comprehensively surveyed on the islands but due to the harsh environment it can safely be assumed that the coast offers better opportunities for looking at animals. There is, however, a stunted form of Soemmerring's gazelle on Dahlak Kebir, which has adapted to the climate and lack of water.

Dolphins are comparatively numerous and can be seen from the mainland, swimming alongside the boat on a trip to the islands or around the islands themselves. Of interest to marine folk for centuries and also living amongst the islands is the dugong, upon whom many say the legend of the mermaid is based.

Fish

Fish are of interest in two respects, for divers and from a commercial point of view – restarting an ancient tradition of fishing in the islands and on the coastline is a major governmental priority.

Fish diversity is high and a wide variety can be viewed from any of the islands that are already regularly visited by the boats available in Massawa.

Levels of endemism are also high in the Red Sea, extending to more than 50% in some fish groups such as butterfly fish. Perhaps the most talked about Red Sea fish species is the shark, but recorded shark attacks are very few and far between and often those reported are exaggerated or even absurd. In one recent study it transpired that three separate attacks were actually the same one; in another that the 'attack' actually took place in the boat, after a fisherman had hauled in his catch and was bitten by the shark in the bottom of the boat.

For many centuries sharks in the Red Sea have 'enjoyed' an infamous reputation. Anyone who wants to read more should try *Red Sea Explorers* (Immel Publishing), a marvellous book on exploration in the area. The authors, Peter Vine and Hagen Schmid, state 'Red Sea sharks are no more dangerous than those of other areas but for many years the area had a reputation for extremely vicious attacks'. Suffice it to say that if snorkelling or diving you should be as careful as you would be in other diving locations in the world, but no more so.

One of the best books on the whole subject is Dr John E Randall's *Red Sea Fishes* (Immel Publishing), which includes 325 species, of which 58 were described by Peter Forsskal, a Swede, who died during an expedition in 1762. In addition Andrea Ghisotti and Alessandro Carletti's *Red Sea Diving Guide* (Swan Hill Press) contains an up-to-date, if not very detailed, account of recent dives off Seil (east of Dissei), Dibrein and Mojeidi.

Current records for coral fish include 40 species in 24 families on stressed coral patches near Massawa and over 250 species in 49 families on outer coral reefs. The species are many and varied; most belong to the following families of fish:

angelfish	Pomacanthidae	squirrelfish	Holocantridae
wrasses	Labridae	surgeonfish	Acanthuridae
parrotfish	Scaridae	butterflyfish	Chaetodontidae
barracudas	Sphyranidae	blennies	Blenniidae
pipefish	Sygnathidae	triggerfish	Balistidae
puffers	Tetradontidae	gobies	Gobiidae
damselfish	Pomacentridae		

Pelagic (open-sea) species include sharks, tuna, barracuda and caranx. Also often visible are turtle species such as hawksbill, green and leatherback: a large proportion of the sandy beaches on the islands (when these occur) are used by turtles for laying their eggs. I have seen both turtle and barracuda within 50m of Gurgussum beach, although I think this was lucky.

Corals and shells: the invertebrates

Sharing the habitat is a great variety of coral and shells. A good book on these is *Red Sea Invertebrates* by Dr Peter Vine (Immel Publishing), which states 'the Red Sea reefs are among the world's greatest wonders'. Again, no description of mine will do this subject justice; go and see for yourself!

A survey in 1988/89 by R Pronzato, R Manconi and A Melles catalogued the invertebrates in the Massawa area. Many of these are in the collection of the Ministry of Marine Resources. Among the more common types of coral are:

Stylophora	Acropora	Favia	Porites
Fungia	Ecinopora	Favites	Lobophyllia
Pavona	Pocillopora	Galaxea	Tubipora musica
Platigyra	Tubinaria		

The most common shells to be seen when swimming off the coast are:

cowries panther cowrie (endemic)
  camel cowrie (endemic)
  Arabian cowrie
  thrush cowrie
Cypraea exhusta (endemic)
conches spider conch
  Strombus tricornis
  Gibberulus alba
cones
nurex
tibia
top shells

On the beaches you can easily find mud snails, moon shells, nerites, sundials, olives and bubble shells. Bivalves and others include clams, oysters, cockles, Venuses, mussels, asphis, scallops, Ark shells, cuttlefish (very common), sand dollar, starfish, sea cucumber, crabs and sea urchins. In the summer in particular the beaches are renowned for being a seething mass of hermit crabs on the move.

Commercial fishing

Unfortunately this virtually came to a standstill during the war and the toll in terms of lost expertise and the decimation of the number of boats in use makes depressing reading. This is, however, an area where the Ministry for Marine Resources is already making active progress. The US$4m Semhar project, in conjunction with the UN, aims to make significant headway in revitalising the industry with new boatbuilding facilities being planned, extensive training facilities and suitable arrangements for landing, storing and distributing fish.

According to the only available sources, even 25 years ago there were some 500 *houris* (indigenous craft), 70 with outboard engines, in operation along the coast, and over 300 dhows. Ten years later this number had fallen to 130 craft in total and by 1992 it was estimated that of the remaining boats counted, one third were out of service and the average age was eight years. The total fishing population has obviously dropped dramatically; indeed, the whole population on the coast may, according to some estimates now be as low as 70,000 (Massawa alone once had a population of 100,000).

The revival of commercial fishing will bring a much-needed source of income and protein to the coast. Any stimulus that it could provide to Massawa would be a particularly welcome boost in bringing the town back to life. While *sambuks* and fishing boats are seen here they are not in large enough quantities to enable the town to recapture its former character, or for the fishermen to assume the ability to support themselves.

OTHER MARINE INDUSTRIES
Salt production
This is another formerly important industry on the coast which made efficient use of natural resources. Extensive salt flats still exist in the Assab region, in Massawa, on the Buri Peninsula, and inland adjoining the Danakil Depression. Salt was exported inland to Senafe and Tigray and overseas to the Arabian Peninsula. This industry is also already being revived. In Massawa production took place over an 11km^2 area (4,400ha) with a peak production level of some 130,000 tonnes per annum; currently 25% of the ponds are back in operation, making about 40,000 tonnes per annum.

Prospects for oil
The prospect of extracting oil in commercial quantities could be a dream come true for the Eritrean economy. A Department of Energy report in 1993 stated that 'all the factors necessary for an attractive potential are at least locally present... the hydrocarbon potential of the Eritrean Red Sea is promising'. Despite a certain amount of exploration during the 1990s, no conclusive evidence, or lasting stability, has led to any oil companies committing themselves to extensive drilling in Eritrean waters or on shore. Suffice it to say that work continues in this field, drawing upon previous surveys over the past sixty years and upon new work. Petroleum was detected off Massawa as early as the 1920s and there was extensive drilling in the islands between 1938-40. It appears that the last serious, but none too successful, attempt at exploration was by Mobil in 1969 when a well blew out with gas.

ACCESSIBLE ISLANDS AND HOW TO REACH THEM
There is a vast choice of cruising among the many Eritrean islands. Permission to visit the islands (except **Green Island**) should be obtained from the **Eritrean Shipping Lines** office (tel: 552475; fax: 552391) next to the Imperial Palace on Taulud Island, if you are travelling to the islands on your own or in a group. If you are on an organised tour through an official operator, the permits should be arranged for you. A fee of US$20 is payable (in US dollars only) for three-day visits, and US$10 for each extra day. Inquire with Eritrean Shipping Lines as to which Islands are most accessible or suitable for your interests and also if you wish to hire diving equipment.

As an old Ethiopian guide to the islands points out, 'serious underwater work can best be carried out from aboard a boat'. In time there will be considerably more operators plying the route to the islands with tourists, but at the moment the choice is limited. Given the number of tourists, availability does not yet present a major problem. However, prices for boats, given their scarcity, are wholly non-negotiable. More operators should be a feature sooner rather than later. The places to try are:

Eritrean Shipping Lines (ESL) Massawa; tel: 552475; fax: 552391; Asmara; tel: 120402; fax: 120331. **ESL** provide organised boat trips to Dahlak Island (round trip US$295); other islands (US$175–320 – check with their price list, as it's liable to change); diving US$15/25/30 for 1/2/3 dives, US$45 for equipment; fishing US$16/hour.

Another option is **Mohammed Gaaz** (tel: 552667) who speaks Italian and a little English. The crew is very friendly and can also provide a picnic lunch. Diving equipment is not provided here; your boat is basically an off-duty fishing boat.

Eritrean Diving Centre Tel: 552688

Dahlak Hotel on Taulud Island just by the causeway to Massawa Island; tel: 552818; fax: 552782

Travel House International in Asmara; tel: 552818

The inner islands

Apart from the description of the general topography above, a record of the names and general characteristics may be helpful, although any skipper will help in advising which islands to visit if you specify what it is that you are looking for. Here is a small selection of the inner islands; these are currently the most regularly visited.

Sheikh Said Island (or Green Island) is just opposite Taulud, the first of Massawa's islands reached by crossing the first causeway. It is ideal for a day trip/picnic and not too expensive to reach. The coral is not exceptional but if you get there early in the morning the visibility is better than later in the day and it makes for a good alternative to the other islands if your budget is really tight. Remember to take your own snorkeling equipment, which can be rented from Eritrean Shipping Lines or the Dahlak Hotel. In the 1930s there was an Italian restaurant on the island, some traces of which can still be found (bottles etc). There is still a small ruined mosque at the end of the jetty. The island consists mostly of mangrove and sandy beach.

Dissei is a hilly island with rocky headlands and beaches. From its northern shore runs an underwater ridge of coral gardens and sand several kilometres long, ending with **Madote**, certainly one of my favourites, with 'Caribbean' blue water and white sand. There are no massive corals at Dissei but many small, delicate, branching corals, and lace, mushroom and branch coral. Diversity is good although visibility, particularly in the winter months, can be a problem due to the turbid water and large concentrations of plankton. A huge hotel complex was planned for Dissei, but it seems unlikely that anything will be built in the near future. South of Madote lie wide flat reefs with better visibility in 2–4m of water. Madote's makeshift lighthouse is usually home to a family of ospreys.

Dur Ghella and **Dur Gaam** are low, flat islands with some trees, mangroves and good beaches. They are 32km north of Dissei and are therefore northwest of the largest island, Dahlak.

Dahlak Kebir is the largest island and has a government hotel by the name **Luul**. Bungalows cost Nfa165/297/347 for one/two/three persons in a bungalow. However, prices must be paid in US$. Despite it being coined as a luxury hotel the restaurant is not well stocked and the beach nearby is far from idyllic. To the south is the ancient capital of the islands, which has a large ancient necropolis. The tombstones in the graveyard are inscribed with Kufic characters. There is a collection of these in the National Museum in Asmara. Near the necropolis there are also the famous water cisterns previously used to collect rainwater.

They are cut out of the coral limestone. James Bruce and Henry Salt, English travellers in the islands in the last century, both mention them as one of the wonders of the ancient world. Dahlak Island encompasses the lagoon of Ghubbet Mus Nefit. At the lower end of this, near Khor Amrac, lies the wreck of the 7,000-tonne liner Urania which was scuttled there as a result of damage in World War II. Nokra, in the mouth of the lagoon, has the remains of an old Italian prison and a more recent Soviet naval base. There are plans to turn this island into a museum.

Dugong

Through Denkalia: Massawa to Assab

Denkalia is the name of the inhospitable volcanic and rock desert that stretches from the Red Sea far into Ethiopia and, in Eritrea, separates Massawa from Assab. As the crow flies the distance from Massawa to Assab through this territory is about 500km; the border with Ethiopia is seldom more than 60km inland from the Red Sea. Eritrean Denkalia thus forms a long finger southeast of Massawa. It is home to the infamous tribal group, the Afars (of whom the Danakil are just one sub-group), whose reputation for ferocity is legendary. While there are a number of accounts from the expeditions of the Portuguese Jerome Lobo (1624), Fr Giuseppe Sapeto (1851), Munzinger (1867 and 1875), Pastori (1906), Nesbitt (1928), Franchetti (1928) and Thesiger (1930s), many others did not live to tell the tale – such as two Italian expeditions in the 1860s. Many of these expeditions were in territory that today lies in Ethiopia. Nowadays the journey is far from treacherous and instead offers some of the most extraordinary environments you are ever likely to see on earth.

If you decide to explore the region beyond the main Massawa to Assab road, then you should be sure to have a guide who knows the area well. This can be arranged through a travel agent in Asmara or, if you're lucky, you might find a local guide when you get there. Try consulting Afars in the isolated settlements along the way, and giving them lifts if possible. The inhabitants of Denkalia can wait up to a week for such a lift to visit their kin elsewhere, or to pick up supplies, so any help you can provide will be much appreciated. English, or any other European language, is very rarely heard in Denkalia, and regional administrators may just wonder what you are doing here. If you are experienced in making trips of this nature elsewhere on the continent then you can probably make do just with the assistance of local guides and administrators.

The journey through Denkalia is one of the most magnificent opportunities on offer in Eritrea. It is a journey into wild, harsh terrain that is still made by very few travellers. Mostly it is not desert in the sense that many people perceive a desert: it is not miles of rolling sand dunes, but more rock, rugged mountainscapes and volcanoes. En route you can see more wildlife than in any other area in Eritrea, vast salt flats worked by the Afars (Buri Peninsula), a volcanic lake (Lake Badda), spectacular beaches, and a way of life pursued by

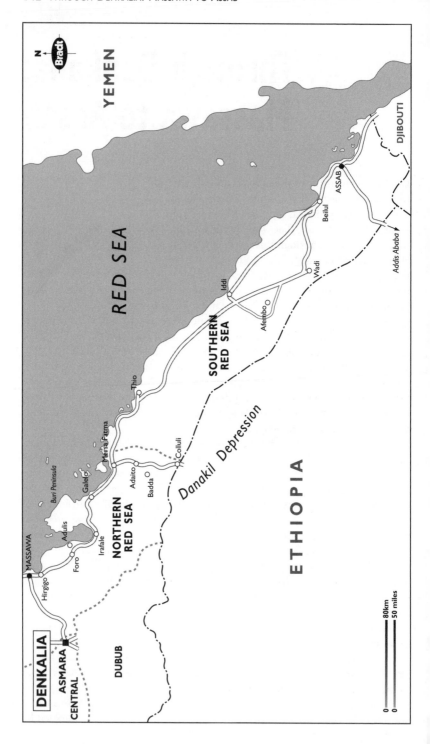

ROADS AND MAPPING

Until recently the only route linking Massawa to Assab by land was a very poor road that was only navigable by the hardiest of travellers. It took at least two days to complete the 700km journey, as it was then, but since 1998 the government has embarked on an extensive upgrading and rerouting of this road, which is nearly complete. There are still some sections that are very rough, but most of the journey can be spent at 120km/h on unsealed, but very smooth road. This has meant that the journey from Massawa to Assab is now little over 600km and takes about ten hours. If you include the Massawa to Asmara leg, the journey from Asmara to Assab is now possible in one day, though you would have to start very early. However, the improved road should not encourage whistle-stop tours of Assab from Asmara. Instead it offers even greater access to the breathtaking environments of the Denkalia region and any trip should include extensive exploring around this region to get the most out of your time there.

It is very important to note that accurate maps for this region do not yet exist and despite significant improvements in the main road, there still remain considerable shortfalls in the mapping of the region and its roads. It is advised, therefore, that you should always ensure you know where you are headed by seeking advice from locals or other travellers where possible. This is particularly important on the unmarked stretches of road linking the smaller villages, but also applies to travelling on the main road, where better conditions have allowed faster speeds, which in turn can lead to missing important junctions or side-roads.

The roads marked in this book for this region are accurate to the best of my knowledge, but should only be used as a guide and not taken as being a perfect indication of the current routes. There are many unmarked side-routes that criss-cross this region and, providing you have reliable local knowledge, are probably worth venturing onto if you are in search of adventure – but be careful, especially in the wet season when these roads become treacherous and impassable.

the Afar for many centuries. The area has always been famous as a trade route, not just for the fish, salt and mineral deposits, but longer ago for slaves, ivory and skins.

WHEN TO TRAVEL

The weather in Denkalia does not vary greatly throughout the year. It is never cool; instead, variations range from searing heat to comfortable warmth. Denkalia is home to the Danakil Depression where, at depths of up to 120m below sea level, temperatures are among the hottest on earth. It is hence worth considering the timing of your trip according to the time of year, as to attempt a journey to Assab in the middle of the summer could be little short of torturous. However, in the winter months, from October to February, the weather is quite pleasant with cooling winds and milder temperatures. The rains on the coast are from December to February, and July to September, though they hardly match those that fall in the highlands. Asmara, for example, has an average rainfall ten times that of Assab.

GETTING THERE

There are three ways of experiencing Denkalia, two of which are far preferable to the third. The most popular is to hire your own four-wheel drive. This can be easily arranged through most car hire agencies in Asmara (see *Car hire* on page 97). Drivers can be included in the price and are essential, unless you have a lot of experience with a four-wheel drive. Make sure to have a driver who is very familiar with the region and, preferably, knows some Arabic or Amharic, which should be more useful than Tigrinya in most areas south of Massawa. Another option for getting to Denkalia is through an organised tour. Falcon or Travel House International, in Asmara, offer tours to this region and can be contacted either before you arrive in Eritrea or from their respective Asmara offices (Falcon: P O Box 3659; tel: 126467/120238; fax: 120801; email: falcon@cts.com.er; Travel House International: PO Box 5579; tel: 201881/2; fax: 120751; email: thi@eol.com.er). The alternative, which should only be considered if you are seriously short of cash and have a lot of time to waste, is the public bus. There is, unbelievably, a bus that leaves Asmara for Assab every Tuesday and Saturday, taking two days. It is an arduous journey, surely ranking amongst the world's most appalling, though it has improved a great deal in the past two years. If you decide to take this option, then take all the supplies you need, including plenty of water (at least three litres a day). Buses are scheduled to leave Asmara twice a week, but services are erratic and you should go to the bus stop to inquire at least several days before you plan to travel.

Equipment

Even Eritreans will raise their eyebrows if you mention a journey to Denkalia, such is its mystique; few would choose to make the trip voluntarily. But this is a reaction to the unknown; in practice, the myth is much worse than the reality.

There is much to see along the route from Massawa to Assab and it is well worth stopping at the many little villages along the way. Unless you specifically want to traverse the whole route, or vice versa, you can just head as far south east as Thio and then return to Massawa. While the southern half is different topographically it harbours fewer of the more spectacular sites.

Now that the road has been improved travelling the whole distance from Massawa to Assab does not require much specialist equipment other than a reliable four-wheel drive, two spare tyres, a full tank (or tanks) of petrol, plenty of water and some extra food rations. Any foray inland into Denkalia south of Foro should only be undertaken if you are fully equipped for tough terrain and desert travel; it must be stressed that this is not an expedition guide but the following are amongst the basic essentials:

- compass and/or satellite navigation system
- fuel (up to 200 litres for a 5-litre petrol Land Cruiser, or 150 litres for a 2.5-litre turbo-diesel Land Rover)
- water (up to 5 litres per person per day, excluding what you may require for cooking and washing). Even in winter temperatures in excess of 35°C are common, and it is important to avoid dehydration.
- spare parts (as you would carry for a trans-Africa trip)
- all food
- spade, and preferably sandplanks plus towrope, for extricating your vehicle from the sand
- minimum of two spare tyres

If you are unsure what constitutes an appropriate list of spares and supplies, consult a guide such as the updated *Africa by Road* by Charlie Shackell and Illya Bract (Bradt Travel Guides), *The Travellers Handbook* by Wexas, or *Africa Overland* by David Brydon. If something goes wrong you may have a very long time to wait if you are not able to extricate yourself independently, and the cost of being 'rescued' could be substantial.

Two last words on safety – although the landmines have now been cleared from this region it is important to remain vigilant and be aware of the dangers that could still persist. Any areas that present a threat should be clearly marked. If you want to walk about do so where you can see that other people have done so, or on terrain that is obviously unsuitable for mines (eg: solid rock areas). From the end of 2001 a Temporary Security Zone (TSZ) was established by the UN along the entire border of Eritrea and Ethiopia, 25km inside Eritrean territory. It was to remain until February 2002, but this has been extended to September 2002. Nonetheless, you should be careful not to travel too close to the border, as it is likely only to raise unnecessary suspicion and could result in problems with the authorities in the region.

The Afars

Thesiger commented that 'no Danakil man may wear a coloured loincloth, a comb or feather in his hair, nor decorate his knife with brass or silver until he has killed at least once'. In addition they had a disconcerting custom of making necklaces strung with their victims' testicles. The Afars are no longer to be as feared as they were, even just prior to World War II. But the people have lived largely in isolation even since then, and your presence is unusual for them. Be even more respectful about taking photographs (or simply refrain if it is clear they do not want to be photographed). Take some provisions that are likely to be welcome – coffee, tea, sugar, cigarettes and sweets will always go down well – if you want to ease communication. Some will refuse point blank to look at you, let alone talk to you; respect for their privacy and way of life is a must. I make no apology for emphasising this. There has already been one nasty incident in Denkalia when a photographer paid an Afar girl a large sum of money to pose nude. The authorities found out, and the photographer was deservedly thrown out minus his film, which is probably at the bottom of the Red Sea.

Such insensitivity runs the risk of making travelling in the region less enjoyable for those that follow, and possibly more dangerous.

THE ROUTE
Distances

These are going to vary quite considerably depending on which way the track meanders at different times of year. The distances (see box below) should be treated as approximate as you are likely to tailor your own route depending on your interests. If you are travelling in the rainy season the routes are also subject to changes depending on the watercourses.

There are as yet no good maps of Denkalia, but this should change with time. There are a couple of mildly useful maps available in Asmara with some of the place names on, but these are seldom consistent, so be sure you know exactly what you are aiming for. No map currently available shows the route that the new road takes, hence the need for a competent guide. All the times stated below are for travelling in a four-wheel drive. If you are travelling by public bus, you can expect to at least double these times. The road to **Hirgigo** (Arkiko), the first village, runs to the south of Massawa from the start of the first causeway, passing the big Agip fuel depot after 4km. Hirgigo (9km from Massawa), with its distinctive minaret, boasts the ruins of one of the oldest mosques in the country. It is over 150 years old and can be found next to its more modern replacement. Hirgigo had a terrible experience during the struggle and at the end of 2001 still looked a very sorry sight, but development is promised and since the near completion of the new power station directly between the village and Massawa, there should be a certain degree of assured

DISTANCES FROM MASSAWA AND ASSAB

Town	km from Massawa	km from Assab
Massawa	0	600
Hirgigo	9	591
Foro	50	550
(Adulis is 7km from Foro)		
Irafale	75	525
Galelo	128	472
(Badda is 127km from Galelo)		
Thio	250	350
Iddi	372	228
Wadi	484	116
Beilul	538	62
Assab	600	0

income in the future. The power station, along with Asmara airport, was a key target for the Ethiopian Air Force during the recent war and progress on constructing the power station was severely set back by the attacks. However, it is now near completion and will provide Eritrea with over half of its energy requirements from 2002. This will be a great leap forward for a country that is subject to many blackouts and seldom has electricity throughout the night.

Extensive Ethiopian fortifications surround the approaches to **Foro** (pronounced Forro), 50km from Massawa. Formerly a major agricultural centre, the town has a large dam that runs from north to south and is still in use. Foro used to trade with the hinterland and across the Red Sea to the Arabian Peninsula; the inhabitants are a mixture of Saho, Tigre and Tigrinya. Driving time from Massawa to Foro is now only about 50 minutes. The plain on which it lies is of importance as the site of Adulis, the ancient Axumite port, which can be reached by turning towards the sea just after you pass over the dam, taking the track towards Zula. Access to Adulis may be restricted if excavations are underway; check at the National Museum in Asmara before you plan a visit, where you will need to purchase a permit. The National Museum will also be able to tell you the name of the guide in Foro who can show you around when you arrive. If you are driving on your own, head towards the only obvious brick buildings, which are Adalet Elementary School, then pass a little further where you will see some mounds of rock and sand on your right hand side. These are left from the many excavations that have taken place here. It is believed that at least 95% of the site still lies unexcavated. Owing to this fact, many visitors, who are not well versed in archaeological expertise, are a little disappointed when they see the site for the first time as little remains of this once magnificent port except a few submerged walls. Nonetheless, it is a fascinating place to visit and as further excavations take place more will be revealed of this important archaeological site. Pottery remains, and coins and porcelain are easily found around the site. Adulis now lies some 4km inland after centuries of silt and debris from the highlands have been washed out to sea here, extending the coastline eastwards. Zula is the current coastal village, which is beyond Adulis.

Irafale (75km from Massawa), a fishing village in the Gulf of Zula, just over half an hour from Foro, marks the start of the Buri Peninsula, one of the most interesting parts of Denkalia. The undulating lava flows create the most captivating scenery. The name Irafale derives from the Arabic phrase *Ara feelum,* which was said to have been uttered by the followers of the prophet Mohammed when they were orderd to go to the Habisha areas (now the Eritrean coast) to escape persecution by the Jews. The phrase literally means 'I can see an elephant', and the oral history of the elders relates that the area was once full of elephants, and while none are to be seen today, the environment still looks very suitable, with the spattering of acacia and other types of trees. If you fork right after leaving the village a road leads southeastwards directly to Badda, but to take this would mean missing Buri Peninsula, one of the most interesting parts of the desert. The first part of the peninsula is very rocky and some parts are very steep. Shortly after Irafale you descend into a large, beautiful bay. The black volcanic sand and the sunbleached driftwood causes a strangely film-negative appearance. The cliffs which back the bay are home for colonies of Hamadryas baboons. Off a sandy spit at the far end there is good snorkelling with as many species of fish as you would find around the islands. It was along these bays that the famous Napier expedition landed in 1868, prior to marching (elephants and all) to Magdala in northern Ethiopia to defeat Emperor Theodore (who had taken a number of European hostages).

Soon after the bay the road turns inland to cross the peninsula west to east. The first Afar villages become visible about 120km from Massawa, this area being known as **Galelo** (pronounced Gall'allo). The administrative centre for North Denkalia is being built here and it is the starting point for seeing the many interesting sights of the peninsula. Being an administrative centre Galelo is quite a large village, with several choices to find food, drink and accommodation, albeit fairly basic. It is a good place to stop for refreshments. The small harbour (really just a jetty) receives fish for trucking to Asmara.

An indication of distances north of Galelo, around the Buri Peninsula, is not relevant because it depends entirely in what order you visit the villages. You should take a guide from Galelo, not least because in some areas there might still be some danger of mines. On the coast, immediately north of the village, is the fishing village of **Doleh** (pronounced Dollo); from here Afar fishermen eke out a precarious existence using traditional *houris* and other indigenous craft. Inland from Doleh there are reasonable numbers of gazelle (Soemmerring's and Dorcas), guinea fowl and ostrich; you may even see jackal or wild ass. These may not be pure wild ass, which are rare, but they are certainly not donkeys; the Wildlife Department is currently making a study of this hybrid so more information should soon be available. North of these bare plains lie the vast salt flats of Buri, some 20km northwest of Galelo. A dramatic backdrop is provided by the still-active volcanoes Mount Doleh and Mount Erca. The flats are a truly astonishing sight; in the sun they shimmer like an oasis stretching as far as the eye can see. We saw them on a day when only three Afars were working, sitting on their haunches chipping away at the salt with the backdrop of the huge expanse of the flats. This was one of my more memorable days in Eritrea. The flats are fed by water from the north; the salt, which was exported by the British in World War II, is now mostly trucked to Senafe and other towns in the southern highlands.

Another fishing village worth visiting is **Inghil** on the northwestern shore of the peninsula. The approaches are marked with large numbers of Muslim graves.

The road from Galelo to Thio used to be one of the worst stretches in the whole of Denkalia with speeds of 10km/h seldom possible. It has now been repaired and the vast rocks which one had to drive over or round now lie by the side of the track. This makes this stretch a lot more practicable and enables you to enjoy arguably the most impressive stretch of Eritrea's coastline. The landscape is distinctly lunar here with the only visible vegetation being mangroves and the bushy sandbanks out to sea. Vast tidal lagoons and a view over the distant islands (the larger ones are Howakil and Baka) are features of

ADULIS

The site of Adulis, Axum's ancient port, lies half an hour's drive towards the sea from Foro. It is between the villages of Afta and Zula, and out to sea you can see the island of Dissei. You can recognise the site from the large piles of tailings, resulting from earlier excavations. The most recent of these were by Anfray in the 1970s, the results contained in his book *Les Anciens Ethiopiens*. The town itself is some 4km inland from where the port would have been and nothing remains of the latter. It became obvious from the various excavations done at Adulis since Paribeni's first major study in 1907, that the town was very significant, sitting astride major ancient trade routes (not least the incense route) from Egypt to the Indian Ocean. Vast quantities of artefacts have attested to the richness of life in the town: gold and silver coinage, glass, marble, decorated pottery, etc, although all of this has been removed. Most of the unearthed ruins are constructed in black basalt; there are tombs, a palace, what is possibly an 8th century Christian church and an earlier temple for the worship of the sun. Adulis' importance was eclipsed in the 7th century, probably by a combination of Arab raids and the port silting up. Until further information is collated and available, or unless you are an expert in Axumite history, the site is not visually so impressive as to make a visit particularly memorable, but it is only a short detour from the main track.

the drive. After initially following the coast you can either head inland to Adaito or continue to the small harbour of Mersa Fatma and south towards Thio. **Mersa Fatma** used to be a harbour of some significance. You can still see the route of the railway line that brought potash from Dallol in the Danakil Depression to the coast for export. All that is left of the harbour are bits of military wreckage and three or four burnt-out Italian buildings. This is a desolate spot and it is hard to imagine any rebuilding taking place in a hurry, unless mining in the Depression was restarted. The drive from Galelo to Mersa Fatma is 40km and takes under one hour.

The new road bypasses **Adaito**, instead sticking to the coast as it heads directly for Thio and on to Iddi. To go to Adaito means a detour inland (23km), from where you can reach Badda (43km). The road is not as good as the main coastal road and travelling will take considerably longer along this route. Adaito is a reasonable-sized village; you won't be able to miss it in daylight. The road heads southwest towards Badda and Dallol (and the Danakil Depression). You might be able to find a local guide in Adaito who will take you to Dallol. If you do undertake a trip to Dallol on no account go without a guide, and do not go with just a single vehicle. It is very dangerous territory where sinking in the salt deposits is always possible; if this happens there's no one for a very long way to haul you out. A trip to Badda to see its volcanic lake is as interesting, and much safer.

Continuing along the coastal road from Mersa Fatma will bring you to **Thio**. Thio is 250km from Massawa and 122km from Galelo. In driving time this distance, from Galelo, takes little over one hour, but you should look out for the shining white minaret on the coast or you will miss the town altogether. The main road bypasses the town so you need to take the appropriate turning when you see the mosque. There is quite a substantial fighters' camp here on the end of the promontory and it is one of the only places you might be able to get repairs done if you need; there is a fully-equipped mobile workshop. The village itself is attractive: many coloured huts of wood and bamboo line the shore, draped with fishing nets. It is the biggest fishing village between Massawa and Assab, and if you have an urge to fish from a dhow this is probably the easiest place to try to organise it. It is now perhaps most famous for the very cheap electrical goods you can purchase there, shipped in from the Middle East. The prices are a fraction of those found in Asmara. Although this practice is illegal, it is largely ignored. If tempted to take a swim, think again. Thio's water is fetched from 30km inland so the sea is unfortunately (but understandably) the sanitation system.

The next destination after Thio is **Iddi** (372km from Massawa), about five and a half hours' drive from Massawa. Iddi is a fascinating fishing village, which sees very few visitors and was cut off, on the land side, until the end of 1995 due to mines. It is a good place to camp, but the locals will be only too happy to help you out with providing some foam mattresses or rudimentary bedding. There is a hotel a little inland if you prefer local luxury. Swimming is safe and clean provided you are a reasonable distance from the village's immediate shoreline. There is a picturesque old mosque on the headland, which is one of five mosques in Iddi. The people here survive mainly on fishing and it is therefore a good place to try local seafood. The painted fishing huts and friendly locals make this village rather nicer than Thio.

Soon after Iddi you enter more volcanic country where the ground is formed by a thin volcanic crust, giving the earth an over-baked appearance. The black soil and the bright green bushes, again, give the appearance of being a film negative. As the road reaches the Afar villages of Wadi and Beilul the desert becomes more conventional. Before reaching Wadi you descend into a vast plain, dotted with large flat-topped mountains. It takes about two and a half hours to reach **Wadi** from Iddi (112km). Wadi is marked by its distinct mosque and many ramshackled huts. You can easily find food and a drink here if you are in need of a rest. The journey from Wadi to Beilul takes around one hour (54km) and passes through some remarkable mountain scenery. One dominant feature along this stretch of road is the almost perfectly conical-shaped mountain with a square rock atop it. There are also many signs left from the struggle, including burnt-out tanks and other armoured vehicles. **Beilul** (538km from Massawa), is surrounded by palms and you will most likely be treated as something of a curiosity. If offered *douma* (pronounced doma), an alcohol made from the sap of the palm trees, it is well worth accepting, although beware of its strength! The journey from Beilul to Assab

TOWARDS THE DANAKIL DEPRESSION: LAKE BADDA

Adaito is on the very edge of the famous, or infamous, Danakil Depression which boasts conditions so harsh that no living thing will be seen anywhere near it. Dallol, in the Depression proper, is off limits since the recent war, but it is possible to drive towards Colluli on the Eritrean–Ethiopian border. You can probably find a guide in Adaito to take you this far (but, due to the danger, no further). Even the start of the track to Colluli gives some clue to what lies ahead, with its desolate, almost lunar landscape. Once again one has to admire the enterprise of the Italians in their former colony: there are signs by the track of the old railway built in 1912 to shuttle potash mined in Dallol to the coast. Even some of the old water cisterns along the roadside remain: these were constructed in the 1930s, at 5km intervals, to facilitate road travel – car radiators in those days were not up to the strain imposed by the very high temperatures.

After leaving Adaito in a southeasterly direction you will come to a fork at 12km: the road to the left goes on to Colluli, the one to the right leads to Badda. Badda is a very interesting alternative, and only a two-hour drive from Adaito. If you arrive during the daily sandstorm (13.00–16.00) it is as desolate a place as you can imagine, with people, camels and donkeys all bent double against the wind and sand. Visibility can be less than 10m. When there is no storm, though, it is a hamlet of great charm, and surprisingly fertile as it collects precipitation from the mountains of Tigray in the background. The market is always humming; with agriculture possible and 1,800ha currently under cultivation, Badda is known as the breadbasket of Denkalia. To reach its prime attraction – Lake Badda – you will need to find a guide and expect to pay him about Nfa50 for his troubles. The lake is a striking anomaly in the middle of a desert. The approach, up the side of a large sand dune towards the lip of a collapsed volcano, gives no hint of what suddenly reveals itself: a crater of some 400m in diameter that is over 100m deep according to an old Italian survey. If you hear rustling in the reeds it is most likely cattle, but there is also a jackal family that likes to descend the volcanic south edge to drink. If you plan to visit the lake you must be in Badda as early as possible in order to make the return trip before the lunchtime storm.

(62km) takes just under an hour and is a good stretch of road. The airport is 15km before entering Assab town (600km from Massawa).

If you plan to drive the whole trip allow at least two days each way, especially if you want to make detours to Badda, Buri Peninsula and Ras Terme; and add on a couple of days for recuperation, sightseeing and swimming in Assab.

Assab to Ras Terme

There were places to visit south of Assab (such as Rahaita, on the border with Djibouti, and Halib Island), but since the recent war it is not advisable to travel to border areas. However, this situation might change so ask at the city's administration if you wish to travel further south.

A good excursion from Assab is to Ras Terme (pronounced Ras Terma). Leave Assab as if driving to the airport and take a right turn immediately after the city checkpoint, thereafter driving due north with the salt flats between you and the coast. The drive takes less than an hour: after 27km dunes and mangrove swamps are easily visible, and is an old Italian building atop the headland. The beaches under the headland are magnificent; turtles and porpoises are not uncommon and further out there are obviously rather more, judging by the fishermen's catches that you are likely to see on the headland. Sharks seem to be the speciality, often just caught for the fins to be sold to the Far East for soup. On the tip of the headland is an old fisherman's shrine constructed from sawfish bills. To the north lies a long palm-backed beach, which is a good place to camp, although there is a dearth of firewood. You are likely to wake to see large numbers of flamingoes on the foreshore. Further to the north, a few kilometres away but clearly visible, is a rocky island, which appears to be a nesting place for birds. Living here is very bleak, and any small gifts to ease your intrusion into the community will be welcome, particularly if you want the fishermen to show you around the headland to see their catch. Further to the north, Barra Isole is also meant to be worth a visit, but is only accessible if it is completely dry, or you are likely to get stranded on the salt flats.

Assab and the South Coast

ASSAB

Assab can be reached in one of three ways: by plane from Asmara, by road through Denkalia or, if you are very fortunate, by boat from Massawa. It is located right at the southern tip of Denkalia and is the capital of the Southern Red Sea province. Most people do not visit unless they have a particular reason, due to its relative inaccessibility, but to ignore it for this reason is, in my opinion, a big mistake. Assab has a charm and character unlike any other town in Eritrea. In the same way that the frontier town of Tessenei has a distinctly vibrant Sudanese feel to it, so too does Assab reflect a certain Ethiopian air. Assab expanded rapidly under Ethiopian rule, and therefore feels more Ethiopian than Eritrean. There are also close links with Yemen, so the town has a very appealing multicultural feel to it.

Sadly, Assab was one of the biggest losers in the recent war with Ethiopia. Being Addis Ababa's closest link to the sea and a guaranteed source of revenue and employment for Eritrea, Assab port has major strategic importance for both countries. Many say that the war, despite all the peripheral reasons, was ostensibly about access to the sea. Assab, therefore, was fiercely contested during the conflict and some of the largest battles took place to defend this town from falling into Ethiopian hands. A sad and inevitable result of this conflict is that the port, which is one of the best equipped in East Africa and far bigger than Massawa, now lies idle. The massive cranes that were once so busy unloading so much of the import demands of the Ethiopian state stand motionless. The population has shifted from a large workforce manning the port to thousands of soldiers stationed here since the conflict. The recent war has also meant that the border is strictly closed. Since the end of 2000 it has remained firmly sealed inside the UN's Temporary Security Zone. Although the TSZ is designed to be dismantled in late 2002, it is unlikely that the border with Ethiopia will be open for some time to come. Building enough trust between these two countries to allow the port of Assab to function as Ethiopia's surrogate port is likely to take many months if not years. Until that time arrives Assab will remain a somewhat isolated corner of the country with little to boast but a disproportionate male population and a diminutive but pleasant multicultural flavour.

The town has been an important port since it was purchased by the Rubattino Shipping Company on behalf of the Italian government in

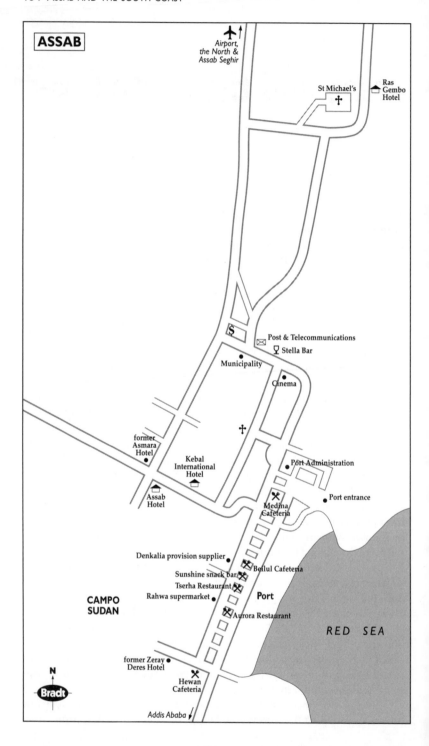

November 1869. From 1882 the government administered it directly. It was therefore the first Italian foothold in Eritrea, from which they expanded northwards to eventually colonise the whole region now known as Eritrea. Owing to its location, it was virtually impossible to attack during the struggle because of its isolation and very heavy lines of defence. You can't help wondering how much its existence prolonged the war with Ethiopia, being its main conduit for military supplies. Sporadic attempts were made to disrupt the port, such as the April 1988 commando raid by the EPLF on the oil refinery.

A hundred years after it was built it was the main port serving Addis Ababa and thrived as a result. In 2001 it is idle, awaiting higher politics to allow trade through its gates once more. A few Italian legacies remain in Assab and the various quarters of the city make for a very interesting mix of cultures and styles. It can hardly be compared with Massawa, but there are parts of the city that mirror the Turkish styles found in Massawa and some interesting old Italian buildings similar to those you might find on Taulud Island. Until recently, the most historic area of town housed many businesses run by Ethiopians. Their absence is marked by the quietness of the town and the boarded up shops and windows.

The town is divided into three parts. **Assab Seghir** (small Assab) is on the shoreline as you enter the town from Denkalia or the airport. In the centre of town is **Assab Kebir** (big Assab), containing the port and city centre. Nestling behind it is the rather ramshackle **Campo Sudan**, once the domain of Ethiopian residents, until they were all deported after the recent war. The latter still has a feel of Addis Ababa about it. However, despite the absence of Ethiopians the area remains the least safe place in town, where you may get hassled by soldiers short of entertainment. Assab Seghir is much more Eritrean in character with its Afar contingent, and has one long main street lined with market stalls selling everything from fruit to samosas and *douma* (palm wine). Heading north from Assab Seghir there are excellent beaches, which are totally deserted most of the time.

There are also extensive salt flats around Assab, which was once the second most profitable industry besides the port. However, production was disrupted by the war and may take a few years before it reaches the success it enjoyed during the mid-1990s, when exports were in the tens of millions of nakfa.

Where to stay

Sadly, the recent war and subsequent redundancy of the port has meant that the number of visitors to Assab has dropped dramatically. This has resulted in a number of hotels in Assab closing. Whether they remain closed is uncertain, but for the near future things are not likely to improve enough to accommodate so many players in the market.

The latest to fall victim are **Zeray Deres** and **Asmara Hotel**. Zeray Deres is an architectural monstrosity at the far end of the port and is singularly unattractive inside as well. The owner seemed resigned to the fact that the hotel would remain closed for some time. Asmara Hotel is opposite Assab

Hotel and is still open as a snack bar but has closed its rooms. It is likely, therefore, that when business picks up the rooms will be reopened.

Upper range
Ras Gembo, formerly **The Port Club** Tel: Assab 661114/660521. Sits on a large, sandy beach (with bandstand) just outside the port area and behind St Michael's Church. Particularly if you have arrived by road it is a welcome haven of creature comforts, but there is little doubt it has seen better days. The restaurant is no longer the culinary haven it once used to be. You'll be lucky to get omelette or *capretto* here now, but you can rely on finding something simple. The service remains abysmal. The manager implied that this situation was going to improve, but judging by the state of the rest of the building it doesn't seem likely. The architecture is definitely 1970s Soviet style and synonymous with so many other hotels built in Africa around this time. Like these, there is the same feeling that it is facing an inevitable demise from lack of maintenance and investment. However, one remains hopeful and perhaps it can be resurrected to its former glory. It would be sad to see it get any worse as the beach and tennis courts make for an ideal setting. The beach is popular among UN workers and the water is much cleaner than Massawa's. The rooms are mostly arranged along the beach. They are a good size, clean and have hot water and air conditioning. There are a whole menagerie of classes and room types to choose from, but simply they come in four classes; VIP/first/second/third. VIP costs Nfa253/329 single/double; first class costs Nfa132/172 single/double; second class costs Nfa88/114 single/double; and third class costs Nfa71/93 single/double. Third class is more than adequate, but still much more than other options in town for the same facilities.

Kebal International Hotel (no telephone available at time of writing). Next to the petrol station opposite Assab Hotel and used to be called Nino's. It has been recently refurbished and is now one of the best places in town, though the bar makes it quite noisy. The rooms cost Nfa165/132/55 first/second/third class. First class has TV, fridge and air conditioning. Second class doesn't have TV and third doesn't have a fridge. It has a central location and is therefore convenient if you like to visit the town rather than spend time on the beach.

Budget
Assab Hotel is by far the best place in the budget range and certainly competitive with the upper-range options if you are in town for a short stay. It is situated on the edge of Campo Sudan on the corner opposite the petrol station and former Asmara Hotel. There are plenty of rooms in two classes. The cheapest are downstairs around the central courtyard for Nfa20 per room (two beds) with shared bathroom and toilet. Rooms upstairs cost Nfa35 for two beds with shower and toilet and air conditioning. Air conditioning is charged as extra if you use it, but there are fans in all rooms. The rooms are clean and the owner very friendly.

Where to eat
A lot of the snack bars and smaller eateries run by Ethiopians have been forced to close since the owners have been deported. This has meant that the variety of options for food or snacks in Assab has decreased. The best Italian food in

town is at **Restaurant Aurora**, still run by a marvellous Italian lady who has stayed the course in Assab, a remarkable feat for even the hardiest of people. Pasta, fish, lasagne and calamari are all available. A meal with drinks will cost about Nfa30 a head.

There are numerous places to eat Eritrean food and other smaller snacks. A good place to look for variety is on the very pretty avenue running westwards along the front of the port from the port entrance. If you start from the port entrance there is **Medina Cafeteria**, followed some blocks down by **Beilul Cafeteria**, then **Sunshine Snack Bar**, **Tserha Restaurant**, **Aurora Restaurant**, then at the very end of the road next to Zeray Deres Hotel is **Hewan Cafeteria**. You can expect to find snacks, local foods and a wide range of drinks at any of these places. **Stella Bar** near the cinema (on the opposite side of the road) also does reasonable food and has a pleasant seated area under the shade of trees.

If you walk up the road past Assab Hotel away from town you will see the many brightly coloured wooden shacks, evocative of West Indian shanties, offering all sorts of goods and services. This is another area where you can get very reasonable local food at local prices.

Shopping

Assab is not a shopper's paradise. There is little to buy here except imported necessities or domestic products. However, if you are after supplies or a return trip to Asmara then head for **Dankalia Provision Supplier/Handler** in the street behind Aurora Restaurant running parallel to the port. This is the mother outlet for the famous Wikianos Supermarket on Liberty Avenue in Asmara and run by a delightful gentlemen who will be able to provide you with just about everything you could ever wish for. If your dreams are not fulfilled and you arrive before Wednesday then you can order other supplies from Asmara through their freight delivery, which arrives on Wednesdays. You can reliably get mineral water, all types of liquors, beer, chocolate, tinned foods, juices and household goods.

In the unlikely event that they do not stock what you are looking for, another place to try is **Rahwa Supermarket**, on the same street but a little further down, almost directly behind Aurora Restaurant.

Other information

Most facilities are available in Assab: post office, bank and open-air cinema. The telecommunications office is largely redundant since the lines were cut during the conflict. In 2001 it was impossible to call Asmara, let alone overseas, from Assab, but this situation should improve in the near future. It is worth asking at the telecommunications building if you need to make an urgent call, otherwise make sure you do this in Asmara before heading down to Assab.

The port

It is possible to visit the port, but you will have to contact the port manager. His office is in the Port Administration building left of the port's main entrance. He might allow you a walk round, depending on the general state of security at the time.

A final word

Assab has experienced an unsettling few years and being so closely associated with Ethiopia has faced a lot of internal scrutiny. With so many residents deported and so many obvious connections with Ethiopia, by the end of 2001 there was a ubiquitous air of paranoia and insecurity amongst residents and businesses concerning 'national security'. This is a very sad scenario, given that the town and its residents depend on the trade they had with their neighbour. For the time being it is best not to enter into deep political discussions in Assab, as this might appear prying or threatening to some and, moreover, you are unlikely to get any honest answers. As things stabilise and when trade begins to flow across this border once more this situation is bound to improve.

THE ISLANDS

There are 30 islands in the Bay of Assab. It is possible to arrange a visit to some of them but it may take time to do so. Asking the Ministry of Marine Resources or the fishermen in Assab Seghir is the best way to start.

Sennabar is the nearest island, a very steep-sided volcanic cone rising sheer from the sea off the north coast of the town. It has a beach on the western side and is used by fishermen.

Another interesting island is **Halib**, 90km (two hours') drive south of Assab. It can be reached via the road to Djibouti and a long causeway across shallow salt flats. The island has extensive mangroves. The road serves a Korean boat-building facility built for the previous regime and now housing the Eritrean Navy.

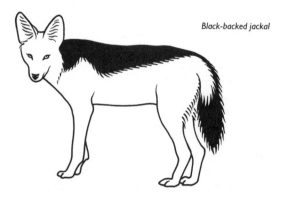

Black-backed jackal

Asmara to Keren and Nacfa

There is a good road covering the 91km to Keren. Buses travel regularly or if you drive yourself the journey will take less than two hours. There are many villages along this stretch of road, some that the road passes directly through and others farther afield. The first one of any significance is **Embaderho** (*Chicken Hill*), 11km from Asmara. After 20km you pass through Weki-Zager where the turning down to Filfil is on the right-hand side. **Adi Teclesan** (42km) is the next village and often a place where people stop for a break between Keren and Asmara, then, as the road begins to follow the riverbed lined by huge mango trees, you soon enter **Elabored** (78km). Elabored is very beautiful, having been a major agricultural centre famous for its oranges, onions and tomatoes. It is surrounded by mountains and therefore appears in a bowl of lush greenery, best seen from the Keren side of town as you drive over the hill out of town. To this day many people use the tins of the Elabored tomato cannery as water containers. While the area is not in anything like full production, plantations are being resuscitated. As you enter Elabored there are also walls of bougainvillaea on either side of the road. As you pass beyond Elabored the slopes of the mountains are intensively terraced, like those seen from the road to Massawa, to prevent soil erosion and retain water.

KEREN

Keren (1,392m) is, by any standards, a beautiful town and is often visited by those wanting a change of scene from Asmara or Massawa. Set on a plateau surrounded by mountains, the name Keren means highland. It is the capital of the Anseba province. The sun rises over one set of peaks in the east and sets over another set in the west. Depending on where you stay, rising for the dawn does not present a problem as the *muezzin* is likely to act as your early morning call. There is a distinctly Muslim feel to the town and it has a much calmer pace of life than Asmara. Of the 60,000 or so residents in the area at the moment, some 55% are Muslim and 40% Christian; the city has plenty of churches and mosques. Keren is also home to the Bilen ethnic group.

Keren has always been attractive to foreigners, starting with the Swiss adventurer Werner Munzinger who arrived here in 1855. It was also a favourite place for Italians because of the temperate climate and the fertile soil – many had

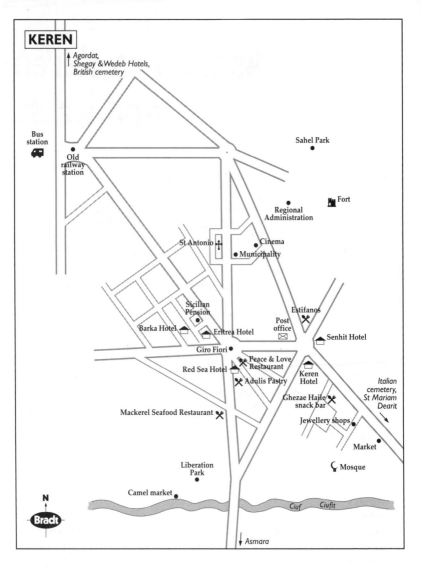

KEREN

Agordat,
Shegay & Wedeb Hotels,
British cemetery

Bus
station

Old
railway
station

Sahel Park

Fort

Regional
Administration

St Antonio

Cinema

Municipality

Sicilian
Pension

Estifanos

Barka Hotel

Post
office

Eritrea Hotel

Senhit Hotel

Giro Fiori

Peace & Love
Restaurant

Red Sea Hotel

Keren
Hotel

Adulis Pastry

Italian
cemetery,
St Mariam
Dearit

Ghezae Haile
snack bar

Mackerel Seafood Restaurant

Jewellery shops

Market

Liberation
Park

Mosque

Camel market

N

Bradt

Ciuf   Ciufit

Asmara

market gardens in the surrounding area, and there is still evidence of this cultivation when you leave Keren heading north on the road to Afabet. At Otala, 2km along this road, were the former Da Nadai estates. Agriculture is being regenerated here and Keren represents a vital agricultural district in Eritrea.

Strategically Keren controls the northern approach to Asmara and the road west to Agordat and the lowlands. The gorge (known as The Keren Pass by the allied forces in World War II) that leads down to the western plains immediately on the outskirts of Keren is a formidable natural defence and has proven impenetrable on many occasions by invading forces. It was here that one of the decisive battles of World War II took place when the allied forces, under General Platt, took four months to defeat the 23,000 Italians defending this position in March 1941. After once being repulsed the allied forces gained a foothold at Cameron's Ridge, on the west side of the present road. The final battle began one month later and Keren was taken on March 27. The victory signalled the defeat of Italy, and their retreat to Asmara only lasted a few days before Asmara was taken on April 1. The Italian surrender was signed in Massawa on 8 April. This provided the allies with secure access through to the Red Sea, whilst also vitally securing Sudan prior to the North Africa campaign. Keren later became an important garrison for the Ethiopians as well. It was substantially destroyed when the EPLF temporarily took the town in 1977, but suffered less damage in the conclusive final assault in 1990.

Although the appearance of the town is predominantly Muslim there are also many examples of the Italian colonial heritage in the architecture. At one time the town boasted not one but two railway stations. Various churches, hotels and administrative buildings clearly reflect Italian construction, the most interesting of which is arguably the regional government offices that reflect a distinctly Turkish style, but which were built by the Italians.

Where to stay
Upper range
Shegey Hotel Tel: 401971. A new hotel situated behind Wedeb Hotel and restaurant on the Agordat road offers singles for Nfa80 and doubles Nfa120. The rooms are clean and despite the rather awkward location Shegey is one of the best options in Keren.

Keren Hotel Tel: 401621/401014. 18 rooms: Nfa60/104 single/double. Like so many other hotels of this era, this is in desperate need of an overhaul. The rooms are not particularly clean and the toilets and showers are no better. It was built in 1977, allegedly, by a Signor Pascuse as his private residence which will come as something of a surprise when you see it, although if this is true it must have been laid out rather differently then. The roof terrace with observation tower contribute to its appearance as something of a folly. Even if you are not a resident the roof terrace is readily accessible and has the best views over the town, with the possible exception of Fort Tigu just to the north. In the evenings there is a bar there, which is a great place for a sundowner. The observation tower appears rather creaky but there are no recorded fatalities. In the downstairs area there is a TV playing CNN most of the day if you need to catch up on international events. The restaurant is at street level but is shielded from the road by a curtain of bougainvillaea. The food is adequate, but not overwhelming.

Budget
There are many local hotels in Keren that offer similar, basic accommodation. In the unlikely event that things are very busy you can try any number of the following, which are all perfectly adequate.
Sicilia Pension Tel: 41059. 17 rooms: Nfa30–50 per room, including singles/doubles/triples. Extra beds can be arranged for Nfa15 each. This was the first hotel in Keren and remains a prime spot to this day. It is next to the Eritrea Hotel and has a pleasant courtyard. It is a reliable favourite for many visitors.

FILFIL – A HIDDEN PARADISE

To the northeast of Asmara lies the *Semienawi Bahri*, or 'Green Belt' region of Eritrea. The area is more commonly known as Filfil and contains the last remnants of Eritrea's once abundant tropical forest, home to an impressive array of birds and mammals. After experiencing the harsh, rugged landscape that characterises so much of Eritrea, it is hard to imagine such dense forest exists in this region of Africa. The forest thrives on the vast, moist escarpment that links the highland plateau with the burning lowland plains, home to the renowned Rashaida people.

Filfil can be reached by a dirt track that leaves the Asmara to Keren road at Weki-Zager, about 32km from Asmara, or from the Asmara to Massawa road about 25km from Massawa. Both routes require the use of a four-wheel drive, though, astonishingly, a bus service linking the villages along the route does ply this road on an irregular timetable. The surface of the road is rough and has numerous unsettling hairpin bends over which the land drops away for hundreds of metres – not a journey for the faint-hearted! The route from high up on the Keren road is the better approach as it offers breathtaking views of the lowland plains and the journey is all downhill. Travelling up from Massawa would be a formidable drive.

Most people tend to approach Filfil from the Keren road and travel an hour or so down the escarpment before turning round and returning the same way. However, the full drive down to the Massawa road, known as the Pendice Orientali, though circuitous, is definitely worth the extra time and effort. The round trip from Asmara will take approximately 7 hours and is a superb one-day excursion.

When approaching Filfil from the Keren road, the track winds through a short stretch of rough, stony farmland before reaching the ridge of the plateau, over which the great lowland plains spread out hundreds of kilometres into the distance. At this point the environment becomes lightly forested with evergreens that dot the landscape, providing a unique and welcome respite from the usual arid and rocky terrain. From a vantage point of 2500m the views of the lowland plains and the forested escarpment below are truly awe-inspiring. On a clear day the Red Sea coast is visible, with the coastal plains spreading as far as the eye can see to the south.

Barka Hotel Tel: 401350. Behind the Sicilian Hotel. Muslim hotel with some food such as meat and *ful*; there is often a barbecue in the evenings. Nfa20/40 for single/double.

Eritrea Hotel Tel: 401298. The bar is a good one, which can limit the attraction of this as a place to stay if you want somewhere quiet. It costs Nfa15/20 for a bed and Nfa40 for a room.

Wedeb Hotel Tel: 401620. On the Argordat road. 13 rooms for Nfa40 each.

Africa Pension Tel: 401117. Right on the Giro Fiori and costs Nfa20/30 for a room.

Yohannes Hotel Tel: 401422. 20 rooms for Nfa40 each.

As the road descends the forest gets thicker and lusher. Native trees and bushes replace foreign species and the bird life becomes incredibly abundant. It is well worth stopping the vehicle for a walk to appreciate the calls and songs of the many different birds and to view their varied and magnificent colours. As well as the rich bird life that includes all manner of hornbills, weavers, canaries, owls, eagles, orioles and many more, there are also considerable numbers of mammals to be seen in the forest. Vervet monkeys and baboons are common and other, more rare, species have been reported. These include gazelle, bushbuck, kudu, warthog and even leopard.

As the road crosses a riverbed, about three and a half hours from leaving the Keren road, it reaches Filfil proper, with its ancient trees and a permanent source of water. The trees that skirt the river's hem are bold and beautiful, reflecting the nature of the region perfectly. It is a great place to stop for a break and walk around, soaking up the rich forest environment and listening to the wonderful array of bird song.

Shortly after this spot the road splits, with the right hand fork leading to the Massawa road, at least one hour away. As the road reaches the bottom of the steep escarpment following various rivers and creeks that carve their way to the sea, the rough, rocky track soon becomes smooth and sandy, making the ride much lighter. The terrain changes dramatically here, offering equally fascinating sceneries that include banana plantations, dry riverbeds (depending on the season) and great tracts of desert. The sandy track reaches a sealed road that links the route to the main Massawa road after half an hour or so. This final stretch is flat and barren, tracing a route across the lowland plains dotted with small villages consisting of clusters of neat round huts. The vast mountains stretching northwards to the Sahel region provide a commanding backdrop as they form the last stretch of the mighty Rift Valley that scars the continent's eastern flank.

Ghatelai, a small settlement sits at the junction with the Asmara to Massawa road where you can purchase much-deserved food and drink before ascending the full 2500m back up to Asmara or, alternatively, driving the short distance to Massawa and cooling off in the Red Sea.

Senhit Hotel Tel: 401042. Opposite Keren Hotel, has 7 rooms for Nfa20 each.

Where to eat

There is not a wide variety of food available in Keren, but the situation is improving rapidly. The most recent addition to the restaurants is the excellent **Mackerel Seafood Restaurant**, which serves many different seafood dishes at a very reasonable Nfa16 for a main dish. It has a pleasant seated area outside or a good terrace overlooking the mosque. Another reliable option is the **Senhit Hotel**, opposite the Keren Hotel, which serves local dishes and good

TERRACING AND DEFORESTATION

Eritrea was once extensively covered by virgin rainforest. It is estimated that a century ago 30% of the country was forested; now it is just 1%. The last significant remnant of this can be seen in the area around Filfil, north of Asmara. To see this last remnant of a once vast forest that covered the entire Eritrean-Ethiopian plateau, and was home to a rich variety of flora and fauna, is a bitter reminder of how man's exploitation and neglect has degraded the environment. The Eritrean highlands are now almost entirely bereft of trees. The process of deforestation can be attributed to a number of different causes, all of which are likely contributors, but none of which can be disproportionately blamed. The traditional building method used to construct the *Hidmo* is particulary resource intensive. The *Hidmo* is a traditional dwelling constructed using thick tree trunks as supports to prop up a roof that is also made from tree trunks or branches and covered in layers of soil and grass. The walls are usually made from stone. Each *Hidmo* is said to require over 100 trees in its construction. This method has obviously had a negative effect on the environment and is now banned. Another cause of deforestation is the demand for fuel, construction materials and farm land after the Europeans arrived in Eritrea. The consumption of native forests during this period has been well documented. In addition to this, the Europeans introduced widespread hunting of animals for pleasure and contributed significantly to the unsustainable depopulation of wildlife in Eritrea. 'The struggle' also contributed to deforestation, especially in the Sahel region, where bombing, construction of trenches, need for firewood and deliberate clearance to deprive soldiers cover from the air has led to little or no

breakfasts for around Nfa10–17. Senhit also has a terrace, which serves as an ideal spot from which to enjoy a quiet drink. **Peace and Love** on the Giro Fiori serves good local food and pasta for around Nfa14–18 and is another safe bet. The **Eritrean and Yohannes Hotels** also provide reasonable local food.

There are numerous eating places serving *ful* (bean stew with onions, tomatoes and egg), *shiro* (lentils) and *zigini* (stew) around the market area. The best place for a breakfast, especially *ful*, is the **Ghezae Haile Snack Bar** behind Keren Hotel overlooking the fruit market. **Adulis Pastry**, just before entering the Giro Fiori on the right-hand side, has good pastries and yoghurt for breakfast. **Liberation Park** and **Sahel Park** are ideal if you fancy a drink and some peace and quiet.

For a drink in the evening there are a number of bars to choose from, as well as most of the aforementioned restaurants. **Red Sea Hotel** on the Giro Fiori serves draught beer (when it is in town) and has a pleasant outdoor area under the trees. The **Eritrea Hotel** is also a popular spot, with lively music. The area around the **Senhit** and **Keren Hotels,** which includes **Estifanos**, is also good if you prefer something quieter.

significant vegetation in some areas today. An ongoing demand for wood lies in its use for fuel. This is now strictly regulated, but still the demand is high. Diet and cooking techniques are equal contributors in this respect, with the cooking of *injera* being extremely energy intensive. More efficient methods of cooking and preparing are being investigated to alleviate this demand.

Previous attempts at reforestation have varied in their success. The Ethiopian regime introduced eucalyptus, which they had imported to Ethiopia from Australia at the end of the nineteenth century, and saved Addis Ababa from being forced to move through lack of firewood, while also being a potential source of oil for export. However, the eucalypt does little to aid vegetation on the forest floor, drains the soil of much of its water content and the imported species in Eritrea does not produce oil. There is now a concerted effort to encourage native regrowth, but to do this first requires a programme of building up sufficient topsoil.

This has been a feature of government policy for some decades. In an attempt to prevent soil erosion and water runoff there has been an intensive programme of terracing. On many trips around Eritrea, particularly to Massawa and Keren from Asmara, you will see entire mountains terraced and resembling life-sized topographical maps with each terrace marking a contour. Nowadays teams of school children are required to fulfil their 'summer service' for one month of their summer holidays by continuing to construct these terraces. The vast areas that have been constructed so far reflect an awesome achievement. It will take many years or even decades before these slopes might again be carpeted in forest, but there are signs that this might be starting in some areas.

What to see

The market, churches and mosques in Keren are well worth visiting. The speed of life is best exemplified by the fact that camels still outnumber cars. Among the more interesting sights are the following:

Just to the northeast of the town centre (the **Giro Fiori**, or 'Circle of Flowers') is the Turko-Egyptian fort, **Tigu** (1,460m). From here, the views of the surrounding country and mountain ranges are superb. At the southwestern foot was the old Imperial Palace but this was destroyed in 1977 and only the ruins are visible. If you want to climb to the top for the views over the town just ask at the buildings at the bottom.

St Mariam Dearit is a small shrine set in a baobab tree about 2km out of town to the northeast. From the market head to the Italian cemetery. Leaving that to your right continue to the edge of town; in the distance you will see a long straight avenue of tall trees and a rather inappropriate row of lights resembling the landing lights of an airport. This leads directly to the shrine. The festival is on May 21. To the north the shrine looks out onto beautiful orchards and countryside.

The British Cemetery, immaculately kept like the Italian one, is 2km from the town, just off the Agordat, before the road starts to descend from the Keren plateau. There are 440 burials in the war cemetery, 35 of which are unidentified, and a Cremation Memorial to commemorate a further 285 Sikh and Hindu soldiers whose remains were cremated in accordance with their faith. There is a visitor's book here, which is an interesting read.

The Italian Cemetery, just north of the market, sits on the side of a small hill from which there are good views of the town. The cemetery is in pristine condition. The graves of Italian soldiers are named and separate from the unmarked graves of local *Askaris* who fought alongside the Italians in their various military campaigns.

If you want to visit the hospital, ask the hospital administrator. It was apparently built by a much-loved American benefactor called Mr Hugh, another who fell for the charms of Keren. The hospital is about 300m north of the Keren Hotel, opposite **Sahel Park**, which is a good place for a drink in the evening.

Another park that is worth a visit is **Liberation Park,** next to the camel market. This is best approached by retracing your steps from the Giro Fiori as if heading back to Asmara. When you come to the bridge over the River Ciuf-Ciufit, descend to the river bed and walk for 100m before turning right. You will see, depending on the time of day, the **wood** and **camel markets** in the riverbed which attract as many as 100 camels a day, bringing their loads of wood from as far as three or four days' distance. If you like camels this is one of the best places to get up really close. Liberation Park is on the riverbank behind the wood market.

Among the many churches and mosques, Keren boasts the oldest church in Eritrea. **St Michael's** church on the eastern slopes of the mountains to the west of town is reported to have been built in 1874. It is well worth the walk. Another more obvious church is **St Antonio's**, the Catholic church opposite the administration building and with a similar but miniature bell tower to Asmara's central cathedral. It was built in about 1925 and has an interesting interior. Due to a burgeoning catholic population, construction of a new St Antonio's is underway right next door, which will considerably overshadow its older namesake. **St Mariam**, the principal Coptic church, is to your left as you are heading out of town on the Agordat road. The **central mosque** is situated to the southeast of the town centre.

For railway buffs the old main **railway station** is a typical example of Italian colonial architecture and now acts as the bus station, complete with café. It is about 350m to the northwest of the Giro Fiori on the route to Agordat.

The **market** area lies behind the Keren Hotel, between it and the Italian cemetery. It is a hive of activity. In the centre are the fruit, vegetable and spice stalls, while surrounding this area are numerous tailors and other craftsmen sitting cross-legged in front of their shops. At Nfa6 per gram silver is cheaper in Keren than in Asmara, although the range of items tends to be more limited. To find the best silver shops, pass between Senhit and Keren hotels and turn

HALHAL

Halhal (1,878m) is 45km from Keren and can be reached by bus from Keren in about three hours, or half the time by car. The drive is a spectacular one. The road goes directly to the town, ascending a particularly steep stretch between 33km and 37km. The Halhal Front was one of the major fronts in the war, partly controlling access to the western plains. There are also Axumite ruins at Aratu, close to the town. Ask for directions.

right before the slight slope leading to the grain and wicker markets. Further down the slope you will find a wide range of baskets and other straw products, as well as many pottery items. It is quite a good place to find souvenirs, though the prices do not differ greatly from Asmara.

KEREN TO AFABET AND NACFA

Buses do run from Keren to Afabet and Nacfa, taking about eight hours in total journey time, but you should check well in advance in Keren, as there is only one bus plying this route and during the rains the service is severely disrupted. If you decide to break the journey in Afabet it can be difficult to find a connecting bus, so allow a day or two, or alternatively try hitching. By car the whole trip can be done in easily under four hours.

Leaving Keren on the road north you pass through the old market gardening area on the outskirts. Although this is not what it once was it is still a very beautiful stretch of road. Oranges, onions, tomatoes, lettuce and a great variety of other produce are grown using water from the Ciuf-Ciufit river, which is a tributary of the Anseba, the main river of the region. Just 3.5km out of Keren there is a meat factory to your right. The village 8km from Keren is called **Sabab**, which means 'narrow'; this can be used as the landmark for the fork to the left to Halhal (11km from Keren).

About 13.5km from Keren the huts on the hill, mostly to your right, mark the village of **Ona**; in 1970, this was the scene of a massacre by the Ethiopian army, during which the 750 villagers were all stabbed or burnt in their huts. A little further on, 17km from Keren, the road crosses the Anseba River at **Genfalu**, one time the front line in the conflict with Ethiopia, facing the hills surrounding Keren. During the dry season it is hard to imagine the torrent that flows down this valley during the rains.

As you reach the peak of the hill and begin the descent into the next plain, 26km from Keren you see one of the unusual sights on this stretch of road: baobabs stretch the full length of the valley, not in great numbers, but enough to give the impression almost of an army on the march. **Gz'gza**, at 33km, marks the end of this area, known as Messalit. The large village 46km from Keren is **Gwai**; with the riverbed on the left the area is usually green. At 56km you climb over the rise to descend into the plain of Afabet. The views of the plain from this point are spectacular. You arrive at Afabet 68km after leaving Keren.

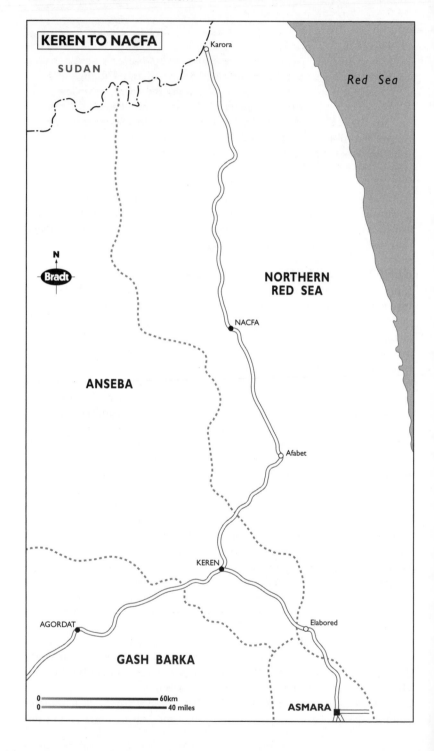

AFABET

Afabet (1,000m) has faced a remarkable recent history. The town was the site of the Ethiopian strategic reserve and as such was the largest military base in the country during the struggle. Its capture by the EPLF in 1988, in what was one of the most stunning offensives ever carried out by a liberation movement, led to the total destruction of the town and over 18,000 Ethiopian soldiers were killed or captured in the battle. However, Afabet has risen from the ashes and now stands as one of Eritrea's largest towns with a population of approximately 20,000. The extensive rebuilding is evident by the vast areas of new suburbs that now skirt the old town centre. When the road from Massawa is complete this town will doubtless further increase in regional and commercial importance.

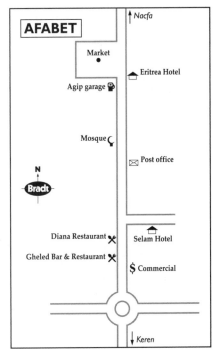

The approach to Afabet is marked by the avenue of little, white-brick tree surrounds, which protect the new saplings from the ever-rapacious goats. The trees, like so many new avenues in Eritrean towns, are *Nim* trees. They are hardy trees that require very little water and care. They also grow quite fast making them an ideal urban tree, providing vital shade. As you enter the centre of Afabet the Commercial Bank is on the right. From here the minaret of the mosque in the main street is clearly visible as the landmark for the town centre. The main street runs north to south and has most of the amenities you are likely to need. The market and petrol station are at the north end of town.

Where to stay

Opposite the market is the **Eritrea Hotel**, which has six rooms with four beds in each. Beds cost Nfa10. Another place to stay is **Hotel Selam,** just off the main street on the right hand side as you enter from Keren, with beds for Nfa10. Both places are basic but they more than suffice for a night or two.

Other useful information

The **post office** is on the right hand side just pass the turning for Hotel Selam and the **mosque** is a little further down on the left. There a number of places to eat along this street, all providing the usual assortment of local dishes. The **Gheled Bar and Restaurant** is a reasonable place at the south end of the

THE RORAS

Rora means 'high place' in Tigre. The Roras are plateaux north of Keren at an altitude of 2,100–2,700m, stretching over an area of 50km by 6km. Nacfa, to the east, is the nearest town. They are sparsely inhabited (population c12,500), with vegetation only able to grow because of nocturnal condensation rather than rainfall. They are of particular interest from an archaeological point of view. Rora Habab, one of the more famous, lies to the west and southwest of Nacfa. Animal etchings, a part of an inscribed stela and two sculpted lion statues, are evidence that in the past Rora Habab supported extensive civilisation, and was an important link between Axum and the coast. Literary evidence supports this. Fr Giuseppe Sapeto, one of the first Italians in Eritrea, mentions the remains of churches and the ruins of an 'Abyssinian' city; other Italian historians such as Terzi found evidence of Axumite settlement in the northern Eritrean borderlands; Fattovich states that Axumite traders would have used 'the traditional route crossing the Rore and Haggher regions'. The principal villages where preliminary studies have been carried out are Bakla, Endlal and Laba. Although the land is now marginal, it is interesting from an environmental point of view that even in the 1930s Italian records show there was an abundance of gamebirds, and even gazelle and wild pig species.

main street. It might have rooms available in the near future. Another satisfactory place is the **Diana Restaurant** just a few blocks north.

After leaving Afabet for Nacfa, the valley 11km away is important. Here, at **Adishrum**, the lead tank of the Ethiopians (fleeing south after the EPLF broke out of Nacfa in 1988) was knocked out, preventing those behind it from proceeding to Afabet. The Ethiopians, fearing the capture of a huge quantity of hardware, called in an airstrike on their own forces trapped in the valley. Despite this brutal self-sacrifice some 70 vehicles were taken intact. The remains of this massacre are still very evident and the naked, peppered carcasses of the armoured vehicles lie twisted beside the road. Passing through this serene valley, it is haunting to imagine the carnage that must have been dealt here.

There is a **Turkish fort** in the hills to your right at **Kub Kub** (19km from Afabet), which was also used by the Italians. Kub Kub is also the junction for the road that leads to **Karora** on the Sudanese border. Shortly after turning right at this junction you will arrive at three **Ottoman Turkish mausoleums** a few hundred metres off the road on the right-hand side. The mausoleums are surrounded by a number of graves with Arabic inscriptions. Further on, the road passes through the town of **Narrow** before following the coastal plains to **Karora**. Travelling along this route should only really be considered if you have a guide who is familiar with the territory and you are well equipped. During the rainy season this route is practically impossible due to the many watercourses that filter down from the Sahel mountains, making the road impassable.

Continuing to Nacfa from Kub Kub you cross the **Moga River** (22km) and begin to climb towards Nacfa through some stunning valleys and riverbeds. It is this stretch of road that makes the journey hazardous during the rainy season (late July–September), as the road follows the course of the riverbed for some 30km. **Denden** (2,500m), the centre of the 400km EPLF trench network of the Nacfa front, is visible high up to your left (58km) as you begin the ascent to the plateau on which Nacfa lies. After climbing the steep road to the plateau, Nacfa is a further 5km away. Just before entering the town the river crosses the **Meo river**, source of most of Nacfa's water.

NACFA AND ENVIRONS

Nacfa (1,780m) is where the hearts of many fighters belong, as it is the symbol of their resistance to the Ethiopian occupation. It was no coincidence that the town was chosen as the location for the third EPLF Congress at which the front formally dissolved itself, and then reconstituted itself as a fully-fledged political party, the PFDJ (People's Front for Democracy and Justice), in anticipation of elections scheduled for 1997, and which are still hotly awaited. Nacfa was totally destroyed in the war, being under continuous bombardment. No building except the mosque was left above two or three breeze-blocks high. However, like Afabet, the town has had an ambitious master-plan drawn up for it and reconstruction is well underway. The regional and city administrations, hospital, airport, hotels and town centre are complete and a central street plan has been laid out with many residential and commercial buildings already constructed. The town plan is based around the main street, which runs from the mosque up to the regional administration buildings on the hill overlooking the town. In front of this complex is an elaborate roundabout, which marks the centre of town. It was originally planned that an entirely new town would be built nearer the airport, but it remains to be seen whether such a development will be necessary or feasible. It would seem dependent on the road from Massawa to Afabet reaching the

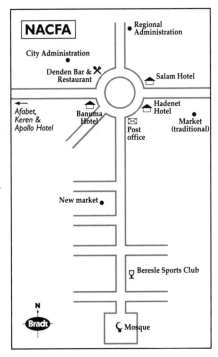

town, thereby providing a valuable and vital transport link to the northern Red Sea region. The chances of this happening in the next 5 years seem very slim.

Where to stay

There are several hotels around the central roundabout offering basic accommodation.

Banuma Hotel, **Salam Hotel** and **Hadenet Hotel** all have rates of Nfa10 for a bed in three-bed rooms and Nfa20 for a single room. They all serve local food. Salam appears the most attractive of the bunch, with a pleasant inner courtyard and less of an obsession with playing load music until the electricity goes off. **Apollo Hotel**, Nfa115/155 for single/doubles, is on a hill overlooking Nacfa town and is the only hotel that provides any degree of luxury. It was a much-awaited development, but it remains a bit obscure, seldom offering food or other services unless a visiting tour group is in town.

Where to eat

For food, Nacfa has a limited range. **Den Den Bar and Restaurant**, on the opposite side of the roundabout to Hadenet, has good local food, or try any of the hotels. **Beresle Sports Club** (don't be misguided by the name) at the mosque-end of the main street shows videos and news from Arabic TV in the evenings, which are extremely popular as other entertainment is limited.

Other useful information

It is not difficult to 'find a friend' in Nacfa, and to find the places worth visiting nearby a guide is necessary. Closest to the town, and particularly for those who are interested in the military history, are the trenches of Denden. The climb to the peak of Denden is well worth the effort (about one hour from bottom to top) just for the view. To the south you can look back down the valleys towards Afabet or east over the ridge to Narrow and the coastal plains beyond. The peak just to the south of Denden is **Harena**, which repeatedly changed hands in the conflict; it afforded an excellent view of Nacfa town but was notoriously difficult to defend. To the southwest is the plain known as *Furnello* or 'Furnace', so-called because it was under continual bombardment. Needless to say all this countryside is denuded, both from bombardment and from the need to construct trenches. Despite an initiative to preserve some of the trench-lines for historic reasons, large sections have been dismantled by the locals to use the wood for fuel or their own construction needs. Standing in the trenches atop Denden you look straight down on the remains of the Ethiopian frontline some 400m away. It is impossible to imagine how grim it must have been. EPLF fighters often served stints in the frontline of up to 18 months without a break. All wood, food and trees for the bunkers had to be carried up the mountainside. For long periods the shelling would be so intense that it was impossible to see the person standing next to you. Shell, bullet and even napalm casings still litter the ground.

Further north from Nacfa, **Tsabra** underground hospital and the old **Winna Technical College** are both good examples of the fighters' resilience.

Both are built into mountainsides that rendered them virtually impregnable. Tsabra, although on a smaller scale than the hospital at **Orotta**, was capable of providing patients with major operations in remarkably good conditions. Today the Hospital and the Technical College have been relocated in town. Winna Technical College has six faculties for 120 of the top students in Eritrea – automotive, electrical, machine workshop, woodwork, surveying and metalwork. You pass the college on your left as you enter Nacfa from Afabet.

If you wish to continue north to **Agra** and **Karora**, the road is usually passable (depending on the rains). It is a rough drive through the mountains, and you won't see much that you can't see in the immediate environs of Nacfa. If, however, you do wish to do this trip, or the round-trip heading north and then back along the coastal road to Kub Kub, be sure to have a local guide, a reliable four-wheel drive and plenty of supplies.

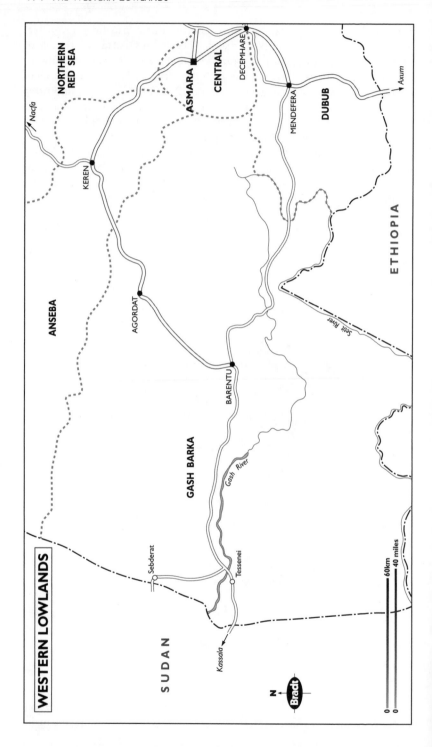

The Western Lowlands

Buses run from Keren to the major towns in the west, but if you want to explore off the beaten track and visit the more interesting spots then a car is essential in the west. North of the road linking Keren to Tessenei is very inaccessible, and does not have any sights of major historical or natural interest. Accommodation along the road westwards becomes very basic: hotel rooms generally have four to eight beds and, depending on the time of year, there is often no running water. Due to the temperature, which in the summer can be searing, many people sleep outside (at any time of the year); if you need privacy then it is normally possible to rent the whole room. The food is all Eritrean, though in Tessenei it is largely Sudanese, and English and Italian are hardly spoken. For those travelling by car, petrol and diesel are usually available in the major towns but ensure you always travel with as much fuel as possible. If you are ever in trouble or you just need some advice, the town or district administration office is usually the best place to ask. The best time to visit is in October and November, just after the rains, when the areas close to the rivers are at their most productive and the dust stays where it belongs – on the ground. The countryside is also stunning at this time of year as the plains are a carpet of green – hard to believe during the height of the dry season. However, a word of caution if you are travelling after the rains; mosquitoes are rife at this time of year and malaria in this region (especially around Tessenei) is the most prevalent in all of Eritrea, so be sure to take the necessary precautions.

KEREN TO AGORDAT

Leaving Keren on the Agordat road to the west you pass the British War Cemetery at the start of the pass and then descend through a tight gorge, which leads immediately to the plains that stretch, more or less, all the way to the border with Sudan. At the bottom of the hill there is a church to your left and a small village; this whole area is known as **Bogu**. As you drive towards Hagaz keep an eye on the impressive saddle-shaped **Mount Jibher** to the north of the road. **Hagaz** (16km from Keren) is the first village of any note. It is a bustling market town with one main street and an attractive church and mosque. The market itself is off this to the south. Food and accommodation can be found at the Yosef Hotel, Hagaz Hotel and Barka Hotel along the main

FESTIVALS AMONG THE NARA AND KUNAMA
with thanks to the Ministry of Information

In the past the most important festivals among these ethnic groups were Kina Farda (the ploughing holiday) and Mashkela (the holiday of the cross). Kina Farda does not have a fixed date, but depends on the coming of the rains. The Nara, unlike the Kunama, celebrate this in all villages simultaneously. The instigators are the elders known as Farda Nama (Kunama) or Log Nama (Nara). At festival time everyone is expected to be in their home village; livestock is then slaughtered on an altar facing east. The Nara traditionally kill a black heifer, the Kunama preferring a reddish goat or a white sheep. A prayer is then offered to Anna, a celestial power who is asked to bless the harvest. Among the Nara the Log Nama are assisted by four first-borns, who receive more meat and hide from the slaughtered beast than others. The spot where the animal is killed is known as Adaga, and is usually the home of the Log Nama.

For Mashkela, people prepare their torches and wait in their doorways until the elders pass, at which point they can light their torches and fall into line in the procession. Outside the village all the torches are piled up and dancing takes place around the bonfire. Once this festival has finished, and only then, the harvest can be gathered. Then a drink is made with the newly cut grain and this is taken to the ancestral tombs as an offering. Once this task is complete the villagers can eat from the new harvest. Among the Nara these rituals are more commonly associated with another festival, Uwa, which falls after Mashkela.

The extent to which such festivals take place varies from place to place.

street. Just beyond it is a large tree, which marks the bus stop. Continuing west you reach **Aderde** (28km from Keren) and 3km further on the old railway line is easily seen just to the north of the road. It once ran as far as Agordat. The **Barka River** crosses the road 41km from Keren, and after a further 12km you reach Agordat.

AGORDAT

Agordat (615m) lies between the Barka and Gash rivers, hence its former importance as an agricultural area. Sizeable exports of every type of produce from bananas to peppers used to go to the Middle East. It has one main street which doubles back from the main road and ends, after the marketplace, between two hills. On these hills are the hospital and the administration centre. The hospital is an extraordinarily atypical building, looking as though it was parked on the hill having arrived from another planet. It was built in 1963 and was once the pride of the health service. The city's administration

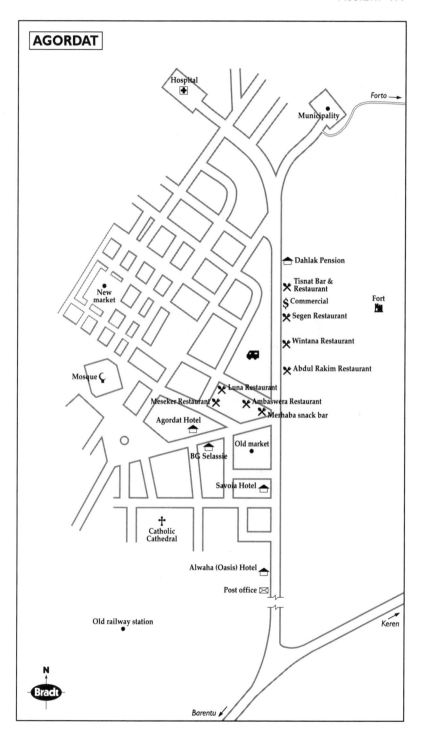

building is a bit more agreeable, from an aesthetic point of view. If you carry on walking past the administration building the road winds up the back of the hill to the *forto* at the top, from where you have excellent views of the town and surrounding countryside, particularly the river.

Agordat is another city undergoing a transformation, not least because of the arrival of a vast number of refugees now permanently housed in settlements to the west, almost doubling the size of the town. If you are not in a hurry there are some interesting sights in Agordat – the **old railway station**, the *forto*, the river, the plantations on the far side of the river, and the market. From wherever you are in town the green-domed **mosque** with its towering minaret dominates. If you need a bank, the **Commercial Bank** is in the centre of the main square.

If you have a few days in Agordat one very interesting walk you can do is along the riverbed, where you are bound to meet many local children and experience the comings and goings of daily life. The riverbed is used as the main highway, so finding a spot under the shade of a tree is the perfect place from where to see many activities and all sorts of people. The birdlife here is also worth seeing. There are many birds of prey, including some very large eagles.

Agordat can be extremely hot. As in Massawa and Assab, the local population combat this by restricting activity to the early mornings and late afternoons. This pace of life gives Agordat a relaxed and pleasant atmosphere.

Where to stay

There is a selection of available accommodation in Agordat. The following have been checked and provide a reasonable cross-section. As you enter town from the Barentu road a new hotel called **Beilul** is opening up near the main junction, which is probably worth trying. Soon after this, you pass the **Alwaha (Oasis) Hotel** with rooms for Nfa15/18 without/with shower. This is a reasonably comfortable place to stay, albeit a little out of town. The next hotel is the **Savoia Hotel**, Nfa20/30 for one/two beds, which has a pool table. The colour and style of the building is attractive, but that's about as far as it goes. In the centre of town is **B G Selassie**, tel: 711066 (or **Belamberas**), which is a favourite amongst most travellers owing to the more than affable owner, Almaz. She is sure to look after your every need and will make you feel more at home than in any other place in Eritrea. The hotel (named after her father) is also her family home and has private and dormitory-style rooms for Nfa60/20. On the other side of the road is the noisy and less attractive **Agordat Hotel**, with beds for Nfa10/30, outside/inside. **Dahlak Pension** on the main road heading towards the hospital has beds outside for Nfa8.

Where to eat

Meseker Restaurant next to the Barka Photo is very popular and serves excellent local dishes. Other places tend to be based around the main square and the choices are pretty much the same whichever one you choose. They include **Abdul Rakim Restaurant** (excellent yoghurt), **Tsinat Bar and Restaurant, Ambaswera Restaurant, Luna Restaurant, Zula Restaurant, Merhaba Snack Bar** and **Wintana Restaurant**.

Leaving Agordat for Barentu you cross the **Katlay** riverbed, 71km after leaving Keren. Anywhere in this area you may see Nara people; for example they are the main inhabitants of **Mogolo** (81km from Keren). A winding road up an incline (95km) marks the approach to Barentu. The peak is at 97km from where you can see Barentu (99km from Keren).

BARENTU

Barentu was occupied by Ethiopian forces during the recent conflict, so remains under tight security. As a result you will probably need a pass to enter the town, or any areas further west. This can be obtained from the Ministry of Information, though it is worth first visiting the Ministry of Tourism in Asmara to see if this permit is still necessary. As the situation improves and stability becomes more assured, this policy will no doubt be scrapped.

Barentu (980m) is in the heart of Kunama territory and is not a particularly remarkable town, but it is the new seat of the regional Gash Barka administration. It has always been something of a target for missionaries of various denominations and it does have an interesting atmosphere owing to its large Kunama population. Quite why Barentu was chosen as the focus of the missionaries' efforts is not clear, but it could have something to do with the fact that the Kunama are Eritrea's only animists and therefore rich pickings for those seeking to convert them. Barentu has one main street that starts after crossing the river when coming from Agordat and stretches for some 2km to beyond the bus station at the western edge of town. The occupation of the town by Ethiopian forces meant that several scores have been settled during the time they were here, which has resulted in certain businesses being destroyed. Among the casualties were the large Gash Hotel, the Asmara Hotel and the Wegahta Hotel. These may be rebuilt, but it will take some time. The **Commercial Bank** is due to open shortly, after also facing destruction during Ethiopian occupation.

Where to stay

Remaining accommodation options are quite limited. The best is the new **Merhaba Hotel** (tel: 731101) opposite the bus station, which miraculously escaped the dynamite. Rooms with two beds cost Nfa60/70/85 for a single/shared bath/en suite. Other options are all fairly basic, but the following list covers most reasonable options. If you want to be near the bus station for an early start, your best choices are **Mereb Hotel**, Nfa25/30, or **Seshebit Hotel**, Nfa10. Halfway between the bus station and the centre of town is the **Freselam Hotel**, which is basic and quite noisy. On the roundabout near the centre of town are the **Hotel Hamasien** and the **Tolul Hotel** with beds for Nfa15/10 respectively. One of the better options in the basic range is the **Selam Hotel**, further down the road, with beds for Nfa10 each. It has a quiet

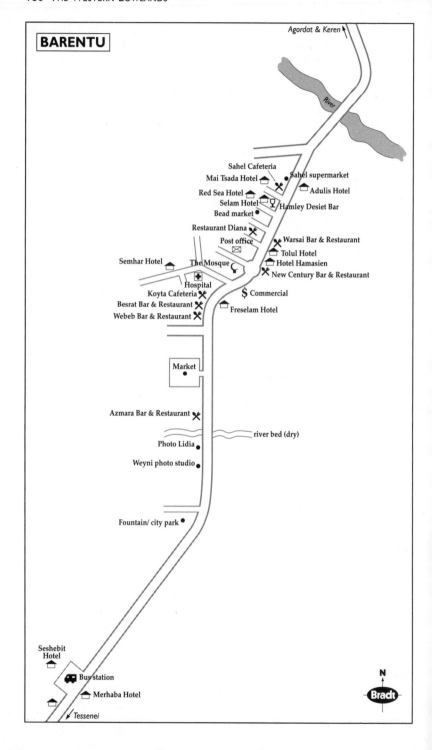

Above Camels awaiting new owners at Keren's famous camel market

Left A plentiful selection of produce on offer at one of Keren's many markets

Below Tigre girls enjoying being a part of the wonderfully colourful Nacfa market

Above left A family in Narrow
Above right The familiar sight of preparing for a coffee ceremony, Assab
Below left Carefully harvesting the delicious but prickly beles fruit
Below right The beles flower

inner-courtyard. Another reasonable place, which also serves good local food, is the **Adulis Hotel**. Rooms cost Nfa30 for two beds. Other options, though perhaps less tranquil, include the **Semhar Hotel**, the **Red Sea Hotel** and the **Mai Tsada Hotel**.

Where to eat
The only place to find pasta and a reliable source of cold drinks is at the **Merhaba Hotel**. For local food there are a number of good options, which are easily found by taking a stroll up the main street. Some pointers include the **Sahel Cafeteria** for good *ful* and delicious local fresh yoghurt, **Adulis Hotel**, **Restaurant Diana**, **Besrat Bar and Restaurant**, **Wedeb Bar and Restaurant** and **Koyta Cafeteria**. For a drink, the **Azmara Bar and Restaurant**, just by the Weyni and Lidia Photo Studios, halfway between the bus station and the centre of town is a good place. **New Century**, **Hamlay Desiet** and **Warsai** are reasonable lively local bars.

Shopping
If you wish to buy any souvenirs there are some interesting beads used by the Kunama to make jewellery. The best stalls for these can be found opposite the entrance to the Selam Hotel and in the market behind this area. Behind the main market there is also a Tigrinya market selling a wide range of baskets and other wicker ware at very reasonable prices. If you are after more luxury goods, such as mineral water, try the Sahel supermarket next to the Sahel restaurant.

SOUTH OF BARENTU
The area south of Barentu was entirely occupied by the invading Ethiopian forces in 2000 and, as a result, has faced massive internal upheaval. The situation is still far from normal and many thousands of people have not been able to return to their homes because of pillaging or the threat of mines. Although the Eritrean authorities and many NGOs are doing their best to improve the situation it will be some months, if not years, before any sense of normality can be returned to this region. Not only has this caused a horrendous human tragedy, but there also remains a deeper mark at

THE NARA
The Nara are a semi-nomadic, Nilotic people, numbering about 60,000. The word 'nara' in Nara language means 'heaven'. All are Muslims, in common with almost everyone to the west of the highland plateau. Much darker than highland Eritreans, and often wearing combs in their thick hair, they are distinctive, although they can be mistaken for the neighbouring Hedareb tribe. The centre of Nara territory is Mogolo, whose main market is on Tuesday. Among the products on offer you are likely to see items for which the Nara are famed: saddles and basketry.

community level where whole villages have been razed, and the agricultural land is now heavily mined in certain areas. Theoretically it is possible to travel to these areas, but there is little sense in doing so as you cannot travel off the main roads and the communities that once attracted visitors are still largely displaced. In addition to this, much of this region currently lies in the UN's Temporary Security Zone and so further permits are required to enter these areas (this time from the Eritrean Commission to the United Nations Mission to Ethiopia and Eritrea; see *Chapter 3* under *Bureaucracy,* page 51). These permits seem to be randomly checked. Although checks are seldom applied, it is better to be safe than sorry and get a permit before entering the TSZ.

Given that the TSZ is designed to be dispensed with by late 2002, and that the process of re-housing internally displaced peoples continues as it is, the situation in this region should improve in the near future. If this is the case, then the following information may be used as a provisional guide to some of the areas of interest.

Heading west from Barentu the road forks after 5km at a place known as **Prima Canteri**. There is a small café here, mainly patronised by fighters. Taking the left fork you travel along riverbeds in a southerly direction and through some of the more varied and beautiful countryside in this region towards Tocombia. Some 29km from Barentu you cross a large riverbed with the Kunama village of **Dase** on the far bank. You are now in the heart of the Kunama territory proper. The word '*Kunama*' in their own language is said to mean '*natural*'.

Tocombia is quite a large town (44km from Barentu) on the banks of the Gash, but there is only likely to be water in it at this point in the immediate aftermath of the rains. The main attraction of the town is its market on Tuesdays, which brings in people from far and wide, and can be found about 4km to the west of the town. The cattle section is reached either by fording the river or by negotiating a precarious wooden walkway. There is a fascinating mix of the lowland peoples in this region – Nara, Kunama, Beni Amer (Tigre), Saho, and even migrant Nigerians (known as Tokharir). Unfortunately, due to the destabilising effect of the Ethiopian occupation, it will be some time before the markets are able to thrive as they did prior to the war.

The next town is **Augaro** (84km from Barentu) where there are still old mineshafts and machinery from the days when the Italians mined gold here. Mining commenced in May 1932. Like Tocombia, Augaro had a lively, although rather smaller, market on Mondays selling everything from fresh produce to daggers. From here on, **Antore** (117km from Barentu) is the only village before you reach the **Setit River**, the only Eritrean river to flow all year round. The road then follows the river east to the village of **Sittona**. The change in this otherwise arid part of the country makes a welcome break. The approaches to the river are particularly beautiful after the rains, and the riverine environment supports a great variety of wildlife. Unless the water is low and crystal clear, do not swim here, as there is a danger of crocodiles. The undergrowth can also be very thick, making some passages difficult going, and tracks that may have been clear and obvious in the dry season may have disappeared altogether. You definitely need a guide for this section south of Augaro.

Barentu to Mendefera (Adi Ugri)

If you wish to return toward Asmara from Barentu by a different route to the Agordat–Keren road, turn back east from Barentu and turn right immediately after the check point at the edge of the town, heading almost due east. The journey to **Mendefera** is 210km. The road is currently being re-surfaced and, when complete, will provide the main access route from Asmara to the western lowlands. However, this is not due for completion until 2002 at the earliest. This route passes through **Mai Laham** (18km from Barentu), scene of a famous attack on the EPLF by Ethiopian airborne troops. The next settlement is **Binbina** (39km) with its imposing church on the hill. Next is **Shambuko** followed by **Arezza** (168km). The latter is a particularly beautiful town with two major churches, one on the hill and one further to the east. The whole route is an interesting loop into southern Eritrea; it is sparsely populated.

Barentu to Tessenei

If you take the right fork 5km west of Barentu instead of going south to the Setit, you are on the road to Tessenei, 107km to the west, and the border with Sudan. The road from Barentu to Tessenei is not yet sealed, and therefore can be quite heavy going, especially during the raining season. The bus takes about six hours while in a car it should take well under three hours. About 28km from Barentu, there is a large Catholic church on the right at **Adi Keshi**. The village of **Haicota** sits beside the road 70km from Barentu. After 95km, you see one of the more extraordinary spectacles on this route: two huge mounds of what looks like rubble, except that, owing to their colossal size, they cannot possibly be manmade. Approaching Tessenei, on the banks of the Gash, there is a noticeable increase in greenery. The bridge is in the part of the town, occupied by some Nigerian inhabitants, the Tokharir, whose forebears settled here generations ago on their way to or from Mecca. They are often to be seen fishing in the water below, even catching and skinning crocodile. You also pass six Italian-constructed irrigation ducts on the way into town, formerly used to irrigate the cotton plantation.

TESSENEI

Tessenei (585km from Asmara) has a real frontier feel to it, especially now that the border with Sudan is open. In the main square in front of the mosque, there is a real cultural melting pot. The town is abuzz with many kinds of different trade, including tailors, cafés, bars and other shops. On the outskirts of town to the north are a couple of hills from which there are exceptional views of the lowlands and the mountains inside Sudan. Unfortunately, as with Barentu, Tessenei faced occupation by Ethiopian forces and has suffered as a result, but nowhere near as badly.

WILDLIFE OF GASH SETIT

While one cannot pretend that the banks of the Setit are suitable for scrutiny by major safari companies, wildlife is more abundant here than in most of the rest of the country. To date, Eritrea has not officially created any national parks, so you may ignore the so-called 'wildlife reserves', which may be marked on out-of-date Eritrean maps: their inhabitants were, in most cases, killed or driven out by the war. It remains an urgent priority to create protected reserves if Eritrea is to hope to have any significant wildlife in the future. This area around the Setit would undoubtedly be one of the prime sites for such a reserve. In the 1930s, hippo, crocodile, giraffe, elephant and leopard were common. It is known that a small herd of elephant still roams this region. What remains unknown is to what extent this herd is genetically different from other African elephants. There is speculation that they could be the descendants of a cross-breed between Indian and African elephants when Lord Napier brought his expedition in the 19th century, but nobody has got close enough to count their toes – the one distinguishing feature between African and Asian elephants.

The following other mammalian species have been identified:

ground squirrel	Abyssinian hare
pale fox	black-backed jackal
common jackal	genet
African wild cat	vervet monkey
Anubis baboon	Emini's gerbil
warthog	Soemmering's gazelle

There have also been unsubstantiated sightings of lion, leopard, greater kudu and Tora hartebeest.

Birdlife

Birds are also in abundance. The following have so far been catalogued by the Ministry of Agriculture:

cattle egret	grey wagtail
great white egret	yellow wagtail
guinea fowl	marabou
sandgrouse	black kite
bee-eater	hooded vulture
Abyssinian roller	African hawk-eagle
grey hornbill	lesser kestrel
swift	lanner falcon
barbet	black-headed plover
Abyssinian nightjar	spotted eagle owl
honey-guide	hoopoe
chestnut-wing starling	

Where to stay and eat

There are a number of places in town to find food or accommodation. The **New Africa Hotel**, between the Telecom building and the Commercial Bank, is arguably the most reasonable at Nfa10 per bed outside, or in rooms around a pleasant courtyard. Opposite **Selam Park** are the hotels **Freedom** and **Shefray** with beds for Nfa10/20 outside/inside. A slightly better option is the **Luna Hotel**, with rooms with two beds for Nfa30/40 shared bath/en suite. The hotel also serves reasonable food. Around the bus station, there are a number of basic hotels, all providing beds for Nfa10 each. These include **Warsay**, **Barka**, **Keren**, and **Aletena**. The most interesting place to find food is undoubtedly the **Soog Al-Sha'By** (public market) where a whole range of Sudanese food can be found. There are many different stalls along this market area, but the best of these places is **Selam**, which serves excellent *ful* massala. The fresh milk and fruit juices, which are widely available in Tessenei, should also be tried.

Around Tessenei

The further you are from Asmara, the more you are going to need to rely on other people to show you the sights: making friends is useful. The nearest place to visit outside of Tessenei is the area surrounded by cotton plantations, called **Ali Ghider**, 10km from Tessenei and the Hedareb tribe's villages. Ali Ghider is an old Italian frontier village, still containing a few Italian relics, including an airport. The village was extensively sacked by the Ethiopian forces and there is a plan to entirely re-locate the village 2km south of its current location. It is the last settlement before reaching the Sudanese boarder. South of Tessenei, you can reach **Golluig** (46km from Tessenei) and **Om Hager** (98km) on the Ethiopian border. Both of these villages were destroyed by Haile Selassie in the 1960s and again by Ethiopian forces during the recent conflict. Their existence remains bleak. This area is also inside the Temporary Security Zone at the time of writing, and is probably not worth the trouble to visit.

All along this route south from Tessenei, Sudanese influence is strong, and the drive an interesting one. If you happen to be here during the **Khamsin**, the winds in February to May, you will be treated to spectacular sandstorms; the sun is not usually visible until about mid-day if it blew hard the previous day. There are also a staggering number of camels being herded around this region.

Ground squirrel

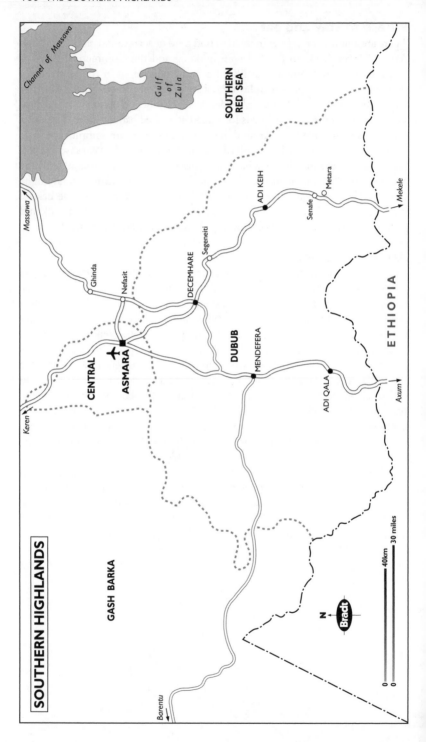

The Southern Highlands

Two main roads leave Asmara for the southern highlands. One runs through Decemhare and reaches the Ethiopian border at Zala Anbesa (pronounced Zall'anbesa), south of Senafe. The other, further west, follows a route through Debarua, Mendefera (Adi Ugri), and Adi Qala, meeting the Ethiopian border and the Mareb River at Ghundet. It is possible to cross from one road to the other about a third of the way to the border, via a track between Decemhare and Teramni.

The south is interesting for a number of reasons. Being one of the major agricultural areas in Eritrea it is also the most densely populated region. Although the whole area is at comparatively high altitude there are great sweeping plains and panoramic mountain views. There are also some of the most important archaeological sites in Eritrea, although all are only partly excavated and information remains scarce.

ASMARA TO SENAFE

The first village after leaving Asmara is **Adi Hawisha**. Just before it, 13.5km south of the capital, a road branches to the right to an area in which gold was mined by the Italian Barantanti. This area was the EPLF front line in 1977 before the Soviet Union began backing the Mengistu regime and pushed the EPLF back to the Sahel mountains. It is incredible to see how tantalisingly close they were to Asmara before having to retreat and wait a further 14 years before finally entering the capital victorious.

The road from Asmara to Decemhare is plied by racing cyclists. If you are travelling early in the morning you will see them in their groups speeding along the roads in training. Cycling is one of Eritrea's most loved sports and is another legacy of Italian influence. Many young men become involved in racing in order to reach the ultimate prize of international success. Eritrea even sent a cycling team to the Sydney 2000 Olympic Games.

After 18km you reach **Zigib** from where you can see Mount Ad Hannes (2,855m) – one of the tallest peaks in Eritrea – far in the distance to your left. **Waha** (27km) has a striking Coptic church with four towers, on the hill to your left. The views from this hill down towards the coast are magnificent. The descent into the plain of Decemhare (2,060m) begins after 34km; the town itself stretches out along the road for some 4km, between the 37km and 41km markers. Right at the beginning of the town the road to Teramni forks off to the west. Before this junction, on the outskirts of town, a big rock lies beside the road with a large Italian inscription to commemorate the building of the road. There are a number of such chiselled inscriptions in this region. Two can be found between here and Teramni, and another is several kilometres along the Tsorona road from Decemhare. At the far end of the town another road forks left and heads north again to Nefasit and the Asmara–Massawa road (the distance is around 40km). This route is a spectacular drive through some of Eritrea's most fertile country, and a very pleasant day trip from Asmara.

Decemhare

Decemhare itself was a favourite settlement of the Italians and by all accounts was a beautiful 'secondo Roma', although this is impossible to imagine now. It was originally designed to be the transport hub of the entire Italian Empire in the Horn of Africa, hence the rudimentary links to Massawa via Nefasit, Gondar via Tsorona and Addis via Senafe. It was one of the primary agricultural areas for the Italians, where they grew grapes for their wine and many other fruits and vegetables besides. Now it is hard to envisage this town as being the planned centre of an empire. What remains is a dilapidated legacy of a once prosperous past. The town was substantially destroyed prior to the final assault on Asmara by the EPLF in spring 1991. The Red Sea General Mills is one of the few traces of the high level of agro-industrial development formerly found on this plain.

During the fascist period, the town was designed with the same racial separation in mind as Asmara. The northern part of town is where the native population lived, which is still very evident today. Further south remains much less crowded, and the buildings considerably more grand, although now somewhat tired. It is hard to say which part of town is the centre today, but the southern part has a central piazza with a cinema and the city's administration, which makes for a more appropriate civic centre. The northern part of town, as in Asmara, is where the town's heart beats: where the shops, boutiques, barbers, bus station and markets are.

It is worth stopping in Decemhare to have a look around, if only to see what remains of this once proud town. There are a number of interesting buildings worth looking at. In the central piazza the **cinema** dominates the surroundings with its bold façade and buttress columns. If you look directly north from here you see the **Catholic cathedral** on the hill, which has a pleasant inner courtyard on its west wing. Further south from the cinema there are some fine, quintessentially Italian apartment buildings in a sorry state of disrepair. One used to be a hotel and the markings of 'Albergo' still remain on the columns beside the entrance. A number of interesting buildings line the main street. These include the **Commercial Bank** of Eritrea, the Plaza Hotel, and others that have ceased to be occupied.

Where to stay and eat

There are several small hotels if you want to stop here, including **Sellas** (south of the telecommunications building) and the **Plaza Hotel** on the corner at

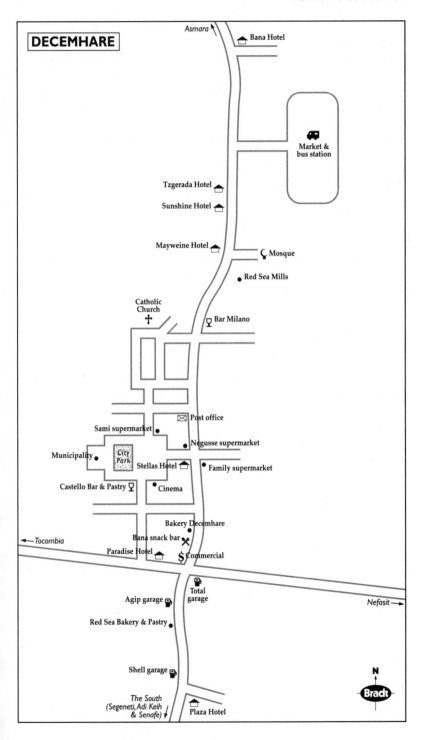

the southern end of town, both with beds for Nfa30. The best bets are the **Paradise Hotel** just off the main street on the Tsorona road and the **Bana Hotel** (tel: 641089) at the very north of town. Paradise has rooms for Nfa50/70 single/double and Bana Nfa30 for a room with shower. Both are very clean and serve excellent local food. Paradise does good pasta dishes too. On the main road near the bus station are a number of local hotels all very much in the budget category at around Nfa10–20 for a bed. These include **Tzegereda**, **Sunshine**, **Akeleguzai**, **Oasis** and **Mayweine.** For a light snack or drink, try **Castello's** in the main square, just across the road from the cinema, which is a central and popular haunt. Another good place is **Bana Snack Bar** on the main road just up from the Commercial Bank.

Beyond Decemhare

Two large churches dominate **Afelba** (47km), one Catholic and one Coptic. In 1894 Afelba was sacked for refusing to take part in a regional rebellion against the Italians in the first years of their occupation. **Segeneiti** (2,203m, 61km), the next town, is a lush fertile area and home to the best *beles* in Eritrea. Beles are the cactus fruit that come into season between July and late September. Originally imported by the Italians from Mexico, they are now considered a local delicacy and collected and sold in vast quantities in the highlands. Segeneiti is also where the best honey in Eritrea can be found. Segeneiti has two forts, high on either side of the pass, which guard the entry to the town. The views from these hills are excellent and some of the buildings have interesting Italian inscriptions. The other famous feature to be found around Segeneiti is the group of huge sycamore fig trees, known as *daaro* (*Ficus vasta*), to the south of the town. It is certainly worthwhile walking along this road to see these as such enormous trees are rare by any standards, let alone in Eritrea. The trees are greatly revered by locals, as they form a place where the community can assemble for discussion or debate, as well as providing ample shade. Such is the status of these trees that the largest has been immortalised on the five-nakfa note. The name Segeneiti derives from the founder of the town, who, being very tall, was given the nickname '*Segen*', which in Tigrinya means 'ostrich'.

Shopping for Tigrinya cloth

If you wish to purchase some Tigrinya cloth (*netsela*) or even ceremonial dress whilst in Eritrea, then there is a superb small-scale manufacturing project run by the Copuchimi Sisters of Mother Rubato. The project was established to provide work for the many war widows and to train them in the art of cloth-making, embroidery and weaving. All the products are manufactured on site, including the thread that is used to weave the large sheets of cloth. There are over 50 women employed by the project and the sale of their products helps support their families and children. The products here are cheaper than those you will find in Asmara and, being handmade, likely to be much better quality. The nunnery is set in the grounds of an old Italian church and is a haven of tranquillity. It is a short distance off the main road to the east.

QOHAITO

The plain of Qohaito (2,600m) lies to your left, 121km south of Asmara and about 11km south of Adi Keih. It measures 2.5km wide by 15km long. There are sharp descents on either side and views to the south of Mount Ambasoira (3,013m), the highest peak in Eritrea, and to the east to the Red Sea. If you want to enjoy these views try to reach Qohaito in the morning; it tends to cloud over later in the day. The plain is inhabited mainly by Saho pastoralists, who trade with other Saho in the Irafale region on the coast south of Massawa. You cannot make the same descent by car as they do on foot or camel. The ruins of Qohaito, a large dam (Safra's dam), the ruins of the palace of King Saba and various pillars and other buildings lie 11km from the main road. The inscription at Safra is, at 79 words, the longest yet found in the ancient religious language of Ge'ez. Little is known about the exact history of this settlement and how long it was of importance – the only certainties being that the dam is indeed a dam, the inscription is in Ge'ez, and the ruins are pre-Axumite and Axumite. There are also some prehistoric cave paintings in the area. Qohaito was thus an important staging post between Axum and Adulis. Even without much information on the history of the ruins the plain is well worth visiting.

Digsa (74km) is the only town between Segeneiti and Adi Keih, although, if you are interested in wartime history, the EPLF hospital used during the assault on Decemhare, and ultimately Asmara, is at Maiweni (signed to the right of the road after 75km). The hospital is no longer in use.

Adi Keih

Further on you come to Adi Keih, the staging post for visiting the archaeological sites at Qohaito and Toconda.

Where to stay and eat

There are a number of places to stay in this important market town. The best hotel is the **Adi Keih**, next to the hospital, where a room with shared shower will cost Nfa50/80 single/double. Right in the town centre the **Keste Demena**, **Kokob**, **Expo 64**, and **Quahaito** hotels are all much of a muchness with beds/rooms costing Nfa10–30. They are basic, though the Expo 64 and Quahaito are a cut above the other two. On the western side of town are four good alternatives: **Garden**, **Sami**, **Aregash** and **Midre Ghenet**, all with rooms for Nfa30. All hotels serve good local food, albeit usually limited in variety. Other options for food can be found at the **Beylul Bar and Restaurant** and the **Red Sea Restaurant**.

There is not a great deal to see and do in Adi Keih itself, though the Catholic church and the mosque are quite interesting. The church has 14 tablets on the

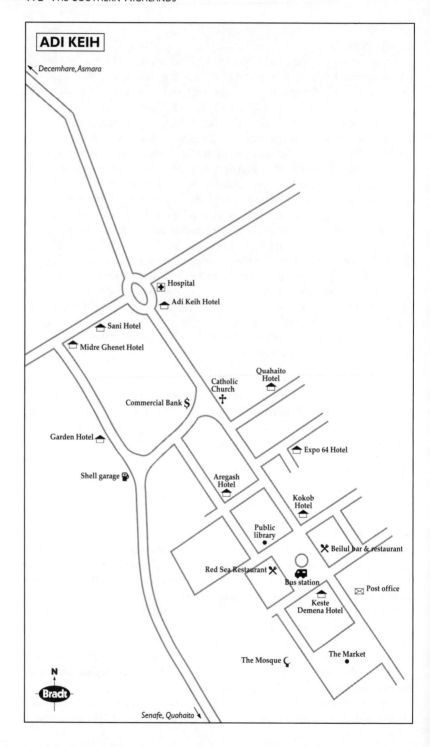

wall depicting Christ's crucifixion. To reach the archaeological sites, continue south on the road to Senafe.

Toconda, the other Axumite site in the Adi Keih region, is 4km south of Adi Keih, but it is not as impressive as Qohaito. There are also some 25 separate locations of ancient rock paintings in the Adi Keih region, but you will certainly need help finding them.

Senafe

From Adi Keih the road proceeds to **Senafe** and the border with Ethiopia. The word *Senafe* derives from '*San'a fen*', which in Arabic means 'Where is San'a?' This is said to have come from the question asked by Middle Eastern (Yemeni) traders who used to pass through this area and climb the high escarpment to try and see their home – San'a. To get to Senafe you will need to enter the Temporary Security Zone if it is still in operation, and to do this will require a permit from the Eritrean Commision to the United Nations Mission to Ethiopia and Eritrea (UNMEE) (see *Bureaucracy* in *Chapter 3*, page 51). Senafe (2,400m, 135km from Asmara) is the last Eritrean town of any size before you reach the Ethiopian border. Like Barentu and Tessenei, it was occupied during the recent conflict, but was dealt a much harder blow than the other two towns. Many homes and official buildings, including the large telecommunications building and hospital, have been destroyed and thousands of people made homeless. This is marked by the refugee camps that still surround the town.

Nonetheless, work is well underway for rehousing these displaced people and many residents of the town are rebuilding their homes and businesses with the enthusiasm and passion which has become such a characteristic of this country.

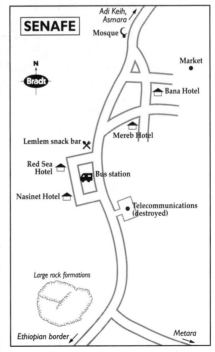

Just 2km to the south of town is the site of the ancient Axumite city of Metara. The plain on which Senafe sits is one of the more attractive on this route from Asmara and is dominated by the huge rocks on the southern boundary of the town. If you want to climb to the top of the largest of these it is worth it for the views but you should ask someone to show you the easiest way, as it is not a simple climb. At the foot is one particularly large tree with 12 branches, one supposedly bearing

METARA

One of the more obvious features of the city, until very recently, was a 5m *stela* (obelisk) with an inscription that has been dated to the 3rd century. On the top is a symbol of a south Arabian divinity, a disc over a crescent. Sadly, this ancient relic was deliberately destroyed by the Ethiopian army and dynamited. It now lies on the ground besides the road where it once stood. It will no doubt be mended and re-erected in time, but it remains a testament to the pettiness of war. The site covers about 10 hectares, and is known variously amongst locals as Balaw Calaw, King Kaleb's remains and the Gate of Axum. The common type of structure is a central building surrounded by secondary dwellings within an enclosing wall, and a staircase. In all, five compounds of this type are visible, one being rather different from the others: a large staircase to the west leads to a paved way which, in turn, leads to the central part of the building. There is a theory that this is actually a Christian church dating back to the 6th century, but this was denied by the National Museum. Under this building a large grave was discovered. In the compound next to this there is a staircase leading straight down into the ground; again legend has it that this is the start of a tunnel that connects Adulis to Axum, via Metara, although there is no concrete evidence yet that this existed. I met a girl on the coast who claimed that her brother had actually walked the tunnel; either I totally misunderstood or it was a rare example of Eritrean hyperbole. One of the more remarkable things, here and at the other archaeological sites, is that the cement that binds the bricks shows no sign of weakening even after some 1,400 years, a fact which is unlikely to be true of the stuff manufactured today. Metara has been identified by the historian Kobishchanov as the Axumite city of Koloe, which currently seems to be a more accepted theory than the one put forward in the 1890s by Bent, that Koloe was Qohaito.

fruit for each month of the year, which is strange seeing that the Orthodox calendar has 13 months.

Where to stay and eat

For those who plan to stay in Senafe there are a number of basic hotels, which all serve standard local fare. The standard was higher than it is at present as just about every hotel in town was destroyed. Rebuilding has only just restarted. Next to the bus station are the **Red Sea Hotel** and the **Nasinet Hotel,** with rooms for Nfa20/30 and Nfa10/20 respectively. The Red Sea had a reasonable restaurant and the manager even boasted that hot water would be available all day and night once he had installed the solar panels! Other basic options include **Mereb Hotel** and **Bana Hotel** with rooms for Nfa20. The **Lemlem**

Snack Bar by the bus station serves reasonable food. The distance by bus from Asmara to this border town is about four hours and costs Nfa13.5. As you leave the town to return to Asmara you pass through the frontline trenches of the Eritrean Defence Force from the recent war. After the first hairpin bend you can see the trenches on the hillside to your right, then as the mountains behind Senafe come into view the trench line along the ridge of the largest mountain becomes clearly visible.

Around Senafe
The only place of interest south of Senafe is the monastery of **Debre Libanos**, the oldest monastery in Eritrea, though getting to it with the current situation on the border is not likely to be possible, as the only road access is from Ethiopia. However, should the situation improve you can inquire at the Orthodox headquarters in Asmara on how to reach it. It is approachable from the village of **Hamm**, which is about 24km from Senafe, on the border with Ethiopia. A road is planned from Tsorona to connect Hamm from the Eritrean side. Hamm has a very old church, which makes a welcome change from the rather more modern architecture of Eritrean churches. Debre Libanos lies in a valley at the bottom of an extremely difficult descent from Hamm village. It will take about an hour down and one-and-a-half hours to return. Do not tackle it unless you are sure-footed and reasonably fit. Information is scarce, but the monastery, spread far and wide across the valley, probably dates to the 6th century, founded by St Mata (or Libanos). There is an important library here, rock paintings and a large number of mummified bodies, which are still in the process of being dated (best estimates are 4th century). The site is considered to be one of the most important in Eritrea and is already attracting archaeologists. Check at the National Museum for the latest information. You will certainly need someone to help you find the way to Hamm; from there one of the villagers will take you down to the monastery, although as it lies over a large area, with difficult terrain in between the different parts, you will not be able to visit the whole site in a day. Some parts are also not accessible: this is still a working monastery. The scenery, dramatic peaks and valleys, and views south into Ethiopia make the walk well worthwhile. In addition, many parts of the monastery are set into the overhanging cliffs, with great fronds of grass sprouting from cracks in the cliff, which are formed by the nocturnal moisture.

ASMARA TO GHUNDET
The other way to experience the southern highlands from Asmara is by heading to Adi Qala. Just out of Asmara on the eastern side of the road is the new **Kelete Hotel**, which is used ostensibly by Asmarinos wishing to get out of the big smoke for an afternoon. It is a pleasant place to get a drink and to feel like you are in the countryside. This road used to provide the other official route to Ethiopia, through Debarua. If you chose to go down one southern road and back along the other there is a good 28km track connecting Decemhare with **Teramni** (south of Debarua). Both the roads to Adi Qala

and across to Decemhare from Teramni are very beautiful and if you are travelling after the rains, you will see some of Eritrea's most fertile land. Agricultural activity is everywhere and the harvesting in October/November is a delightful sight. There is a hotel at Teramni called **Green Island** (tel: 162212), which used to have a good swimming pool, though whether it is working or not appears to be quite random. It has 38 rooms. The old airport at Gura, dismantled by the British, lies to the south of this road 8km from Decemhare. **Debarua** (1,930m) is the first town of any size that you come to south of Asmara, 30km from the capital; it was formerly a copper mining town. **Halhale** (33km south of Asmara) was a very large Italian farming area as you can easily see from the ruined buildings, which, not for the first time in Eritrea, make you wonder whether you aren't in southern Italy.

Mendefera

Further south is Mendefera (Adi Ugri, 1,980m, 54km from Asmara), capital of Dubub province. You will often see the name Adi Ugri used as the title for this town, but it is believed that both Mendefera and Adi Ugri were smaller villages along this road and have since merged. Mendefera is now regarded as the town's official name, which derives from the Tigrinya meaning 'nobody dared', after the resilience shown by the locals when they defended themselves on the hill against the Italian advance. Since being designated as the new capital of the Southern Highland region above Adi Keih (the old capital) there has been a wave of activity and development in Mendefera, which looks set to stay for some time. The new regional offices have been built and dominate the town on the eastern side, giving a rather grand civic feel to the town. The town itself is a pretty garden town with plenty of greenery and flowers to be seen, if you happen to be there during the right season. The town is dominated by two hills on either side of the main road. On the western hill sits the old Catholic church school, with its white belltower, which looks a little like a miniature version of Asmara's. You can visit this school very easily and the views from the hill are quite rewarding. Facing this on the eastern hill is the more modern Orthodox St Ghiorgis Church, which is in an extraordinary style and distinctly sci-fi in appearance.

Where to stay and eat

There are hotels a slight cut above the rest in the south. All hotels will provide some sort of restaurant facility, though the selection is likely to be determined by whatever is in the pot at that moment. The **Red Sea Restaurant** offers a good selection and is centrally located. There is also the lively **St George Bar and Restaurant** a little further up the road.

Upper range

The Mareb Hotel Tel: 611636. 25 rooms. Nfa60–100 per room with TV, en suite and telephone. The hotel has a good restaurant and very modern facilities. It is on the very south of town and therefore quiet. Probably the best the town has to offer.
Cherhi Hotel Nfa50–70 per room. Overlooking the town from the *forto*, this older hotel is in a picturesque spot.

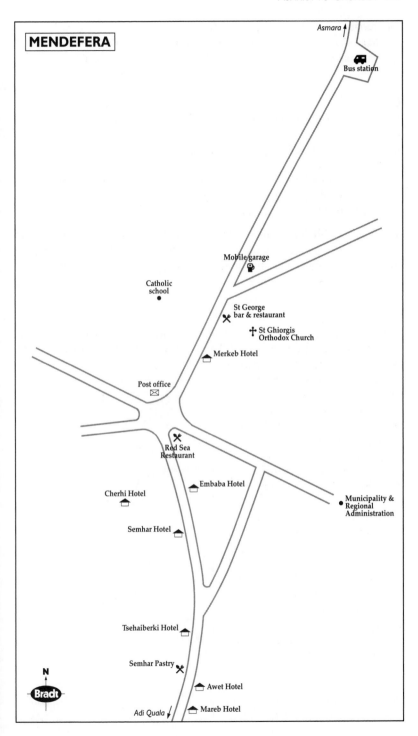

Mid range

Semhar Tel: 611356. 9 rooms. Nfa30/40 double/twin beds. Set around a very attractive courtyard on the main road underneath the Cherhi, the Semhar provides good food and a pleasant atmosphere.

Others

Awet Tel: 611063. 19 rooms. Nfa30 for twin rooms. Reasonable hotel with a local bar at the front.
Embaba Hotel Nfa20/30 single/double. Local hotel with a lively bar, but satisfactory rooms.
Tsehaiberki Hotel 6 rooms. Nfa20 for a twin room. This is a budget hotel with a local bar. Not bad if you are on a tight budget.
Merkeb Hotel Nfa20/30 single/double.

The village of **Sheka Eyamo** (76km) is typical of the area and is approached via a plain. The wells just at the start of the village are often a seething mass of livestock and locals, and an interesting example of life in this part of the country.

Adi Qala

Adi Qala (2,054m, 86km from Asmara) is another fair-sized market town, and the market lying just to the east of the main road is worth wandering around. As with so many of Eritrea's markets, this one is a good example of old and new. Due to the government policy of upgrading the markets in all of Eritrea's towns, in Adi Qala there now lies a brand new market area with surrounding stalls, surrounded again by the old corrugated shacks used by the previous market. Despite their unruly state, there is certainly something endearing about the older shacks, though of course the modern market is what everone wants. Adi Qala, like Mendefera, is a pleasant town with plenty of greenery. Most of the hotels have inner courtyards that are thick with vegetation and provide very pleasant and necessary shade.

One thing that is worth doing during a visit of a day or more in Adi Qala is the walk to the **Italian**

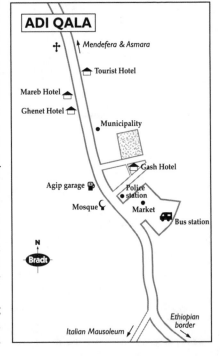

Mausoleum on the hill to the south of the town. It is a fair walk (about 6km), but well worth it, as the path goes through some fine agricultural land with superb views of the neighbouring escarpments. However, the finest views await you after you reach the mausoleum. It overlooks the agricultural plains of Eritrea and the Ethiopian Highlands far to the south. The mausoleum itself is an impressive memorial. It stands atop the hill and is the resting place of some 8,000 Italian troops lost at the disastrous battle of Adua on March 1 1896, when Italy first tried to make inroads into Ethiopia. It marked the first major defeat by an African army against the Europeans and thrust into question the Italian presence in Africa, causing them to change their colonial policy towards Eritrea. The mausoleum was built during the fascist era and boasts some impressive if not distasteful fascist symbolism with the numerous well-maintained Roman '*fasci*' depicted around the memorial.

Also of interest is the maximum-security prison (west of the bus station) which, like that on Nocra Island in the Dahlaks, was built in the early years of the colonial period to house Eritrean dissidents. Adi Qala is the last town before the Ethiopian border, which lies after the village of Enda Ghiorgis (103km from Asmara).

Where to stay and eat

There are a number of good places to stay in Adi Qala, offering the same sort of standards of accommodation and food. Most have very attractive interior courtyards and provide double or twin rooms.

Tourist Hotel 10 rooms. Nfa25. Each room is en suite and the courtyard is excellent. Currently used by the UN, so may be booked up.

Mareb Nfa20; Nfa 10 per extra bed. Very attractive courtyard and good rooms. Centre of town.

Ghenet Nfa15/30 single/double. Next to the Mareb, this offers a very similar standard of accommodation. There is a billiard table in the front bar.

Gash Nfa10–40. Four classes of accommodation to cover every conceivable option (in this price bracket). Set back two blocks from the main road, this hotel has a quiet atmosphere and a good courtyard. The restaurant is also very good.

Vervet monkey

MEASUREMENTS AND CONVERSIONS

To convert	Multiply by
Inches to centimetres	2.54
Centimetres to inches	0.3937
Feet to metres	0.3048
Metres to feet	3.281
Yards to metres	0.9144
Metres to yards	1.094
Miles to kilometres	1.609
Kilometres to miles	0.6214
Acres to hectares	0.4047
Hectares to acres	2.471
Imperial gallons to litres	4.546
Litres to imperial gallons	0.22
US gallons to litres	3.785
Litres to US gallons	0.264
Ounces to grams	28.35
Grams to ounces	0.03527
Pounds to grams	453.6
Grams to pounds	0.002205
Pounds to kilograms	0.4536
Kilograms to pounds	2.205
British tons to kilograms	1016.0
Kilograms to British tons	0.0009812
US tons to kilograms	907.0
Kilograms to US tons	0.000907

5 imperial gallons are equal to 6 US gallons
A British ton is 2,240 lbs. A US ton is 2,000 lbs.

Temperature conversion table

The bold figures in the central columns can be read as either centigrade or fahrenheit.

°C		°F	°C		°F
−18	0	32	10	50	122
−15	5	41	13	55	131
−12	10	50	16	60	140
−9	15	59	18	65	149
−7	20	68	21	70	158
−4	25	77	24	75	167
−1	30	86	27	80	176
2	35	95	32	90	194
4	40	104	38	100	212
7	45	113	40	104	219

Appendix 1

LANGUAGE

The working languages in Eritrea are Tigrinya and Arabic. Italian is also spoken, particularly by the older generation in Asmara. Tigrinya, spoken by at least half the population, has its own script derived from the ancient language Ge'ez, now only used in the Orthodox Church. The script has over 200 characters or letters, each representing a different sound. It is not an extremely difficult language to learn. The following is an attempt to provide some of the basic words and phrases for a visitor. I am very grateful to Glenn Burks, who has compiled the list of words and phrases. It has been 'tested' with Eritreans, but all regional or dialectic variations cannot be taken into account. Above all it is intended to be user-friendly. Eritreans are well aware just how difficult their language is at first for foreigners and you will find that if you can say hello, thank you, or order food, the pleasure this will give to the recipient far outstrips one's linguistic ability. Do not be afraid to have a go.

Alphabet

The Tigrinya alphabet might at first appear to be a daunting script to understand, but it is relatively simple to master. Each consonant has its own character which itself has seven derivatives, one for each of the seven vowel sounds that accompany it. Although this makes the Tigrinya alphabet intimidating at first sight (having so many individual characters), once you are able to recognise each of the consonants it becomes very simple to apply or identify the necessary vowel sound.

Pronunciation

aa	long a, sounded in the back of the throat
<u>aa</u>	almost the same as above, except that it is pronounced as two separate, but almost indistinct syllables
a	long a as in *hard*
ee	long e, same as in English
i	same as ee
e	short sound, as in *bed*
<u>e</u>	long e, sounded in the back of the throat
<u>er</u>	er sound, as in English, but sounded in the back of the throat
ai	I, as in the English pronoun
oo	as in *cool*
<u>o</u>	long o, sounded in the back of the throat
u	ew, as in *few*

y̱	a constricted u, made in the back of the throat
r	r's are always slightly rolled
g	hard g, as in *guttural*, sounded in the back of the throat
ḵ	hard k, sounded in the back of the throat
ts	as in *pits*, pronounced at the tip of the tongue
ṯ	hard t, pronounced emphatically at the tip of the tongue
ḥ	hard h, sounded in the back of the throat

Greetings

Hello	*Selam*
Goodbye	*Selamat*
	Dehaan waal
How are you?	*Kemayla-ha? (male)*
	Kemayla-hee? (female)
	Kemayla-hoom? (male or mixed plural)
	Kemayla-hen? (female plural)
Good morning	*Dehaan haudir-ka/kee/koom/ken*
Good afternoon	*Kemay wyl-ka/kee/koom/ken*
Goodnight	*Dehann hd-er/ee/oo/a*
Good evening (parting)	*Dehaun ams-ee/i/oo/a*
(greeting)	*Kemay amsee-ha/hee/hoom/hen*
How were the last few days?	*Kemay kenye-ha/hee/hoom/hen?*
Where are you from?	*Kabey ig-aa/ee/oom/en metsi-ka/kee/koom/ken?*
Where are you going?	*Nabay tygey-id/ee/oo/a?*
Thank you	*Yekanyelay*
Please (rarely used)	*Beja-ha/hee/hoom/hen*
Yes	*Uwa/uway*
No	*No/Aylonen*
Good	*Tsebuk/tsebo*
OK	*Dehaun*
Bad	*Hmak*
Good (more positive than *tsebuk*)	*Tsebo alo*
What is your name?	*Men shem-ka/kee/koom/ken?*
My name is Edward	*Shemay Edward iyu*
I live in London	*Ab London yeneber*

In practice the key exchange to master is to say hello (*selam*), how are you? (*kemayla-ha*), I'm fine (*tsebuk*). Note that in Arabic-speaking regions, *keff* is also a common greeting.

Numbers

1	*Haade*		12	*Aserte-kilte* etc
2	*Kilte*		20	*Esra*
3	*Seleste*		30	*Salasa*
4	*Arboate*		40	*Arba*

5	*Hamushte*	50	*Hamsa*
6	*Shuduste*	60	*Susa*
7	*Shuate*	70	*Seba*
8	*Shomonte*	80	*Semanya*
9	*Teshuate*	90	*Tesa*
10	*Aserte*	100	*Miti*
11	*Aserte-haade*	1,000	*Sheh*

Room number 11 *Koosari aserte-haade*

At the market, eating food

market	*Idaga*	mango	*Mango*
potatoes	*Dnish*	lemon	*Lemon*
tomatoes	*Pommidere*	guava	*Zetoon*
onions	*Shoogurti*	water	*Mai*
carrots	*Caroti*	beer	*Birra*
green pepper	*Go̲*	mineral water	*Mai gas*
chili pepper	*Berbere*	tea	*Shahi* (like 'shy')
green beans	*Fajoli*	milk	*Tsaba*
peas	*Ayne-ater*	oil (cooking)	*Zayti bile*
zucchini	*Zucchini*		
garlic	*Tsada shoogurti*	delicious	*Te̲-e̲rm*
cabbage	*Caolocabucchi*		(two syllables)
bread	*Bani*	sweet	*Mookoor/muooze*
rice	*Rooze*	spicy	*Marir*
beef	*Syga kepti*	bitter	*Metsits*
	(literally 'cattle meat')	cheap	*He̲rsoor*
chicken	*Dorho*	expensive	*Keboor*
fish	*Assa*	How much is it?	*Kenday iyu wagu,*
cheese	*Formaggio*		usually just *kenday?*
orange	*Oranchi*	Do you have	*Shoogurti ali-ka/kee/*
banana	*Banana/mooze*	onions?	*koom/ken-do?*
papaya	*Papaya*		(one word)

Colours

black	*Tselim*	yellow	*Beecha*
white	*Tsada*	green	*Ke̲telia/hamlai*
red	*Ke̲yeh*	orange	*Aranchonay*
blue	*Semayowi*		

Useful adjectives/adverbs

hot	*Wa̲a̲i*	beautiful	*Tsebuk*
cold	*Koori/zahali*	new	*Haudish*
big	*Aabi* (male),	I am thirsty	*Te̲miay*
	aabai (female)	I am tired	*Ana̲y degimay,*
small	*Nyi̲shto*		or just *degimay*

I am angry	*Handikay*	left	*Tsegam*
I am sad	*Hazinay*	right	*Yeman*
I am happy	*Hagusiny*	this	*Izi*
		that	*Iti*
fast	*Keltuf*	here/there	*Abzi/abti*
slow	*Medenguai*		
	(four syllables)		

Useful words and phrases

many	*Buzerh*	It is important	*Agadasi iyu*
very	*Betoamee*	Do you	*Teredioo-ka/kee/koom/*
few	*Wooherdt*	understand?	*ken?*
only	*Tyrayai*	I understand	*Terediuni*
for	*Nγ*	I don't understand	*Ayeteredanen*
both	*Kelete en*	What is this?	*Izi entai iyu?*
too much	*Azeyoom buzerhat*	No problem	*Sheguryelen*
again	*Degam*		
all right	*Harai*	Help me	*Hagezaynee*
nothing	*Waala haude*	Show me	*Ahreyene*
which one?	*Iyenai?*	Give me	*Habenee*
in/inside	*Wushtee*	I want	*Deleeay*
out/outside	*Wetsaiee*	There is	*Alo*
		Wait a minute	*Haansab tshanee*
Who?	*Men?*	Enough	*Backa*
What?	*Entai?*	The same	*Kooloohaade*
Where?	*Abay?*	I know	*Felete*
When?	*Maas?*	I don't know	*Ayefelton*
Why?	*Nementai?*	Beautiful day	*Tsebo maalti*
		Not here	*Abzi yelen*
Please speak	*Kesayil-ka/kee/koom/*		(or just *yelen*)
slowly	*ken tesar- ab/ee/oo/aa*	No more	*Yelen* (*yelen* is widely
I have a car	*Anay makina alinee*		used, for example
I need a car	*Makina yedeleyini*		even if a restaurant
Are you tired?	*Dagim-ka/kee/koom/*		has run out of
	ken dig-a/ee/oom/en?		something)
It is difficult	*Tsegem iyu*		

Days of the week

Monday	*Senui*	Friday	*Arbi*
Tuesday	*Selus*	Saturday	*Kedam*
Wednesday	*Robo*	Sunday	*Senbet*
Thursday	*Hamus*		

Time

See also the note on the calendar, page 10

What time is it?	*Saat kenday koyenoo?*	today	*Lommi*
Four o'clock	*Saat arboate*	tomorrow	*Tsebah*
Quarter past four	*Saat arboaten-rebyn*	day before	*Kedemi timal*
Half past four	*Saat arboaten-feregan*	yesterday	
Quarter to five	*Saat hamushte-reby-godel*	day after tomorrow	*Dehuri tsibah*
		three days ago	*Kedemi kilte maalti*
day	*Maalti*	always	*Kooloo gezee*
minute	*Dekik*	never	*Befertsom*
hour	*Saat*	every day	*Kooloo maalti*
week	*Semoon*	impossible	*Atse gami*
month	*Werhee*	maybe	*Yegewoon*
year	*Amet*	now	*Heji*
		next/later	*Daharai*
yesterday	*Tamali*	this week	*Izi semoon*

Warthog

Appendix

FURTHER READING

Abeba Tesfagiorgis *A Painful Season and a Stubborn Hope* Red Sea Press, Trenton, New Jersey

Cliffe, Lionel and Davidson, Basil *The Long Struggle of Eritrea* Red Sea Press, Trenton, New Jersey

Connell, Dan *Against All Odds* Red Sea Press, Trenton, New Jersey

Doombos, M *Beyond the Conflict in the Horn* Red Sea Press, Trenton, New Jersey

Eritrea at a Glance available in Asmara

Firebrace, James and Holland, Stuart *Never Kneel Down* Red Sea Press, Trenton, New Jersey

Habte Selassie, Bereket *Eritrea and the United Nations* Red Sea Press, Trenton, New Jersey

Keneally, Thomas *Towards Asmara*

Kutschera, Chris *L'Érythrée 1984–94* Edibra Press, Paris

Markakis, John *The Nationalist Revolution in Eritrea* Journal of Modern African Studies, Volume 26

Papstein, Robert *Eritrea: Revolution at Dusk* Red Sea Press, Trenton, New Jersey

Pateman, Roy *Eritrea: Even the Stones are Burning* Red Sea Press, Trenton, New Jersey

Semplici, Andrea *Eritrea* Clup Guide, Milan

Trevaskis, G K N *Eritrea, A Colony in Transition* Oxford University Press

Wilson, Amrit *The Challenge Road: Women and the Eritrean Revolution* Red Sea Press, Trenton, New Jersey

Websites

There are many websites available from where you can pick up good travel advice, or news on Eritrea. The various Eritrean communities overseas have many different sites representing their activities and events. Some of the larger community sites include:

www.asmarino.com A news agency site that has a wide range of articles and opinions from a broad readership. Probably the most objective source of information.

www.awate.com The voice of the opposition ELF party.

www.dehai.com A members-only news site, but with a broad readership.

www.eritrea.org Operated by the Eritrean Network Information Center. Has not been in operation for some time.

www.edf.org The Eritrean Development Foundation site.

www.eritrea1.org The site representing those currently seeking reform in Eritrea.

www.hafash.com A good source of local and regional news and links to other related sites. Also has on-line discussions.

www.shabia.org The ruling party's (PFDJ) official site.

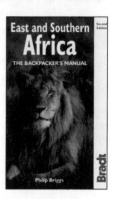

Index

Page numbers in bold indicate main entries, those in italics indicate maps.